# CRIME IN THE PROFESSIONS

*For M.C.M.*

# Crime in the Professions

*Edited by*
RUSSELL G. SMITH

**Ashgate**

Published by
Ashgate Publishing Limited
Gower House
Croft Road
Aldershot
Hants GU11 3HR
England

Ashgate Publishing Company
131 Main Street
Burlington, VT 05401-5600 USA

Ashgate website: http://www.ashgate.com

**British Library Cataloguing in Publication Data**
Crime in the professions
    1. White collar crimes  2. White collar crimes - Prevention
    3. Professional ethics
    I. Smith, Russell G.
    364.1'68

**Library of Congress Cataloging-in-Publication Data**
Crime in the professions / edited by Russell G. Smith.
        p. cm.
    Includes bibliographical references.
    ISBN 0-7546-2291-6
    1. White collar crimes--Australia.  I. Smith, Russell G.

    HV6771.A8 C75 2002
    364.16'8'0994--dc

                                                                    2002016499

    ISBN 0 7546 2291 6

Printed and bound in Great Britain by Antony Rowe Ltd., Chippenham, Wiltshire

# Contents

# Contributors

**Mr Sitesh Bhojani**

Until his appointment on 6 November 1995 as a Member of the Australian Competition and Consumer Commission, Mr Bhojani was (from 1992 to 1995) a barrister with a general commercial and civil litigation practice at the independent bar in Western Australia. In 1994 he was appointed an Associate Commissioner of the Trade Practices Commission and has also been Deputy Chairman of the Law Council of Australia, Business Law Section's Trade Practices Committee.

From 1986 to 1992 he was a barrister and solicitor with the Commonwealth Attorney-General's Department, Perth office, and also with the Trade Practices Unit of the Australian Government Solicitor/Federal Court and Tribunals Registry.

In June 1991, and subsequently in June 1994, Mr Bhojani completed the Negotiation Workshop and the Advanced Negotiation Workshop respectively at the Program of Instruction for Lawyers at Harvard Law School, Harvard University.

He holds a Bachelor of Science (Monash) and Bachelor of Laws (Monash). In 1986 he was admitted as barrister and solicitor in Victoria and Western Australia. He has also tutored in trade practices law at the University of Western Australia.

Mr Bhojani's responsibilities on the Commission include its enforcement activities (as Chairman of the ACCC's Enforcement Committee), the professions, the health sector and small business initiatives. He regularly represents the Commission in negotiations and mediation of ACCC litigation.

**Ms Sophie Curzon Blencowe**

Sophie Curzon Blencowe is a Research Fellow at the Key Centre for Ethics, Law, Justice and Governance at Griffith University, in Queensland. She holds the degrees of BA (Hons) and LLB (Hons) from the University of Melbourne and received the 1992 Jessie Mary Vasey Prize for her honours thesis in women's history. She was also awarded the Dwight's Prize for the Final

Examination in Arts, School of History in 1992, and the Sir George Turner Exhibition for Constitutional and Administrative Law in 1993. Together with Charles Sampford, she is the author of 'Educating Lawyers to be Ethical Advisers' in Economides, K. (ed.) 1998, *Ethical Challenges to Legal Education and Conduct*, Oxford University Press, Oxford.

## Mr Graham Brooks

Graham Brooks is a lecturer in community justice in the School of Social Work and Social Policy at the University of Birmingham, England, where he teaches trainee probation officers. Previous work has included research into the effectiveness of local, social juvenile programs to reduce offending; the relationship between drinking/drug habits and violence; and measuring the success of probation service employment schemes to reduce recidivism. Whilst such research is diverse, a personal leitmotiv of his work is the social control of the 'body' and the 'elective affinity' between work and discipline. Recently this interest has moved away from offenders to look at the construction of 'professional deviance' and the control and regulation of 'criminal justice practitioners'.

## Ms Anne-Louise Carlton

Anne-Louise Carlton has worked for State Departments of Health and Community Services in both New South Wales and Victoria since 1978. Her qualifications include undergraduate degrees in Arts (majoring in Psychology and Law) and Social Work, from Sydney University, an MBA from Monash University and, more recently, a Bachelor of Science (Clinical Studies) from Victoria University. Her work in the public service has included almost 20 years in the Intellectual Disability field, both in line management and policy, where she was actively involved in closing institutions such as Caloola, and in managing the state-wide establishment of community-based programs.

More recently, Ms Carlton's work as Manager of the Practitioner Regulation Section has included reviews of occupational regulation legislation under National Competition Policy, including reviews of Victorian legislation governing optometrists, chiropractors, osteopaths, physiotherapists, medical practitioners and nurses. She has been responsible for the research and policy development work that led to the passage of the Victorian *Chinese Medicine Registration Act 2000*. She is currently responsible for implementation of that Act, as well as reviewing the Victorian Pharmacists Act, the Medical

Practice Act and the Nurses Act. Since starting work on a review of Chinese medicine, Ms Carlton now deals with many of the policy issues that arise in relation to complementary therapies.

## Ms Margaret M. Coady

Margaret Coady is a Senior Lecturer in the Education Faculty at the University of Melbourne. She has held positions as Visiting Research Scholar at the Centre for Human Values, Princeton University, the Rockefeller Research Center at Bellagio, Italy, and the Joseph and Rose Kennedy Institute of Ethics at Georgetown University. Her research interests are in professional ethics, in rights of children and in state regulation of groups such as families and professions which demand a degree of autonomy. She has read papers on these topics at a number of universities in the United States, England, China, Singapore and South Africa, and has published on these topics in international journals. She is the Program Manager in Professional Ethics for the Australian Research Council Special Research Centre in Applied Philosophy and Public Ethics.

## Ms Carla Day

Carla Day is currently completing doctoral studies on compliance and decision-making in complex organisations at the Australian National University. She was previously Director of the Fraud Control Policy and Ethics Directorate within the Inspector General Division of the Australian Defence Organisation. Her role there was to manage a Defence-wide awareness program in ethical resource management, conduct research, and develop and implement fraud control policy within the Defence organisation. She is a registered psychologist who is a trained facilitator and has a broad background in health administration, management, counselling, and social and educational research.

## Mr Andrew Dix

Andrew Dix graduated with a combined Arts/Law degree from the University of Sydney in 1977. After a period in private legal practice, he became involved in the field of medical law in the early 1980s as the in-house lawyer for the New South Wales branch of the Australian Medical Association. Following his involvement in the drafting of far-reaching amendments to the NSW Medical Practitioners Act, he was appointed as Registrar of the NSW Medical Board, the position which he currently holds. Mr Dix is co-author of *Law for the Medical Profession in Australia* (Butterworth Heinemann), now in its second edition.

### Ms Kathryn Dwan

Kathryn Dwan holds a Bachelor of Science (Hons) and Bachelor of Arts and is currently a doctoral candidate at the University of Queensland. Prior to commencing her doctorate, Kathryn worked in the Queensland Health Department for five years as a Senior Policy Officer. She is currently a research assistant for Emeritus Professor John Western on the 'Reshaping Australian Institutions—Professions Study'.

### The Honourable Justice Kenneth Hayne

The Honourable Justice Kenneth Hayne is a Justice of the High Court of Australia, having been appointed on 22 September 1997. At the time of his appointment he was a judge of the Court of Appeal of Victoria, having been appointed one of the foundation judges of that court in June 1995. He graduated in Arts and Law from the University of Melbourne and, having been elected Rhodes Scholar for Victoria in 1969, graduated in 1971 as a Bachelor of Civil Law from the University of Oxford. He was admitted to the Victorian Bar in 1971 and appointed Queen's Counsel in 1984 practising in State and Federal Courts principally in commercial, constitutional and general civil matters. He was appointed a Judge of the Supreme Court of Victoria in 1992.

### Dr Julie McMillan

Julie McMillan is a Research Fellow at the Australian Council for Educational Research. Prior to this she held research positions at the Australian National University and the University of Queensland. She has been involved in the Professions in Australia study for a number of years, examining issues such as the nature and characteristics of the professions, determinants of status and earnings within the Australian legal profession, and the recruitment and retention of medical practitioners to rural areas. Her current work, based upon the Longitudinal Surveys of Australian Youth project, focuses on the influences on educational attainment and early labour market outcomes of young people.

## Dr Toni Makkai

Toni Makkai is Director of Research at the Australian Institute of Criminology and program director of the Drug Use Monitoring in Australia (DUMA) project. Prior to this she has held university teaching and research appointments in England and Australia. Her research interests include drugs and crime, regulation and compliance and the professions. Her most recent publications have included 'Harm Reduction in Australia: Politics, Policy and Public Opinion' in Inciardi, J. and Harrison, L. (eds), *Harm Reduction: National and International Perspectives*, Sage Publications, Thousand Oaks, and 'Drug Trends and Policies' in Chappell, D. and Wilson, P. (eds), *Crime and the Criminal Justice System in Australia: 2000 and Beyond*, Butterworths, Sydney.

## Mr Tim Phillipps

Tim Phillipps is the national forensic partner for Deloitte Touche Tohmatsu, based in Sydney. He has an extensive background in law enforcement and corporate regulation and has been responsible for some of Australia's largest corporate investigations. He has a strong interest in technology-based investigations.

## Ms Leanne Raven

Leanne Raven is Chief Executive Officer at the Nurses Board of Victoria in Melbourne, Australia. For the last 12 years she has worked with three nurse regulatory authorities in two states in Australia. With an undergraduate degree in science, a postgraduate diploma in education and a masters degree of nursing studies, she is currently working with a team of researchers in the field of gerontic acute nursing care. She is the Deputy Chair of the Australian Nursing Council and sits on the Nurse Practitioner Implementation Advisory Committee and the Victorian Secondary Schools Nursing Program Advisory Committee for the government in Victoria. In 1996 she was instrumental in the establishment of the Asia-Pacific Regional Regulatory Forum which now has met on three occasions. At the last meeting held in Bangkok there were

150 delegates from 21 countries. The next meeting is to be held in Hong Kong in November 2002. Leanne is a fellow of the Australian College of Nurse Management and the Australian Institute of Company Directors.

## Professor Charles Sampford

After gaining a double first in politics and philosophy and the Supreme Court Prize in Law from the University of Melbourne, Charles Sampford won a Commonwealth Scholarship to Oxford to pursue his studies in law, being awarded a DPhil in 1984. He returned to the University of Melbourne to teach law before being seconded to the Philosophy Department in 1990 to help establish the Centre for Philosophy and Public Issues where he became Acting Director then Deputy Director and Principal Research Fellow, leading several projects including one on 'Law, Ethics and Business'. Griffith University's research committee invited him to apply for the Foundation Deanship and in March 1991 he set about the task of establishing what is widely regarded as the most innovative and most successful of the new law schools with Professor Sampford's curriculum receiving particularly high praise (including Sir Ninian Stephen referring to it as the 'second revolution' in Australian legal education).

While Dean he founded the National Institute for Law, Ethics and Public Affairs (NILEPA), an elite research unit which he later directed. In 1999, NILEPA joined two other centres to form the Key Centre for Ethics, Law, Justice and Governance, of which he is Foundation Director.

Foreign fellowships include the Visiting Senior Research Fellow at St John's College Oxford (1997) and a Fulbright Senior Fellowship to Harvard University (2000).

Professor Sampford has written over 60 articles and chapters in Australian and foreign journals and collections ranging through law, legal education and applied ethics and has completed 16 books and edited collections. He has also won over seven million dollars in grants, consultancies and awards for research work he has led. At the same time he has pursued a successful career as a part-time company director, gaining insights into the operation of Australian and international business that are valuable in work as an applied ethicist.

Professor Sampford has been consulted by business, government and three Queensland Parliamentary committees—the Parliamentary Electoral and Administrative Reform Committee, the Ethics and Privileges Committee and he is the advisor to the Scrutiny of Legislation Committee. In the UK he has advised the Nolan Committee on Standards in Public Life and the Lord Chancellor's Committee on Legal Education and Professional Conduct. His advice was followed and his contribution has been publicly acknowledged by Lord Nolan. This approach has now been adopted by the OECD. In September 1998, he went to Indonesia on a special mission for the World Bank to advise the Indonesian government on governance reforms to deal with corruption.

### Dr Russell G. Smith

Russell G. Smith has qualifications in law, psychology and criminology from the University of Melbourne and a PhD from the Faculty of Laws, King's College, University of London. He is admitted as a Barrister and Solicitor of the Supreme Court of Victoria and a Solicitor of the Supreme Court of England and Wales. Dr Smith practised as a solicitor in Melbourne for a number of years before becoming a lecturer in Criminology at the University of Melbourne in 1990. He then took up a position at the Australian Institute of Criminology in 1996 where he is now Deputy Director of Research. He has written widely on aspects of computer crime, fraud control and professional regulation. His books include *Medical Discipline* (Clarendon Press, Oxford, 1994), *Crime in the Digital Age* (Federation Press, Sydney, 1998, written jointly with Dr Peter Grabosky), *Health Care, Crime and Regulatory Control* (Hawkins Press, Sydney, 1998), *In Pursuit of Nursing Excellence* (Oxford University Press, Melbourne, 1999) and *Electronic Theft: Crimes of Acquisition in Cyberspace* (Cambridge University Press, Cambridge, 2001, written jointly with Dr Peter Grabosky and Dr Gillian Dempsey).

### Emeritus Professor John Western

Emeritus Professor John Western has a first-class Honours BA degree in Psychology from the University of Melbourne, a first-class MA in Psychology from the same university and a PhD in Sociology from Columbia University in New York. He is a Fellow of the Academy of Social Sciences in Australia, a Board member of the Swiss Academy of Development, the Director of the Social and Economic Research Centre at the University of Queensland and a one-time Commissioner of the Criminal Justice Commission in Queensland. He has been President of the Sociological Association of Australia and New Zealand and the Australian Sociological Association. He is the immediate Past President of the Asia-Pacific Sociological Association.

He has 30 years experience of basic and applied social research with an emphasis on the professions and work, class and social stratification, urban and regional development, the criminal justice system, social impact assessment and program evaluation. He has worked in south-east Asia and China as well as in Australia. In Asia, his work has been supported by UNDP, IDP, the World Bank and AIDAB and in Australia by the Australian Research Council, the Criminology Research Council and a variety of government agencies.

## Mr Andrew Williams

Andrew Williams has long-term experience with a number of specialist insurance broking firms, particularly in relation to the effect of litigation on professions and occupations. Mr Williams has been directly involved with the creation and administration of affinity programs for professional and occupational liability insurance for the commercial, legal and medical professions.

## Mr Peter Willis

Peter Willis is a Barrister and Director of Transparency International Australia, a non-governmental organisation dedicated to combating corruption in government and international business. He holds the degrees of BA (Hons) and LLB (Hons) from the University of Melbourne and was awarded the Supreme Court Prize. Previously a Ministerial Adviser to the federal Attorney-General, partner of law firm Mallesons Stephen Jaques and Chairman of the Law Council of Australia's International Trade and Business Committee, he is now a barrister practising in commercial, administrative and international law, based in Melbourne.

## Ms Beth Wilson

Beth is the Health Services Commissioner (health ombudsman) in Victoria, Australia. The Commissioner receives and resolves complaints from consumers of health services about health service providers with a view to improving the quality of health services for all. Prior to becoming the Commissioner, Beth was the President of the Mental Health Review Board. She is a lawyer by training, specialising in medico/legal issues, and has an interest in law, medicine and ethics.

# Foreword

*On Monday 21 February 2000, the Australian Institute of Criminology's conference 'Crime in the Professions' was opened by the then Minister for Justice and Customs of the Commonwealth of Australia, Senator the Honourable Amanda Vanstone. The following is the text of Senator Vanstone's address.*

In the last population census conducted by the Australian Bureau of Statistics in 1996, there were 1.3 million professionals and 861,000 associate professionals identified. All of the professions have a vital role to play in Australia's economic and social development. The ability of professionals to apply knowledge to real world problems, and their ability to change as conditions change, will make them the source of much of our future wealth. If the ethical standards expected of the professions are maintained, their contribution will be all the more valuable.

In recent times, the professions have been changing. New occupations have sought and achieved professional standing; new technologies are altering what professionals do. Professional work has lost some of its mystique. For example, we can all find out a lot more about our diseases on the Internet, we do not need to rely on doctors for information; and transnational and multidisciplinary professional practices are starting to emerge.

Along with these changes are new opportunities for professionals to act illegally or unethically. In this book, representatives from a number of professional organisations will speak about the nature of professional crime which is taking place at present, and how this will change in the future. The increasing complexity of our financial arrangements means we rely more and more on lawyers and accountants. This provides them with new opportunities to appropriate clients' funds other than in the best interest of the client. For example, one smaller client being advised to invest in a project being developed by a larger client. It need not be a risky project but the question should be is it the best for the smaller client or just acceptable with the side effect of making the bigger client happy.

Doctors are more entrepreneurial. They are more available than ever, but entrepreneurial medicine also creates the opportunity to act unethically for financial gain—for example to over-service.

The public service is less process- and rule-driven. That means that it is more flexible, but creates the opportunity for unethical conduct.

It is not just offences against criminal law which should concern us. In 1989 I raised the issue of drugs in the workplace. Anyone who has suffered the misfortune of a hangover will understand how debilitating it can be. Do lawyers after a boozy lunch settle for less on your behalf than they should? Does an accountant neglect an extra tax deduction you could claim? No one wants a hung-over or drug-affected doctor examining their critical blood tests.

The importance of professionals' jobs, and our reliance on them, means that they have just as great an obligation as a train driver or airline pilot to turn up for work ready to do their best for their clients. Needless to say, recent media reports of the use of cocaine in the legal profession are extremely concerning in this context, and because society rightly or wrongly expects highly paid experts to set an example.

Although members of the public now have a much greater willingness and ability to challenge the power of professionals, there remain problems in providing effective ways in which allegations of impropriety may be identified, reported and investigated. It is clear that we need new enforcement approaches to professional crime.

This book will also consider how crime within the professions can best be dealt with. The problems are significant. The use by professionals of new technologies, for example, has created particular problems for police and regulatory agencies in investigating cases of fraud and dishonesty, as the traditional trails of evidence can be disguised and manipulated with ease. In the future, as technology makes cross-border professional activity a reality, it may become necessary to reconsider the traditional geographical boundaries which govern the regulation of professional activities. Not only national, but also international regulatory measures will be needed as professionals, both new and old, explore the possibilities which the convergence of computing and communications technologies has brought.

The Commonwealth is acutely aware of the importance of the new criminal opportunities that are developing as a result of globalisation and advances in information and communications technology. Fraud is the major criminal offence committed against the Commonwealth. It is a crime that responds quickly to new opportunities. We are updating our fraud control policy, and we have recently introduced a Bill consolidating and updating the Commonwealth's theft and fraud offences.

However, developments to address crime in the professions will need to build on what is good about the professions. You will also be reading about the important role which professional education in ethics can have in preventing illegal and improper behaviour. Although self-regulation through the use of codes of practice can have an anti-competitive aspect, prevention of misconduct is far preferable to dealing with the problem once it has arisen. As a lawyer I am acutely aware of rivalries between the professions. In this book, we can see how professionals can put aside their rivalries to work on professional crime. The continuing role of professions in our society depends on it.

**Senator The Hon Amanda Vanstone**
**(Minister for Justice and Customs, Australia,**
**from October 1998 to January 2001)**

# PART I
# BACKGROUND

Chapter 1

# Crime in the Professions:
# An Introduction

Russell G. Smith

## Introduction

In recent times, the professions have been subject to a number of changes
and challenges. Many new occupations have sought and achieved professional
standing; competition policy has altered the way in which professionals are
required to behave toward other professionals and to members of the
community; new consumer-based regulatory structures have been established
to deal with complaints; professional work has lost some of its mystique due
to the routinisation of tasks and the increasing use of information technologies;
the service basis of professional work has been replaced by a largely
commercial one; and the boundaries between the professions have been
challenged through market forces and globalisation such that transnational
and multidisciplinary professional practices are now starting to emerge. In
all, these changes have given rise to what has been described as a 'crisis of
professionalism' (Hanlon 1999).

Each of these factors has influenced the way in which professionals carry
out their daily work. Each has also created opportunities for professionals to
engage in conduct which infringes ethical principles of good practice, specific
professional guidelines which govern practice within individual professions,
as well as the laws which apply throughout society. This book examines the
nature and extent of crime in the professions and discusses the many complex
issues which arise in attempting to prevent criminality and unprofessional
practice and to regulate professional practice in the most effective way.

The following chapters are based on papers presented at a conference
conducted by the Australian Institute of Criminology entitled *Crime in the
Professions* held at the University of Melbourne on 21 and 22 February 2000.
Representatives from a wide range of professional groups within the private

and public sectors attended along with others from some of the principal professional regulatory bodies throughout Australia.

This book is divided into four parts. The first seeks to define what is meant by professional and to identify which members of the community may be characterised as professionals. Later in this introductory chapter we shall see how many Australians in the labour force claim to be professionals and how the proportion of professionals in the labour force changed throughout the twentieth century. In chapter 2, Kenneth Hayne provides an analytic framework for defining crime in the professions and raises some challenges for those who believe that the topic deserves special attention. In chapter 3, John Western and his colleagues will present some of the findings of the *Professions in Australia Project* which has documented the attitudes of a sample of University graduates between the mid-1960s and today toward their professional careers and work.

Part two looks at the nature and extent of crime and misconduct committed by professionals by considering those who practice in three professional groups. Andrew Williams (chapter 4) describes the type of criminal and unprofessional activities engaged in by accountants, while Andrew Dix (chapter 5) and Leanne Raven (chapter 6) look at crime in two of the health care professions, medicine and nursing, respectively.

These chapters raise some common themes. It is agreed that criminal conduct is committed by only a very small minority of professionals, although poor standards of conduct arise much more often. The motivations behind professional crime are similar to the motivations which drive other similar types of crime, although professionals' abuse of their unique position of power often creates specific vulnerabilities. There are particular problems in ensuring that professional crime is reported to the authorities, whether by victims or by professional colleagues. Finally, there seems to be a proliferation of ways in which professionals are now regulated and a duplication of complaint-handing mechanisms.

Part three takes up some of these issues and looks specifically at how crime in the professions is dealt with. Margaret Coady (chapter 7) provides an examination of the role which codes of ethics play in shaping professional behaviour and in preventing crime, while Carla Day (chapter 8) provides an example of how one government department—the Department of Defence—developed and uses its fraud control policies to prevent crime. Tim Phillipps (chapter 9) then considers how consumers of financial services can best be protected from misleading and deceptive practices, while Beth Wilson (chapter 10) examines some key issues arising from the public adjudication of complaints against health care professionals. In chapter 11, Sitesh Bhojani describes ways in which to protect those who report professional crime in the public interest—so-called whistleblowers. Part four concludes with Peter Willis's (chapter 12) account of the history of attempts to prevent corrupt practices being engaged in by professionals.

The final part of the book examines issues which have arisen in regulating certain new professional groups and new types of illegality. Anne-Louise Carlton (chapter 13) presents a report on Victoria's unique initiative to regulate practitioners of Chinese medicine and the problems which have arisen in developing an appropriate statutory regulatory model. Graham Brooks (chapter 14) looks at recent changes which have taken place in the regulation of probation officers in England and Wales and how the Home Office's *National Standards* have restricted the professional autonomy of such officers. Chapter 15 then considers the opportunities for professional crime which the introduction of new technologies has provided. The discussion concludes with a call by Charles Sampford and Sophie Curzon Blencowe (chapter 16) for an integrated approach to be adopted to promote professional values and to avoid crime in the professions.

## Definition of Professionals and Professionalisation

Although the following two chapters will address in some detail the questions of how professionals may be defined and what professionalisation is, we should, nonetheless, begin by seeking to characterise professionals in order that we can understand the scope of the problem being addressed.

The concepts of professional and professionalisation have changed considerably over the preceding century. When Carr-Saunders and Wilson (1933) published their seminal work on the sociology of professions in the 1930s, the number of organised professional groups in society was already beginning to grow and they were able to identify some 30 groups of professionals. All, except nursing, were composed predominantly of men and the oldest professions, such as law and medicine, had established procedures for admission of new members and exclusion of those who were unable to attain the specified standards or who were found to have engaged in unprofessional conduct.

Sociologists examined the concept of professionalisation throughout the twentieth century with a variety of fundamental precepts being identified. Johnson (1972, p. 23) divides the definitions of professional into two types:

trait and functionalist approaches. The former seeks to list attributes which are said to represent the common core of professional occupations, whilst the latter seeks to distil those elements which have functional relevance for society as a whole.

Some of the traits of professionals which are generally agreed upon include: skill based on theoretical knowledge; the provision of training and education; testing the competence of members; organisation; adherence to a professional code of conduct; and altruistic service (Johnson 1972, p. 23; see also Boudon and Bourricaud 1989, pp. 278–80).

The latest Australian Standard Classification of Occupations published by the Australian Bureau of Statistics (1997) distinguishes between professionals and associate professionals. Professionals are defined, using a trait-type approach, as follows:

> Professionals perform analytical, conceptual and creative tasks through the application of theoretical knowledge and experience in the fields of science, engineering, business and information, health, education, social welfare and the arts. Most occupations in this group have a level of skill commensurate with a bachelor degree or higher qualification. In some instances relevant experience is required in addition to the formal qualification (1997, p. 103).

The tasks performed by associate professionals include:

> Conducting scientific tests and experiments; administering the operational activities of an office or financial institution; organising the operations of retail, hospitality and accommodation establishments; assisting health and welfare professionals in the provision of support and advice to clients; maintaining public order and safety; inspecting establishments to ensure conformity with government and industry standards; and coordinating sports training and participating in sporting events (1997, p. 229).

Table 1.1 shows the number of professionals and associate professionals recorded in the 1996 Australian population census.

The numbers of employed persons in Australia in some of the more widely-recognised groups of professionals and associate professionals for the various states and territories are set out in Table 1.2.

In the absence of agreement as to those traits which are fundamental to professional practice, theorists have examined the process of professionalisation in order to determine how professions develop and when they can be said to have achieved professional status. One example is that of Wilensky (1964, pp. 142–6) who describes the following 'natural history of

**Table 1.1     Professionals and associate professionals in the 1996 Australian population census**

|  | Male No. | Male % | Female No. | Female % | Total No. | Total % |
|---|---|---|---|---|---|---|
| Professionals | 641,072 | 48.9 | 668,394 | 51.0 | 1,309,466 | 100 |
| Associate professionals | 511,209 | 59.4 | 349,958 | 40.6 | 861,167 | 100 |
| Total | 1,152,281 | 53.1 | 1,018,352 | 46.9 | 2,170,633 | 100 |

*Source*: Australian Bureau of Statistics 1996

**Table 1.2     Numbers of selected professionals in Australian states and territories, 1996 ('000 employed persons)**

|  | NSW | Vic. | Qld | SA | WA | Tas. | NT | ACT | Aust. |
|---|---|---|---|---|---|---|---|---|---|
| *Professionals* | | | | | | | | | |
| Architects | 5.3 | 1.4 | 1.6 | 1.0 | 1.4 | 0.2 | 0.3 | 0.2 | 11.4 |
| Accountants | 43.2 | 30.4 | 11.6 | 5.9 | 14.4 | 1.1 | 0.7 | 2.2 | 109.5 |
| Computing professionals | 56.3 | 43.8 | 16.7 | 6.7 | 8.8 | 0.8 | 0.6 | 7.9 | 141.6 |
| Medical practitioners | 21.9 | 12.9 | 8.9 | 3.4 | 6.3 | 1.6 | 0.2 | 0.9 | 56.1 |
| Nursing professionals | 57.9 | 45.0 | 29.9 | 12.8 | 15.8 | 4.9 | 2.6 | 2.5 | 171.4 |
| Dental practitioners | 1.8 | 1.6 | 1.0 | 0.5 | 0.7 | 0.3 | 0.1 | 0.1 | 6.1 |
| Veterinarians | 1.2 | 0.3 | 1.0 | 0.6 | 0.4 | 0.2 | 0.0 | 0.0 | 3.7 |
| School teachers | 92.8 | 64.9 | 47.8 | 22.8 | 27.6 | 9.0 | 3.0 | 4.1 | 272.0 |
| Social workers | 3.1 | 2.9 | 0.6 | 1.6 | 0.6 | 0.2 | 0.0 | 0.4 | 9.4 |
| Ministers of religion | 5.5 | 2.0 | 1.5 | 1.4 | 1.5 | 0.5 | 0.2 | 0.5 | 13.1 |
| Legal professionals | 21.2 | 13.3 | 5.2 | 2.0 | 1.9 | 0.7 | 0.1 | 1.6 | 46.0 |
| Journalists | 10.3 | 2.8 | 2.2 | 1.0 | 0.9 | 0.7 | 0.2 | 1.2 | 19.3 |
| *Associate professionals* | | | | | | | | | |
| Financial dealers | 15.8 | 6.5 | 3.9 | 2.6 | 4.9 | 0.5 | 0.1 | 0.5 | 34.8 |
| Chefs | 17.1 | 12.7 | 7.3 | 1.6 | 2.4 | 0.7 | 0.2 | 1.3 | 43.3 |
| Enrolled nurses | 6.5 | 6.6 | 7.1 | 4.3 | 2.7 | 0.6 | 0.1 | 0.5 | 28.4 |
| Police officers | 15.4 | 9.1 | 7.1 | 4.5 | 6.1 | 1.0 | 1.0 | 0.5 | 44.7 |

*Source*: Derived from Australian Bureau of Statistics (1996) *Labour Force Survey Data*

professionalisation': the emergence of a full-time occupation; the establishment of a training school; the founding of a professional association; political agitation directed towards the protection of the association by law; and the adoption of a formal code.

In the context of health care, medicine and dentistry proceeded through these stages a long time ago, whilst nursing has only recently completed its process of professionalisation (Smith 1999b). As we shall see in chapter 13, alternative health care still remains at an early stage in its professional development, at least in Western countries.

Sociologists who favour the functionalist approach have tended to examine professionalisation in terms of its power relationships between professional and client and the purposes for which professional status are sought. Professionalism can also be seen in terms of institutionalised forms of control. In the words of Johnson (1972, p. 45), 'a profession is not, then, an occupation, but a means of controlling an occupation'.

Because professions maintain a specialised knowledge base and are generally self-regulatory, they possess high social standing which is reflected in relatively high levels of income, wealth, power and prestige. This has made the process of professionalisation attractive for other occupations which have taken on the indicia of the long-standing professions in order to enhance their own status (Johnson 1995). The achievement of professional standing was not easily won, however. In the case of nursing, for example, even the achievement of having education based in universities rather than in hospital nursing schools took 50 years of concerted effort by a group of determined women (see Smith 1999b).

Using conventional trait-type definitions of professional, the percentage of professionals in the workforce in Britain increased steadily throughout the last century: four per cent in 1900, to eight per cent in 1950, to 13 per cent in 1966. It was predicted that by 2000, 25 per cent of the workforce would be professionals (Schön 1983, p. 7).

Comparable figures for Australia are 3.5 per cent in 1911, 5.9 per cent in 1947, 9.6 per cent in 1966 and ten per cent in 1976 (Anderson and Western 1976, p. 44). In 1991, professionals and associate professionals made up 22.4 per cent of the total employed labour force. Using the most recent labour force data in Australia, employed professionals made up 17.1 per cent of the total labour force while associate professionals made up 11.3 per cent. Together they comprised 28.4 per cent of the 8.4 million Australians aged 15 years and over in the employed labour force in 1996 (Australian Bureau of Statistics 1996).

In the early years of last century, the conventional wisdom concerning professionalisation was beginning to be questioned with advocates for change such as George Bernard Shaw waging a concerted campaign against the established organisations and professional bodies such as the General Medical Council and British Medical Association (Shaw 1931). More recently, Illich in the 1970s engaged in the wholesale debunking of professional claims to special expertise observing that 'professional cartels are now as brittle as the French clergy in the age of Voltaire' (Illich 1977, p. 38; see also Schön's (1983) account of the crisis of confidence in professional knowledge).

These, and other critics, maintain that professionalism has not always been beneficial to society. Some of its negative effects have been a reduction in competition in the workplace, a reduction in productivity and the adoption of an unnecessarily defensive attitude to criticism or challenge (Boudon and Bourricaud 1989, pp. 278–80).

Invariably the achievement of professional standing requires educational standards to be developed or improved and regulatory mechanisms imposed in order for standards to be set and maintained. At the turn of the twenty-first century, there exists a vast body of professionals who are organised in a myriad of associations, and who are regulated by innumerable agencies. In one sense, professionalisation is everywhere and the activities of professionals over-regulated by both public and private-sector bodies. This idea is not, however, new. Over 30 years ago, Wilensky (1964, p. 143) argued that all occupations were being professionalised but that few would achieve the level of authority which the established professions commanded at the time.

More recently, however, a trend of 'deprofessionalisation' has taken place worldwide fuelled by international initiatives towards free trade, consumer and commercial pressures, and pressures from within professions themselves for increased competition (Paterson 1996, pp. 146–8). Although the recognition of the negative aspects of professionalism has been beneficial in a number of respects, it is a matter of concern that standards of conduct may decline if the professional ideal is eroded too far. In the words of Boon and Levin (1999, p. 67):

> Faced with a considerable reduction in privilege and public trust, professionals can either retreat to the view that their practice is purely a business or they can renew their professional commitments and seek new ways of realising the professional ideal.

## The Changing Nature of Professional Practice

Professional practice has altered considerably in recent years, largely brought about through changes in social and economic conditions in Western democracies (Hanlon 1998). Mention has already been made of the crisis of professionalism, the emergence of the commercialised professional, and the deprofessionalisation of some aspects of practice in recent years. Four important developments, however, have had a profound influence on the nature of professional practice: the introduction of competition policy; the breaking down of barriers between the professions; globalisation; and the use of information technologies in professional work. Each has implications for the nature of crime in the professions in the years to come.

*Competition Policy*

During the 1970s and 1980s, governments throughout the world sought to improve the economy by stimulating competition in the marketplace. This was intended to have a variety of consequences including lower prices for consumers and improvements in the range of goods and services which were available.

In Australia the government introduced a National Competition Policy in 1995 which implemented the recommendations of the *National Competition Policy Review* (Hilmer 1993). In 1995, the Council of Australian Governments agreed to implement the recommendations of the Review and complementary legislation was enacted to give effect to the policy.

From 21 July 1996, the provisions of the *Trade Practices Act 1974* (Cth) were made applicable to individuals, partnerships and unincorporated associations as well as to corporations. This had the effect of making professionals subject to the prohibitions against various restrictive trade practices set out in Part IV of the Act as well as the prohibitions against unfair practices set out in Part V of the Act. For example, individual practitioners now need to take care when making representations about matters such as professional qualifications, experience and fees charged for services. Similarly, restrictive trade practices such as exclusive dealing, price fixing and misuse of market power must be avoided (see Kamvounias 1999).

Under competition policy guidelines, regulatory proposals such as occupational registration that have the effect of limiting the number of persons engaged in an occupation and preventing other people from engaging in certain activities of that occupation are deemed to be restrictions on competition unless specifically exempted. Any new legislation which is enacted must comply with competition policy unless it can be established that the benefits of the restriction to the community as a whole outweigh the costs and that the objectives of the legislation can only be achieved by restricting competition.

The policy did not, however, affect professional licensing arrangements although restrictions on practice imposed by the rules of professional bodies were prohibited unless a new public benefit could be demonstrated. One immediate effect of this was to lessen professional prohibitions against advertising and other restrictive practices, particularly in the legal profession (see Parker 1997). Most professional legislation continues, however, to prohibit unregistered persons from adopting professional titles, despite this having a potentially anti-competitive effect (see Peck 1999).

In 1995, the Industry Commission in Australia estimated that the introduction of competition reforms in the legal profession would result in a 50 per cent reduction in conveyancing costs due to the removal of the profession's monopoly over conveyancing work, and a 13 per cent reduction in barristers' fees through the removal of advertising restrictions (Tonking 1995, p. 42). In fact, a comparison of conveyancing fees between 1994 and 1996 conducted by the Justice Research Centre found that the mean professional fees charged by small law firms decreased in real terms by approximately 17 per cent because of increased competition (Baker 1996).

Reduction in cost was not the only consequence of the introduction of competition policy (see Pascoe 1994). In the legal profession, for example, the removal of solicitors' monopoly over conveyancing meant that some small practices had to become more entrepreneurial and seek other avenues of practice in order to survive. In Britain, solicitors sought and gained extended rights of audience in the higher courts in order to extend their practice following the loss of conveyancing work in the 1980s (Hanlon 1998, p. 94). In medicine in Australia, it has been argued that 'the opening up of medicine to commercial interests and the promotion of economic competition have undermined fundamental values and seriously threaten patient care' (Komesaroff 1999, p. 266). In nursing, competition reforms in the United States and the United Kingdom were said to have changed the nature of the delivery of health care resulting in the number of nursing practitioners being reduced and nursing being further deprofessionalised (Kermode, Brown and Emmanuel 1995).

*Multidisciplinary Practice*

Another important change in the professions which arose as a consequence of competition policy reforms was the destruction of strict interdisciplinary boundaries which existed between different professional groups. The legal profession, for example, has seen the establishment of multidisciplinary practices (MDPs) with other business professionals such as financial advisers, real estate agents, valuers and accountants (see Boon and Levin 1999, pp. 78–86; Gray 1999, p. 88). Although originally, the accounting profession grew out of specialist legal practice (Hanlon 1998), it was for many years unethical for solicitors to enter into unincorporated associations with other professionals. Recently, however, this rule has been relaxed and it is now permissible for solicitors to work within accountancy practices as long as separate accounting procedures are maintained in respect of clients' funds. This obviously has considerable benefits for small rural communities which are unable to support separate practices for solicitors and accountants (see Brown 1999).

The establishment of MDPs has, however, created the situation in which different professionals working within the same organisation may be subject to different ethical rules governing their practice. There are also complex issues to do with the provision of professional indemnity insurance amongst different professionals working within a MDP (see Gray 1999), ensuring that services are only provided by professionals qualified in the appropriate discipline, and that conflicts of interest do not arise (Gawler 1999).

The need exists, therefore, for some harmonisation of codes of practice between professions which enter into MDPs, particularly if they are to have common accounting procedures, have joint committees of management, seek outside capital and have joint incorporation (Boon and Levin 1999, p. 85; Baxt 1994, p. 24).

*Globalisation and Mutual Recognition*

Changing economic conditions, increased competition, international trade and the dependence upon information technologies have resulted in the globalisation of a number of aspects of professional practice. Many professionals now practise internationally in multinational law firms and transnational accountancy and consulting practices. Business professionals now offer advice by telephone or electronic mail and health care is able to be delivered electronically through the use of telemedicine procedures which make use of online video conferencing technologies. In the legal profession, for example, six Australian law firms now practice in China, with China being Australia's third-largest overseas legal services market after the United States and the United Kingdom (Williams 1999, p. 63). International mobility in the medical and academic worlds is also well established.

The principal means by which cross-border professional practice has been regulated is through the mutual recognition of qualifications and registration. In Europe, the Treaty of Rome of 1960 required the free movement of people between Member States and the European Court of Justice has confirmed the right of any professional person who is a national of one Member State to set up in practice in another Member State or to provide a service there from his or her own Member State. Full professional mutual recognition has not, however, been achieved in the European Union with only a small number of professions having achieved mutuality in full or in part (de Crayencour 1982).

In Australia, mutual recognition of professional qualifications has been necessary because of Australia's federal constitutional system. The legislatures of each state and territory have power to make laws for the peace, order and good government of their own state or territory and each state and territory has exercised these powers to establish registration and disciplinary systems in respect of their own professionals.

Under the Commonwealth's *Constitution* (s. 51, pl. xxxvii), parliaments of the states and territories are able to refer matters to the Commonwealth Parliament for it to enact legislation upon, in which case the Commonwealth law shall override any state or territory law to the extent of any inconsistency (s. 109, *Constitution* (Cth)). The use of this reference power has already been used in order to achieve consistency between the laws in the various states and territories in relation to cross-border practice of various professionals.

At the Special Premiers' Conference in Brisbane in October 1990, the various heads of government agreed to establish a system of mutual recognition of standards in order to remove artificial barriers to interstate trade in goods and the mobility of labour caused by regulatory differences amongst the various Australian states and territories.

A consultation process was undertaken in 1991 and agreement was reached as to the creation of a system whereby various professionals, registered in one jurisdiction could have their registration recognised by each of the other jurisdictions. An innovative legislative mechanism was used to achieve the aim of mutual recognition which involved each of the states and territories requesting the Commonwealth to pass a single Act which, once enacted by the Commonwealth Parliament, would override any inconsistent legislation in the states and territories. Each state and territory then formally adopted the Commonwealth regulatory regime by enacting local legislation which incorporated the Commonwealth provisions. Thus, each state and territory was able to achieve uniformity of legislation (see Commonwealth of Australia, *Parliamentary Debates, House of Representatives*, 3 November 1992, vol. 186, pp. 2432–5, *per* Mr Free).

The mutual recognition legislation in each jurisdiction now adopts the provisions of the *Mutual Recognition Act 1992* (Cth) which enables the registration of professionals in one jurisdiction to be recognised by each other jurisdiction (*Mutual Recognition (Australian Capital Territory) Act 1992* (ACT), *Mutual Recognition (Northern Territory) Act 1992* (NT), *Mutual Recognition (New South Wales) Act 1992* (NSW), *Mutual Recognition (Queensland) Act 1992* (Qld), *Mutual Recognition (South Australia) Act 1993* (SA), *Mutual Recognition (Tasmania) Act 1993* (Tas.), *Mutual Recognition (Victoria) Act 1993* (Vic.), *Mutual Recognition (Western Australia) Act 1995* (WA)). In order to be able to practise in another jurisdiction, practitioners must notify the registration board in the new jurisdiction, provide evidence of current registration and pay the prescribed fee. The practitioner then becomes subject to the legislative regime which applies in the new jurisdiction, including its professional conduct controls.

If a practitioner's registration is subject to conditions or restrictions in the original jurisdiction, then any subsequent registration in another jurisdiction will be subject to the same conditions or restrictions. Suspension or cancellation of registration in one jurisdiction also suspends or cancels registration in the other jurisdiction. The effectiveness of this system is obviously dependent upon immediate notification of any orders which affect a practitioner's registration from one jurisdiction to another.

Although the mutual recognition scheme achieves its objective of allowing the mobility of practitioners between jurisdictions, in order for them to be able to practise in every jurisdiction, it is necessary to apply separately to each registration board, comply with the formal requirements and pay appropriate fees. This, in practice, is both time-consuming and expensive.

## *The Impact of Information Technologies*

Because the professions rely extensively on the acquisition and dissemination of information, the use of computers and communications technologies has had a profound effect on the way in which professionals carry out their work. Some effects have been beneficial, while others have created problems for professional people and those in the community with whom they interact. The use of information technologies could, therefore, be said both to enhance and to detract from professionalism. Illich (1977) noted some time ago that technological progress results in specially trained personnel being needed to use more complex forms of technology. At the same time, new technologies are often specifically designed so as to be useable by everyone regardless of technical expertise.

The Internet, for example, albeit maintained by highly trained information technology professionals, now permits individuals to obtain health information which they may use to speak with doctors in what is arguably a more informed way than in the past (see, for example, <www.mediconsult.com/> and <www.healthanswers.com/>). Similarly, litigants now approach solicitors armed with the latest legal precedent—which might or might not be relevant to their case. This technology has, accordingly, empowered consumers of professional services, and at the same time disempowered professional advisers.

Perhaps the greatest challenge for professionals in the twenty-first century lies in their ability to deal with the exponential increase in information which technology has made available. Although this has many benefits, it has also made the task of finding relevant information and assimilating it much more difficult. For example, lawyers now have access to databases which contain most legislation, reported and unreported judicial decisions, and academic commentaries from around the world. Although powerful digital searching capabilities may facilitate the task of finding specific information, the challenge remains in making use of relevant material in an efficient and productive way. Information overload has, accordingly, resulted in considerable demands being placed on professionals.

This will lead, inevitably, to a change in the nature of professional practice. In medicine, for example, it has been suggested that technological developments will change the nature of the traditional doctor–patient relationship:

> The doctor's role will become more advisory, analytic and interventionist. Doctors will need to be experts in assessing information from many different sources and in clinical reasoning, particularly for patients requiring more than a guidelines-and-pathways approach to care (Yellowlees and Brooks 1999, p. 524).

In addition, the use of information technologies, especially in legal and accounting practices, has led to much work becoming routinised. This has enabled less qualified staff to carry out the bulk of tasks leaving fully qualified practitioners time in which to supervise that work and to deal with more complicated problems which may arise. Potentially this is beneficial and could result in costs being reduced, such as has occurred with conveyancing work. The concern is, however, that inadequately qualified staff may be doing work beyond their level of training and expertise. As Boon and Levin (1999, pp. 86–7) observe:

> The capacity to carry out work more quickly reduces the economic return from work; more has to be done for the same return. Additionally, information technology has the potential further to unbalance the relationship between the technical dimension of legal practice and the element of indeterminancy or discretion in professional judgment.

Health care providers have also realised the enormous potential benefits which modern communications technology has for interacting with colleagues and treating patients. The use of computers and telecommunications networks in health care, or what is known as 'telemedicine' or 'telecare' has the potential to be life-saving, especially in remote areas of the globe where consultations may be carried out and treatment provided even where the practitioner and patient are incapable of being present together at the same time and place (Smith 1998).

Electronic communications technologies, such as the Internet, are also enabling consumers of professional services to be better informed about matters which previously lay within the province of professional advisers. Members of the public are now able to conduct their own share dealings online and obtain advice about legal matters. One of the largest English firms of solicitors now provides online information and advice about local laws, regulations and other details to global investment banks operating in Europe, the United Kingdom and Asia for a yearly fee of up to £125,000 for unlimited access to the service (Gray 1999, p. 89).

Patients are also able to locate health information and even buy alleged cures for many health problems electronically. Advice on building your own home is also available online, although few would contemplate constructing a railway bridge on the basis of information obtained from the Internet. This has not only reduced the power and control which professionals once maintained over less qualified people, but has also created a variety of problems for consumers who rely on electronic information in the absence of professional advice.

In addition, the business aspects of professional practice have been transformed through the use of computers. Most professionals now record their client attendances on electronic databases and, in the case of work paid for out of government funds, claims are able to be made electronically and payments received by way of electronic funds transfer direct to the provider's bank account. The collection of revenue from professionals has also been greatly facilitated through the use of computers, and it may become obligatory for them to deal with revenue departments electronically in order to expedite the processing of claims and to facilitate computerised data-matching for risk management purposes. In Australia, for example, a system for the collection of goods and services tax (GST) which commenced operation on 1 July 2000, requires all taxpayers to communicate electronically with the tax office if their annual turnover exceeds A$20 million. Large legal, accounting and health care practices would all come within such a threshold. If electronic GST returns are given they must be in a form approved by the tax office and secured by an electronic signature (ss. 31–25, *A New Tax System (Goods and Services Tax) Act 1999* (Cth)).

Computers are also of critical importance in the financial side of the provision of health care. The Health Insurance Commission, for example, makes wide use of computers in processing health care claims. Claims are made and payments processed through a national network of 226 Medicare Customer Service Centres located throughout Australia and connected online to a central computer at the HIC's central office in the Australian Capital Territory (ACT). During 1997–98 more then 500 million raw service transactions were processed by this network. Over 24 per cent of Medicare claims in Australia are made electronically while some 4,800 pharmacies send over 6,000 computer disks to the Commission each month relating to pharmaceutical benefits claims. The largest volume of claims come from providers who direct-bill the HIC. In 1997–98, approximately 72 per cent of services were direct-billed either through the submission of paper claim forms or electronically using the HIC's 'Medclaims' system following which payment is made either by cheque or by electronic funds transfer direct to the provider's bank account. Some providers also make use of an EFTPOS type of device in order to transmit information to the HIC with payments being able to be made by credit card. At the beginning of June 1998, 2,616 sites were transmitting claims electronically to the HIC accounting for 42 per cent of direct-bill claims (Health Insurance Commission 1998).

An indication of the use of information technologies by three groups of professionals is provided in the most recent survey undertaken as part of the *Professions in Australia Project* (Davies and Makkai 2000).[1] This study began in 1965 when 652 first-year engineering students and 645 law students were interviewed in various universities throughout Australia. In 1967, interviews were conducted with 572 first-year medical students and 1,275 students of teaching. Over the next 30 years, participants were contacted at various points of their careers, the last survey being conducted in 1998. Approximately 30 per cent of the original first-year class had failed to complete their degrees and by 1998, 203 engineering, 191 law and 248 medicine graduates returned completed questionnaires. This final survey included a number of questions concerning their use of information technologies.

Amongst the results it was found that of the 642 respondents from the three professional groups,[2] 71.2 per cent reported using information technology at work (94.1 per cent of engineering, 70.0 per cent of law and 53.1 per cent of medicine graduates). Using word processing for work-related activities either 'all the time' or 'daily' was reported by 68.5 per cent. Law and engineering graduates reported using word processing for work much more frequently than did graduates of medicine. Sixty-eight per cent of all respondents reported using the Internet for work, most of those using it more than once a week. Almost three-quarters of respondents reported using email, with 22.6 per cent using it 'all the time' (41.6 per cent of engineering, 19.6 per cent of law and 9.3 per cent of medicine graduates).

Graduates of medicine also reported relatively frequent use of information technologies in relation to other specific aspects of their practices. Of the more than 240 graduates of medicine who responded, 57 per cent employed frontdesk billing systems; 28.4 per cent used electronic file transfer systems; 26.7 per cent reported using script writing packages; 22.4 per cent made claims electronically to the Health Insurance Commission; and 21.2 per cent used telemedicine technologies.

Each year surveys have also been undertaken of legal practitioners in New South Wales and Victoria. In a 1998 survey conducted of Victorian practitioners, 2,684 responses were obtained out of 8,500 surveys distributed by the Law Institute of Victoria (Kriegler 1999). Sixty-three per cent of respondents were male with the majority aged in the category 30 to 49 years (57 per cent). Forty-four per cent of respondents indicated that they had access to the Internet on their desks, 57 per cent had Internet access elsewhere in their office and 35 per cent at home. Forty-eight per cent of respondents used the Internet for legal research, 57 per cent for electronic mail and 37 per cent for web browsing. Some 74 per cent of respondents were aware of the Law Institute of Victoria's web site (Kriegler 1999, p. 55).

**The Continuum of Deviant Conduct**

The vast majority of professional people carry out their work carefully, conscientiously and in accordance with high standards. In most professions, the proportion of criminal and deviant conduct reported to the authorities is extraordinarily low. In medicine, for example, we shall see in chapter 5 that approximately 1,000 complaints are made to the New South Wales Medical Board each year which regulates the conduct of approximately 22,000 registered medical practitioners in that state (4.5 per cent).

Even smaller proportions of professionals are prosecuted before the criminal courts, although when they are, proceedings invariably attract high levels of publicity (see, for example, the case of Dr Harold Shipman: Carter, H. 2000).

Of course, not every unprofessional or illegal act is reported to the authorities and the 'dark figure' of unreported matters is as problematic in this, as in other crime contexts. Arguably, because of the trust and respect which professionals command, the problem of unreported crime and misconduct is even greater than for non-professionals.

Crime and deviant conduct exists on a continuum which extends from the most serious instances involving criminal homicide or fraud through less serious cases which attract professional disciplinary sanctions such as suspension of registration, to less serious instances of incompetent and unskilled conduct which may require that the practitioner undergo some form of remedial education. At the lowest end of the continuum are cases of rudeness and laziness which may result in complaints being made but would generally not lead to serious sanctions being imposed.

There is also a range of instances of professional deviance which may be categorised as health-related matters in which the professional person's work is affected through addiction to alcohol or drugs, or is caused through mental illness. Some groups of professionals seem to be particularly susceptible to such problems and have established mechanisms to deal with it. In Victoria, for example, the Medical Practitioners Board received notifications of 170 impaired practitioners between 1983 and 1997. Of these, 105 practitioners had a psychiatric disorder, 73 had a drug use disorder, 35 had an alcohol use disorder and 13 had a physical disorder (non-exclusive categories) (see Wijesinghe and Dunne 1999). Where alcohol and drug abuse are involved, the possibility of the practitioner breaking the law is high and involvement with the criminal justice system may result in the practitioner coming to the attention of the registration authorities.

The various approaches to professional regulation must, therefore, be considered in the context of the wide range of professional deviance which exists. Arguably, considerable flexibility is needed in applying formal professional controls to deal with each form of deviant conduct as it lies on the continuum of seriousness.

## Current Systems of Formal Professional Control

In Australia over the last 20 years, the organisation of many professions has been subject to extensive inquiry and reform. At present, professional conduct is governed by a plurality of controls which may be both internal or external to the profession in question. The rules to which professionals are required to adhere are to be found in civil laws, criminal laws and the codes of conduct which statutory professional bodies administer. In addition, professional behaviour is subject to investigation by a variety of consumer-oriented statutory bodies such as ombudsmen and complaints commissions which generally operate in relation to specific professional groups. As such, professional conduct may be scrutinised from a plethora of perspectives.

### Civil Action

Redress through the civil law requires that a particular legal relationship exist between the professional person and the consumer of the service. This may have been created through the parties having entered into a contract, or through a duty of care having been created out of the professional relationship. Professionals who have breached their contractual obligations or failed to discharge their duty of care may be sued for breach of contract or in negligence (respectively). The law of trespass may also be relied upon in various circumstances such as where an assault has occurred or where property has been wrongfully taken from the client or detained against the client's wishes.

Civil action provides a financial sum to successful claimants which aims to place them in the same position they would have been in had the wrongful act not taken place. Normally, an award of damages is aimed at compensation rather than punishment although in rare instances exemplary or punitive damages may be awarded which aim to make an example of the defendant with a view to deterring similar conduct in the future (Collis 1996). Damages are generally assessed by a jury which hears evidence presented by professional experts for both the plaintiff and the defendant in an adversarial setting.

Where death has occurred, health care professionals may be required to give evidence before a coronial inquiry, the outcome of which may be that the professional be charged with a criminal offence or be subject to other civil proceedings.

Professionals who are employed in the military services may also be subject to military law and be required to undergo court martial proceedings if they have acted illegally or in breach of military codes of practice. In the past, adverse findings before military tribunals were automatically referred to registration authorities for investigation of the professional conduct of the individual (Smith 1994).

*Criminal Action*

Professionals are also required to comply with the criminal law and may find themselves facing prosecution for theft, dishonesty, sexual assault, murder or any one of a range of statutory offences (see Smith 1994 for examples of the range of criminal offences which registered medical practitioners in Britain have committed throughout the last 140 years).

In certain jurisdictions of the United States, new offences have been enacted which make sexual contact in professional relationships criminal (see Borruso 1991; Kane 1995). These include situations which would not otherwise be criminal under existing laws of sexual assault and are primarily directed at therapeutic relationships in which there is a power imbalance.

Criminal proceedings aim at punishing the offender in the retributive sense, denouncing the conduct in question and preventing further offending by deterring the individual from engaging in similar conduct in the future while deterring others in the community from offending by making an example of the individual in question. Guilt is determined by a jury in serious cases and statutory criminal compensation may be awarded in certain circumstances.

The penalties which are available to a judge in sentencing an offender include imprisonment, fines, community-based orders and various forms of conditional and supervised release. The extent to which such sanctions are appropriate and effective in deterring unprofessional conduct by so-called white-collar offenders is hotly debated (for example, Tillman and Pontell 1992) and many have argued that more appropriate sanctions should be used such as adverse publicity, financial penalties or further compulsory training in ethics and professional conduct.

Professional legislation generally creates offences for persons who are not registered to practise or who hold themselves out as being registered, provide professional services without being registered, or recover fees or reward for the provision of professional services. Offences are also created in some jurisdictions for persons who are not registered using certain qualifications or titles without authority.

Those who have had their professional status withdrawn, or who have never been properly registered to practise, may be prosecuted for unregistered practice in a number of professions. This area of liability is of particular relevance to practice using information technologies where professionals engage in cross-border practice but do not obtain registration in the appropriate jurisdiction.

*Disciplinary Action*

Professional legislation establishes a system of registration for professionals primarily designed to protect members of the public from unregistered and unqualified practitioners. Those who have attained specified educational standards are eligible for registration which entitles them to engage in specified forms of practice within the geographical confines of the registering authority. Legislative standards of conduct are specified and procedures established for dealing with instances of unprofessional conduct committed, once again, within jurisdictional boundaries.

Although most health care providers now belong to a statutorily recognised profession, some alternative medicine practitioners are not covered by existing registration authorities and thus are not subject to any professional disciplinary controls. Where misconduct occurs in such situations, the patient will only have recourse to criminal and civil action or in some cases to conciliation offered by some Health Complaints Commissioners (see below).

Registration bodies are set up to protect members of the public by providing for the registration of qualified practitioners (see, for example, *Medical Practice Act 1994* (Vic.), s. 1(a)). Boards are under a legal duty to investigate complaints that are made and where allegations are proved, the registration of the practitioner may be restricted in some way or removed. Disciplinary action is not intended to be punitive in the retributive sense, but rather is designed to ensure that acceptable standards of practice are maintained in the profession (see Smith 1994, pp. 55–8). The one exception to this is Boards with jurisdiction to impose monetary penalties or fines which are exclusively intended to be punitive and to act as a deterrent (for example, *Medical Practice Act 1994* (Vic.), s. 50(2) (f)).

Registration Boards are predominantly composed of senior, experienced members of the profession in question, although in recent years the proportion of so-called 'lay members' is increasing substantially. Most Medical Boards now have 25 per cent of their membership non-medically qualified (Smith 1994, pp. 80–2). Formal disciplinary proceedings are now usually open to the public and they are conducted adversarially and with legal representation.

Those who belong to a statutorily regulated profession are required to obey not only laws which apply in the community generally, but also the rules of professional behaviour which are created within the profession in question. Failure to behave professionally may result in the practitioner's registration being withdrawn or restricted either permanently or for a specified period. The practitioner would then be unable to engage in certain specified activities such as being able to charge a fee for work performed, claim to be a registered practitioner or carry out certain activities such as prescribing specified drugs or holding clients' moneys in trust.

Some registration authorities also require practitioners to undergo counselling or further education in order to remedy any deficiencies in their professional skills. The effect of disciplinary action may also be to declare standards of acceptable conduct for the rest of the profession although this is obviously dependent upon the extent to which the decisions in disciplinary cases are widely disseminated to all registered practitioners (Smith 1993).

Systems of professional registration or licensure are invariably restricted territorially in that the registration body only has jurisdiction over those practitioners who are registered with it and/or who practise within a specified geographical area. This gives rise to problems where practitioners engage in cross-border practice, either between different states and territories or internationally as they would be required to be registered in every location where the work is performed. Already this is becoming problematic for a number of professions. In the case of architecture in Australia, for example, it has been estimated that 22 per cent of architectural fees come from services delivered offshore (Peck 1999). In the case of work carried out through the use of telecommunications technologies, this creates various problems of definition and interpretation as we shall see.

The issue of multistate registration raises fundamental questions not only about the role of a modern registration authority but also of states' rights and federal–state relations (see Painter 1998). In the case of health care professionals, the fact that the technology is innately disrespectful of conventional geopolitical boundaries will test long-held and cherished assumptions about acceptable patterns of health care delivery and the regulation of this delivery (see Milstein 1999, p. 561).

*Consumer Complaints Systems*

In recent years many professionals have been made more accountable through the introduction of independent complaint-handling authorities. These bodies operate as a form of coerced self-regulation or what Johnson (1972) has called 'mediated professionalism'. In Britain, the *Court and Legal Services Act 1990* (Eng.) created the post of the Legal Services Ombudsman to oversee the professional behaviour of lawyers (Hanlon 1998, p. 94). Similar reforms occurred in Australia. In Victoria, for example, the legal profession was subject to substantial reform with the introduction of the *Legal Practice Act 1996* (Vic.) which ended its monopoly over the regulation of the profession. Amongst other reforms, the legislation introduced a Legal Practice Board, Legal Ombudsman and Legal Professional Tribunal to regulate the activities of legal practitioners. The legislation made the Law Institute of Victoria a Recognised Professional Association and also made membership voluntary. In New South Wales, the Office of the Legal Services Commissioner also made complaint-handling substantially more consumer-oriented (see Parker 1997, p. 16).

In relation to health care, all jurisdictions in Australia have Health Complaints Commissioners whose functions include the resolution of disputes between health providers and health users arising out of the provision of health services. Commissioners are required to investigate complaints and may resolve them by conciliation which simply means by encouraging a settlement of the complaint by holding informal discussions with the health provider and the health user. Conciliators often do not have training in the profession in question, although they may be professional and legally qualified conciliators. Where necessary, they will seek expert assistance from relevant trained professionals.

Complaints can be resolved by extracting an explanation and apology from the practitioner or by the practitioner's defence organisation paying a sum of money to the complainant. If conciliation fails, the Commissioner may refer the complaint to a Registration Board for disciplinary action.

*The Limitations of Existing Regulatory Approaches*

A number of problems arise out of the current regulatory environment for professionals in Australia. First, not all professionals are subject to the same level of accountability as others and some may not be subject to formal disciplinary controls at all. On the other hand, there is a proliferation of investigatory agencies to deal with instances of unprofessional behaviour which, although having different roles, still results in considerable wastage of resources and delay in investigating and adjudicating any given complaint.

Second, the current regulatory systems are generally confined within geographical jurisdictions, resulting in difficulties of investigation of unprofessional and criminal conduct which crosses state and territory borders—not to mention international jurisdictional boundaries. At present the legal rules which govern geographical jurisdiction of the criminal courts are complex and generally unsatisfactory to deal with many crimes carried out electronically. Hopefully, the reforms suggested by the Commonwealth of Australia's Model Criminal Code Officers Committee of the Standing Committee of Attorneys-General (2000) will solve many of the problems and provide clearer rules for the criminal courts to follow in deciding where online cross-border offences are to be dealt with. Similar reforms, however, are needed for each of the other regulatory systems which deal with the activities of professionals in the digital age.

Third, a range of standards exist with respect to the investigation and proof of allegations of unprofessional conduct in different professions and in different jurisdictions resulting in some practitioners being treated more leniently, or harshly, than others in comparable circumstances. Differences exist between jurisdictions with respect to the composition of tribunals, evidentiary standards, openness of proceedings, and range and use of sanctions, with the result that some professionals are judged according to divergent standards. This means, for example, that a practitioner who has been found not guilty of unprofessional conduct in one state may, possibly, be found guilty of unprofessional conduct if dealt with for the same conduct in another state, whilst a practitioner whose registration has been cancelled in one state may, if dealt with for the same conduct in another state, only have his or her registration suspended. This lack of uniformity weighs heavily against the current state and territory-based system of professional regulation.

The result, then, is that professionals are subject to a wide range of regulatory controls which are highly idiosyncratic in nature depending upon the nature of the profession and the jurisdiction in question. This has the effect of making some professionals overly accountable whilst others remain under-accountable.

## Conclusions

In this introductory chapter we have seen how the professions and professional practices have changed in recent times. On the one hand, the proportion of professionals in the labour force has increased greatly, while on the other hand there has been a trend towards removing some of the regulatory controls which previously governed professional work. The changing nature of professional practice and its regulation has not, however, prevented a number of occupational groups from seeking to achieve professional standing for themselves.

We have also witnessed changes in the way in which criminal and unprofessional conduct is dealt with. Criticism of professional monopolies and self-regulatory practices have led to the establishment of new controls which have removed some of the power of the traditional professions such as the law and medicine. The creation of external forms of control which arose out of the consumer protection movement has been the most dramatic change in this regard and is likely to continue to be of importance in the years to come.

Our discussion also considers how existing controls on professional behaviour are able to deal with the new ways in which professionals behave, particularly those which entail the use of computing and communications technologies which have not only created new ways in which professional practice takes place but brought new opportunities for illegal and unprofessional conduct to occur.

Although the focus of the following chapters is on the worst forms of professional misconduct which involve infringements of the criminal law, many of the issues are relevant to the regulation of less serious forms of professional deviance as well. Having simple and appropriate systems in place is, arguably, the best way in which to identify and to control all forms of professional deviance, from the least to the most serious forms of illegality. In the twenty-first century, however, it will no longer be acceptable for crime in the professions to be dealt with by individual bodies within specific jurisdictional regions alone. Professional crime is now a problem which breaches all jurisdictional boundaries. Its solution will require that some, if not all, of those boundaries be removed.

### Notes

1    Data reported here were derived from Davies and Makkai (2000). The present analysis and interpretation, however, is the sole responsibility of the present author.
2    Not all respondents provided answers to every question.

# Chapter 2

# Defining Crime in the Professions

Kenneth Hayne

Why is it necessary for an entire book to address the question of crime in the professions? Is the problem so large that it warrants all this attention? Are the problems presented by crime in the professions so different that they call for special consideration? Why is crime in the suites different from crime in the streets?

These and similar questions lie behind much of the discussion that follows but it is as well to bring them a little further forward now, so that we may give them some thought. This chapter will not attempt to do more than ask questions and offer a few suggestions that the reader may, in the end, come to regard as no more than blinding glimpses of the obvious. Hopefully, however, they may provoke consideration of some of the basic issues that lie behind the subject of the present volume.

There are many ways in which to classify crimes. The most common classification is by reference to the nature of the offence: crimes against the person, crimes against property and so on. The subject of the present volume is not described in this way. 'Crime in the professions' seeks to classify crimes by reference to the offender rather than the offence. In doing so, it directs attention to why the occupation of the offender should be regarded as a matter of any significance.

There are, inevitably, some questions of definition which should be considered at the outset. What is meant by 'crime in the professions'? Does it refer to any crime committed by any person who pursues a profession? Is it a more restricted field of enquiry? Is 'crime in the professions' all 'white-collar crime'? Are the two fields of crime in the professions and white-collar crime coincident or is one a subset of the other?

For present purposes, it is convenient to begin with a description that has been given to white-collar crime generally, namely, 'crime committed by a person in a position of trust for his or her personal gain' (Reasons 1982, p. 59). That description is very broad. It would apply to any person embezzling from an employer. Most people, however, would understand crime in the professions not to extend to every such case. In that sense, crime in the professions might be thought to be a subset of white-collar crime. But what of the case of a doctor who sexually assaults a patient; is that a white-collar crime? Arguably not. These definitional issues may not seem all that important but there are two elements in the description quoted above which are important in understanding what is meant by crime in the professions and why it may be thought appropriate to study it separately. Those elements are the relationship of trust or dependence and the abuse of that relationship for personal gain.

Next, it is as well to say something about the vexed word 'profession'. The *Oxford English Dictionary* (Simpson and Weiner 1989, 'profession' meanings 1a and b) defines the word profession as being a declaration, promise or vow made by one entering a religious order or, more broadly, any solemn declaration, promise or vow. And although now the word is commonly used to describe '[a]ny calling or occupation by which a person habitually earns [a] living' (*ibid.* 'profession' meaning 6b), the word is one which retains powerful resonances of its narrower meaning of '[a] vocation in which a professed knowledge of some department of learning or science is used in its application to the affairs of others or in the practice of an art founded upon it' (*ibid.* 'profession' meaning 6a). No longer is the word restricted in its application to the three learned professions of divinity, law and medicine (with or without the addition of the profession of arms) but central to its usage are the ideas that the person in question professes knowledge of some department of learning or science and seeks to use that knowledge in its application to the affairs of others or, as the dictionary has it, 'in the practice of an art founded upon it'. And it is because the professional seeks to use knowledge for others that crime in the professions focuses upon the abuse of the relationship of trust or dependence that exists when one seeks to apply knowledge in or about the affairs of another.

Human nature being what it is, the problem of a person abusing a relationship of trust or dependence is anything but new. The problem of the lawyer misusing a client's money, the problem of the doctor taking sexual advantage of the vulnerable patient, are problems as old as the professions. Why then should we spend valuable time looking again at what are age-old problems? Is there something deficient in the way in which society responds to these problems? Is society changing in ways that require us to deal with these problems in a different manner?

Again, it is convenient to mention one aspect of the matter with a view to putting it to one side. Crimes committed by those in the professions are committed by persons who would ordinarily be considered to be well educated, privileged members of society. Their crimes would most often be committed against persons who trusted the offender or who were dependent upon the offender. Many would say that, given these facts, the offending behaviour would often warrant sterner punishment than the punishment that would be inflicted on other criminals. Others would say that the conviction of a professional is, itself, a severe punishment and that, accordingly, punishment should be mitigated. Are these reasons enough to single out the problem of crime in the professions for special treatment and consideration? I doubt that they are, for the issues that are raised by these matters extend well beyond any question of dealing with crime in the professions. They invite attention to general theories of punishment rather than to any consideration special to the offender's position as a member of a profession. That is, they invite consideration of why we punish people and what factors should be taken to account in measuring that punishment rather than to any problem that is special to crime in the professions.

Is the problem of crime in the professions a growing problem? Some crimes by professionals now attract much publicity. Much public attention is drawn to doctors who are alleged to have defrauded the Health Insurance Commission, to doctors who take sexual advantage of their patients, to lawyers who steal from trust funds, to lawyers who assist others in the commission of crime. Although there is much public attention now given to these matters in newspapers and on the television it is not self-evident that there has been some increase in the frequency of these offences or in their gravity. Certainly there has been much publicity given to sexual offences by those in religious callings but we simply do not know whether the increase in numbers of such offences reported suggests that there has been some increase in the frequency of their occurrence.

Whether or not the frequency of offending in that profession has increased, in my own profession it is as well to remember that prominent members of the profession have offended in centuries long before the present. In 1621, Lord Chancellor St Alban was ordered to pay a fine of £40,000, sentenced to be imprisoned in the Tower of London during the King's Pleasure and forever debarred from holding any public office, place or employment on account of his admittedly taking bribes from litigants in cases he was to judge (Campbell 1857, vol. iii, p. 113). His defence that he did not actually allow the bribes to influence his judgment in any case was less than convincing. There may be thought to be a nice philosophical question about which is worse—taking a bribe to fix a case or taking a bribe to fix a case and then not delivering the promised benefit. In the end, it probably does not matter. A judge taking bribes is an unpardonable offence and one not heard of in this country.

Or if that example is not colourful enough, what of Herbert Rowse Armstrong, solicitor of Hay, in England, found guilty in 1922 of murdering his wife by poisoning her with arsenic, but alleged also to have attempted to poison another solicitor in the town who was pressing Armstrong to complete a conveyance in which Armstrong was acting for the vendor (*R. v Armstrong* [1922] 2 KB 555)? Or if medical cases are sought, what of the doctor found guilty of Medibank fraud some decades ago who bulk-billed the repairman installing a television set in his house (Hall 1979, p. 64)? Or, in the United Kingdom, what of the 25 general practitioners charged with fraud during the last year?

The problems are there, but are they increasing? Or are we seeing an increased frequency in publicity rather than occurrence? As previously mentioned, it is not self-evident that offending by professionals is increasing in frequency or gravity.

So far then, several reasons have been given for thinking that crime in the professions may not present any particularly new or different problems. There are, however, at least two relatively recent developments which may be thought to warrant careful consideration of the topic. First, there are the consequences of deregulation and commercialisation of the professions and, secondly, there is the move from profession-based forms of discipline to state-imposed disciplinary regimes. These are relatively new developments whose consequences are by no means fully understood at the present time. In looking at why issues are presented by these changes, it is convenient to take as examples the professions of law and medicine. The issues, however, arise in many other professional areas and it is not only the legal and medical professions that encounter them.

For many years, the professions of law and medicine were immune from any external competitive force. Individual lawyers or doctors built up their own practices as best they could, but the ways in which they competed in doing so were strictly limited. Touting was, after all, regarded as a serious professional offence. Now, of course, lawyers and doctors are subjected to external competitive pressures from all kinds of sources seeking to provide similar kinds of service to their clients or patients. In addition, individual lawyers and doctors are subject to much more active competitive pressures from within the profession. Advertising of services, at least in the law, is now commonplace and clients routinely will ask large firms to tender for their work in competition with others. And these developments have taken place at a time when the notion that a profession is a self-disciplining group has been supplanted by the perception that governmental regulation of all aspects of professional conduct is necessary to protect individual members of the public.

For many years the definition of 'infamous conduct' adopted in medical cases was that stated in *Allinson v. General Council of Medical Education and Registration* ([1894] 1 QB 750 at 760-1 *per* Lord Esher MR):

> If it is shewn that a medical man, in the pursuit of his profession, has done something with regard to it which would be reasonably regarded as disgraceful or dishonourable by his professional brethren of good repute and competency, [then it is open to the General Medical Council to say that he has been guilty of] infamous conduct in a professional respect.

The same test, with necessary adaptations, was also applied to lawyers (see *In re a Solicitor; Ex parte The Law Society* [1912] 1 KB 302). Leaving the gender-specific language aside, it can be seen that professional misconduct was to be understood by reference to the standards of the profession as a body, rather than by reference to any externally prescribed, let alone government-prescribed, norms of conduct. All this is changing or has already changed. More and more, the standards of behaviour of professional people are set by governments and then enforced by government-appointed bodies rather than by the body of professional opinion reflected in honorary disciplinary committees of professional associations.

The consequence of these changes, in the mind of many, is that the professions must conduct their affairs according to the same rules as any commercial enterprise and individual members of professions are to be subject to discipline by state-appointed bodies administering state-prescribed laws. If that is so, why, then, should crime in the professions stand apart from any other form of criminal behaviour? In the ordinary criminal law, society sets norms of behaviour which are then enforced by police and courts owing their origin and powers of enforcement to the state. More and more, the discipline of deviant behaviour in the professions proceeds by closely analogous means: state-appointed officials administer and enforce state-prescribed norms.

In those circumstances, what is it that should set some offending behaviour (namely, behaviour engaged in by members of particular kinds of occupation) apart from any other kind of crime? As I have said earlier, it is, I think, because crime in the professions is marked by a breach of the relationship of trust or dependence for personal advantage. It is this which sets it apart from other crime.

In the end, the engendering of that relationship of trust and dependence and the proper fulfilment of that relationship lies at the heart of the pursuit of any profession. If the pursuit of self-interest (whether economic or any other form of self-interest) intrudes into the practice of a professional, there is a denial of all that lies behind the concept of a profession. Crime in the professions focuses upon the pursuit of self-interest in breach of the proper performance of that relationship of trust and dependence.

Forty years ago, a great Chief Justice of Australia, Sir Owen Dixon (1965, p. 192), said:

> [U]nless high standards of conduct are maintained by those who pursue a profession requiring great skill begotten of special knowledge, the trust and confidence of the very community that is to be served is lost and thus the function itself of the profession is frustrated.

That, of course, remains self-evidently true. And these ideas (which lie at the heart of the meaning of 'profession' and 'professional obligation') will inform much of what follows in this book.

Long before Sir Owen Dixon made those observations, the obligations of a member of a profession were described, with all the flourish of Elizabethan language, in the following terms:

> I hold every man a debtor to his profession; from the which as men of course do seek to receive countenance and profit, so ought they of duty to endeavour themselves, by way of amends, to be a help and ornament thereunto. This is performed in some degree by the honest and liberal practice of a profession, when men shall carry a respect not to descend into any course that is corrupt and unworthy thereof, and preserve themselves free from the abuses wherewith the same profession is noted to be infected; but much more is this performed if a man be able to visit and strengthen the roots and foundation of the science itself; thereby not only gracing it in reputation and dignity, but also amplifying it in perfection and substance (Francis Bacon, *Maxims of the Law, Works*, ed., Spedding, vol. vii, p. 319, quoted by Sir Owen Dixon 1965, p. 134).

The present volume seeks 'to visit and strengthen the roots and foundation' of the science being pursued. The chapters which follow seek thereby to '[grace] it in reputation and dignity' and '[amplify] it in perfection and substance'. In doing so the present work fulfils one of the fundamental tasks of any profession. But while these words have relevance to the present discussion, it is, perhaps, as well to note that their author, Francis Bacon, was later to become Lord Chancellor St Alban.

Chapter 3

# The Nature and Characteristics of Professionals in Australia

John Western, Toni Makkai, Julie McMillan and Kathryn Dwan

**On the Nature of the Professions**

In virtually all advanced industrial societies, three major factors have shaped the structure of the economy in recent times. The first has been a growth in the non-manual component of the paid workforce to well over 50 per cent. In Australia at the present time, non-manual workers comprise around 63 per cent of the workforce, having grown from around 45 per cent in 1966 (*1978– 95 Labourforce*, ABS, Cat. No. 6204.0). The second and related change has been the movement of labour out of primary and secondary industry, agriculture, mining and quarrying, manufacturing and building, and into the tertiary sector. The third has been the increasing casualisation of a great deal of paid work (Brault 1997). As a consequence of these changes, and particularly of the first and second, the middle class has expanded significantly.

This middle class is not a homogeneous group. Those located within it differ in the formal credentials they possess and the autonomy and authority they exercise in carrying out their work. Among this middle class are members of a group of occupations we have come to call 'professions'. While there is little debate about the eligibility of certain occupations for membership in this group, the eligibility of others is far more contentious. In part this is because of lack of agreement about the defining characteristics of a profession, and indeed whether it is appropriate to talk about defining characteristics at all, and in part because of the apparent rapid increase in jobs seeking professional status (Freidson 1994).

Freidson (1986) notes in what is probably the seminal work on the professions in recent years that 'intellectual interest in the professions has a long tradition in the English-speaking world' (Freidson 1986, p. 27). The earliest contributors to this interest were British. Spencer (1896), in *Principles of Sociology*, argued for the importance of the professions in applying specialised knowledge to human problems. Beatrice and Sidney Webb (1917) provided an analysis of the performance of professional associations, which they saw as possible alternatives to capitalism for the control and organisation of work in the public rather than the private interest. The historian Tawney (1920) argued for the professionalisation of industry. These three writers were essentially precursors to what is customarily regarded as the benchmark study of the professions, the book by Carr-Saunders and Wilson (1933) entitled simply *The Professions*.

A major thrust of Carr-Saunders and Wilson's work was to identify common elements in all occupations called professions, and to argue for the positive role of the professions in contributing to societal growth. They saw the emergence of the professions as associated with the application of scientific knowledge to the problems of production, and claimed that 'the rise of the new professions based on intellectual techniques is due to the revolution brought about by the work of engineers and thus indirectly to the coming of science' (Carr-Saunders and Wilson 1933, p. 297). Not only were they able to identify new professions that were technologically based but they were in the forefront of those arguing for the professionalisation of work in general:

> in the long run technical advance implies an increase in the number of those doing more or less specialised work...and while the extension of professionalism upwards and outwards will be fairly rapid its extension downwards, though gradual and almost imperceptible, will be continuous (Carr-Saunders and Wilson 1933, p. 493).

Interest in the professions waned in the United Kingdom in the immediate post-Second World War period but surfaced across the Atlantic in the United States and for a period of around 20 years the Americans dominated the scene. Any account of writings on the professions in North America has to acknowledge the original work of Talcott Parsons. In 1939, Parsons wrote an article entitled 'The Professions and Social Structure' in which he argued that the capitalist economy, the rational-legal social order and the modern professions are contemporary historical developments. The professions were characterised by collegial organisation in which authority rested on functional specificity, that is, the restriction of their sphere of activity and the application of impersonal standards on a universalistic basis without regard to the personal characteristics or circumstances of either professionals or their clients.

Parsons was the stimulus for a great deal of work in the 1950s and 1960s. A number of writers during this period saw as their major task the identification of characteristics that distinguished professions from other occupations. Goode (1960) and Greenwood (1957) were prominent. Goode argued that there were two core characteristics that distinguished professional groups: a prolonged specialised training in a body of abstract knowledge and a collectivity or service orientation. He argued that important benefits follow from the possession of skills and knowledge on the one hand and a recognised service orientation on the other. These have to do with being granted autonomy to practise and having a monopoly over particular services. Both clients and practitioners benefit as a consequence of this situation. Clients come to recognise that they are in the hands of experts and practitioners are rewarded by the services they provide.

How is all this controlled? Greenwood believes the answer lies in an understanding of 'the culture of a profession' (Greenwood 1957, p. 52). The attribute that distinguishes professions from other occupations is their professional culture. This comprises values, beliefs, attitudes, skills, knowledge and behaviours. The culture is transmitted during training and reinforced during social interaction with other professionals following the completion of training. The social values of the professional group are its basic and fundamental beliefs, the unquestioned premise upon which its existence rests. Foremost amongst these values is a belief in the essential worth of the service which the professional group extends to the community. The profession considers that the service is a social good and that community welfare would be impaired by its absence. The separate but twin concepts of professional autonomy and monopoly also possess the force of a group value, thus the proposition that, in all service-related matters, the professional group is infinitely wiser than the laity is beyond argument (Greenwood 1957, p. 52).

This view was to hold sway for quite some time. There was considerable argument as to what were the defining dimensions of a profession, but there was never serious debate that a service orientation was lacking, or that a body of knowledge and a set of skills acquired during a period of prolonged training characterised practitioners.

This somewhat benign view of the professions was perhaps consistent with the mood of the times but it was not to last. In the words of Paul Starr, 'the dream of reason did not take power into account' (Starr 1982, p. 1). The declining legitimacy of so-called consensus theory in sociology (Dahrendorf 1959) was accompanied by a resurgence of interest in class analysis from a neo-Marxist perspective (Wright 1985; Poulantzas 1975). This ideological shift was reflected in a change in emphasis of subsequent theorising about the professions 'away from their role in holding society together and towards issues of conflict and power' (Freidson 1994, p. 3).

Prominent in this change in orientation were Freidson, Johnson and Larson. In both the *Profession of Medicine* (1970a) and *Professional Dominance* (1970b), Freidson emphasised the ideological nature of many professional claims, unjustified aspects of monopolistic privilege enjoyed by the profession and the way in which professional organisations created and sustained authority over clients and associated occupations. Freidson argues that the key feature for distinguishing professions from other occupations was the fact of autonomy, 'a position of legitimate control over work' (Freidson 1970b, p. 82).

Freidson argues that autonomy need not be absolute. It does not have to exist across all zones of occupational activity. Where it must exist is with respect to the content of the work itself. Freidson sees autonomy as the outcome of interaction between political power as exercised by the state, and economic power and occupational representation as exercised by the profession. This interaction, he suggests, is sometimes facilitated by educational institutions and other devices which successfully persuade the state that the occupation's work is reliable and valuable.

Jackson (1970), in *Professions and Professionalisation*, argues similarly. He suggests that it may be useful to look at professions in terms of their monopolies over certain resources (that is, knowledge) which can be used to address certain societal needs. The position which particular professions have established on the basis of their exploitation of these resources will differ. Clearly some professions will be better able to exploit their monopoly than will others.

Writing around the same time, Terence Johnson (1972) defined 'profession' as a method of controlling work, one in which an occupation exercises control over its work. He emphasised the role of power in establishing and maintaining such control. Johnson questioned the existence of a service orientation among professionals, which the majority of those writing from the consensus framework accepted as axiomatic. He suggested that the professions may well be seen as bringing knowledge to the service of power and he argued, as did C. Wright Mills (1959) quite some time ago, that a fusion of knowledge and power has created a new kind of professional technocrat who is at the beck and call of existing ruling elites.

From the same structural viewpoint, Magali Larson (1977) has argued that professionalisation is the process by which the producers of special services sought to constitute and control a market for their expertise. Professions are a particular class of organisation who organise themselves in particular ways to attain market power. Larson argued that 'professionalisation is thus an attempt to translate one order of scarce resources—special knowledge and skills—into another—social and economic rewards' (Larson 1977, p. 17). She goes on to say that the focus on the constitution of professional markets leads to comparing different professions in terms of the marketability of their specific cognitive resources. Larson draws some equation between marketability and competence and suggests that once having established their competence, professionals can secure a monopoly within the market.

This very brief review has suggested several persistent themes: first, that professions are characterised by a service orientation, that professional skills, knowledge, values and behaviours are acquired initially through an extended period of training; second, that professions have a great deal of autonomy both in setting conditions and standards of service and in their work. Professions assert their views about recruitment and training and attempt to protect members from outside or bureaucratic interference as they carry out their tasks. They also set standards of conduct and claim to have means of disciplining members who violate these standards. Associated with the notion of autonomy is the idea of exclusive competence. Professions attempt to ensure that a person who is not trained and not duly certified to membership is not allowed to practise a professional task. Finally, a profession is recognised by its own members, and perhaps by the society in which it exists, as having considerable expertise.

The success of claims by the professions for autonomy, exclusive competence and the right to monopolistic control of a field of endeavour rests on their ability to maintain what Paul Starr has described as 'cultural authority'. Simply stated, cultural authority is the probability that particular definitions of reality and judgments of reasoning and value will prevail as valid and true (Starr 1982, p. 13). For the professions this means wide societal acceptance of their claims to autonomy, exclusive competence and monopolistic control. Patently this is less widespread than it was a decade or so ago.

The watershed was perhaps 1992 when, as part of their microeconomic reform agenda, the Australian government instituted an Independent Committee of Inquiry into the need for a national competition policy. The resulting Hilmer Report (Hilmer 1993) heralded the universal application of competition laws to *all* businesses throughout Australia. In 1994 the Council of Australian Governments (COAG) agreed to enact the necessary legislation and the work of professionals, such as doctors, lawyers, architects and engineers, was made subject to Part IV of the *Trade Practices Act 1974* (TPA) and its counterpart, the Competition Code. The legislation took effect in 1996 and sought to prohibit anticompetitive practices, for example any action likely to lessen competition in the market, any agreements that contained exclusionary provisions and price-fixing agreements.

Not surprisingly, the professions objected that the rules prohibiting anticompetitive conduct should not apply to them on the grounds that the conduct in question was designed by the professions to protect the public (Fels 1997a). The Australian Competition and Consumer Commission (ACCC) remained unconvinced by this argument and in 1997 its Chair, Professor Allan Fels (1997a), was prompted to enquire, 'what was it about the fiduciary relationship which required a professional to engage in actions which contravened Part IV of the TPA?' Given the wide range of matters which constituted a public benefit, the ACCC challenged professionals and their organisations to 'articulate and demonstrate' the putative public benefits of their actions (Bhojani 1997). Earlier that year, in an address to the health sector, which was pleading its special case, Commissioner Bhojani had bluntly stated that the health sector would have to 'learn to live with the TPA' in the same way that other businesses were required to do (Fels 1997b). The professions were learning not to expect special treatment from the government.

Similarly, in the legal arena, doctors were learning that their profession bequeathed them no special privileges. Up until the mid-1990s medical boards and tribunals in each state had regularly suppressed the names of doctors under investigation. However, the right to do so was challenged in a 1997 case regarding a GP charged with sexual misconduct involving a female patient. The medical community was shocked when the Victoria Supreme Court decided that the Victorian Medical Board did *not* have the statutory power to suppress a doctor's name. The comments of the unfortunate doctor whose case prompted this decision and who was subsequently cleared of the charges typified the dismay of the medical profession:

> [So] what the courts have said is that just because you are a doctor you are not entitled to any more protection of your identity than any other person (quoted in Santen 1999).

These examples, regarding expanded government legislation and recent legal rulings respectively, demonstrate that while the professions perhaps deem themselves as special cases, their cultural authority is on the wane. It is not what it once was. Partly this is due to the emergence of competing groups offering similar services, partly it is due to an improved community awareness of the activities of the professions and their declining mystique, and partly it is due to actions of the state spread or spurred on by an ideology of freer markets and economic rationalism.

## The *Professions in Australia* Project[1]

*Overview*

The first systematic investigation of the professions in Australia was called, somewhat unimaginatively, the *Professions in Australia* project, and commenced in the mid-1960s. Incoming students in engineering, law, medicine and teaching at a number of Australian universities (the University of Queensland, the University of New South Wales, the University of Western Australia, Melbourne and Monash universities and the Australian National University) were invited to complete questionnaires in their first week or two of university study. The questionnaires focused on social background, reasons for choice of profession, career plans and attitudes to a variety of professional and social issues. The intention when the study started was to follow the group of students until they left university, either through graduation or dropping out. The major question on which the study focused was: how do recruits to the professions acquire the values, dispositions, preferences and practices which characterise the professions they seek to enter?

In addition to the first questionnaire, further questionnaires were given at the completion of first year. No questionnaires were administered in the second year but in the third, fourth and sixth years for medical students, additional information was collected. In part, we were looking for data which would provide information on attitude and value change and the extent to which we could argue for the emergence of a professional self as a consequence of training. The nature of professional contacts that were made was gauged, the extent to which networks developed amongst student groups was assessed and final performance at graduation was also examined.

A great deal of data was gathered during the course of this study. Much of it has been published in more than 20 papers and three research monographs. The study was initially funded for a six-year period by what was then the Australian Research Grants Committee (ARGC) and it was only through such funding that it was possible to maintain a longitudinal examination of students throughout the entire course of their university education.

It had not been intended to continue the study beyond the early 1970s. However, in 1978, Trevor Williams, who was then at the Australian National University, expressed an interest in the possibility of following up the one-time students of the professions to determine what they were doing in terms of professional work. By 1978, the practising graduates would have been young professionals with most of the traumas of becoming established behind them. The success Trevor Williams had in locating the group provided the opportunity to reopen the investigation. By the early 1980s, around 80 per cent of the original group had been found.

Questionnaires were designed and sent to this group over three successive years. Our focus at this time was to look at the qualifications obtained and the proportion who had additional qualifications. The study also looked at careers in the professions, gender differences and attitudes to a variety of issues confronting the professions. Again a number of papers reporting on this data have been published.

The Australian National University in Canberra is currently undertaking a major research program called the Reshaping Australian Institutions Project. This project involves both research activity and public symposia at which issues pertinent to Australia's future are being addressed. Because we had been involved in a longitudinal research project which is probably unique, we were invited to participate in the Reshaping Project by once again going back to our original participants, or as many of them as we could find, to seek some further information from them about their experiences of professional work and how it has changed over a period of some 25 to 30 years. As a consequence, we undertook a final wave of data collection in 1998 and early 1999.

This was preceded by a quite lengthy period in which we tried to ensure that the information we had about addresses was as up to date as possible. We consulted professional directories, telephone directories and electoral rolls and, in doing so, were able to identify a substantial number of our original respondents. Table 3.1 provides details of our sample sizes at the various time points of the study. As can be seen, over the more than 30 years of the study, the samples reduced to about one-third of the original number.

In longitudinal studies such as this, questions of representativeness inevitably arise. What is this group representative of? Students commencing courses in the four areas in 1965 and 1967? Students graduating in engineering, law, medicine and teaching some four to six years later? Current practitioners who are 50+ years of age? None of these groups?

**Table 3.1     Sample size**

| | Engineers | %[a] | Number of cases Lawyers | %[a] | Doctors | %[a] |
|---|---|---|---|---|---|---|
| Beginning of course | | | | | | |
| 1965[b]/1967[c] | 652 | | 645 | | 572 | |
| End of course | | | | | | |
| 1968[b]/1972[c] | 367 | 56 | 310 | 48 | 333 | 58 |
| 1982 | 302 | 46 | 316 | 49 | 344 | 60 |
| 1983 | 312 | 48 | 288 | 45 | 327 | 57 |
| 1984 | 278 | 43 | 264 | 41 | 284 | 50 |
| 1998 | 234 | 36 | 191 | 30 | 203 | 35 |

a   response rate
b   engineering; law
c   medicine

Over 50 per cent of those initially answering questionnaires completed further questionnaires at a time designated as 'end of course' in Table 3.1. However, not all of those entering in 1965 and 1967 in fact completed their courses. If we turn our attention to those who graduated rather than those who began their course of study, we have indications that around 75 per cent of the graduates completed questionnaires in 1968 or 1972. Considering the medical group for a moment: in 1972 approximately 800 students graduated from medical schools across Australia. Our final sample of 333 medical graduates from the University of Queensland and Melbourne and Monash universities represents around 42 per cent of the total fairly representative sample. Similar relationships exist for the other two groups. Probably we can conclude that the samples are reasonably representative of the original groups from which they came, and representative of graduating groups in 1968 and 1972.

*Social Origins*

Back in 1965 and 1967 the young people entering courses for engineering, law and medicine came from privileged backgrounds. Between 60 and 75 per cent came from homes in which the male bread-winner occupied either managerial or executive positions or worked independently or in an employed capacity as a professional. Less than 20 per cent were in lower white-collar jobs as clerical and sales workers and smaller numbers overall were employed as skilled or semi-skilled manual workers (Table 3.2).

**Table 3.2    Father's occupation at time of student's entry to university (column percentages)**

|                                | Engineering | Law | Medicine |
|--------------------------------|-------------|-----|----------|
| Upper white-collar workers     |             |     |          |
|   Managers and executives | 34     | 37  | 31       |
|   Professionals      | 25          | 38  | 37       |
| Low white-collar workers       |             |     |          |
|   Clerical and sales workers | 16  | 13  | 13       |
|   Manual workers     | 22          | 9   | 15       |
|   Farmers            | 3           | 3   | 4        |
| N*                             | 143         | 151 | 158      |

\*    The numbers refer to persons who answered all questionnaires. In comparing father's occupation of this group with the original samples we find remarkably similar distributions.

Writing in 1970, Anderson and Western asserted that:

in terms of both education and occupational status, compared with the Australian male population generally, students' fathers ranked very high with at least 50 per cent of the fathers compared with 17 per cent of the male population being classed as professionals or managers and 19 per cent compared with two per cent having a university education.

In terms of father's income also it was found that students, especially those studying law or medicine, tended to come from a moneyed elite.

Not a great deal has changed over the years. A report which appeared in September 1999 (Long, Carpenter and Hayden 1999) revealed a very similar pattern. While participation in higher education almost doubled in the period 1980–1994 from 20 per cent to 38 per cent of Year 12 students, differences associated with socioeconomic status were unchanged. Young people from backgrounds of higher parental occupational status, better parental educational attainment and greater family wealth were more likely to have completed Year 12, to have entered higher education from Year 12 and to have participated in higher education by age 19.

Inequalities in access to higher education have been an intractable problem since the establishment of universities in Australia in the middle of the nineteenth century. In recent years, different governments have sought to address the problem in different ways. In the 1950s the Menzies government introduced annual university scholarships. Scholarship holders were exempt from tuition fees and were paid a living allowance that was means-tested.

Slightly more than one-third of university students in the 1950s were in receipt of Commonwealth scholarships, however such an initiative did little to change the social composition of the university student population. Hammond (1956) and Shonell, Rowe and Meddleton (1962) concluded at that time that university students came disproportionately from upper middle class and wealthy family backgrounds.

Partly in response to this situation the first federal Labor government in over 20 years to come into office in 1972 abolished all entrance fees to universities and assumed full financial responsibility for tertiary education. While the total number of students increased rapidly following the changes, the main beneficiaries were older students and women. There was no major change in the socioeconomic composition of the student population (DEETYA 1997).

The situation is not unique to Australia. Blossfeld and Shavit (1993, p. 2) noted:

> Given the long-term process of educational expansion, reinforced in many countries by educational reforms, one might expect a drop in the impact of social background on educational opportunity...surprisingly, however, empirical studies [show] that inequality of educational opportunity between social strata has been quite stable over time.

Results from a variety of studies in a variety of countries suggest that the proportion of people from disadvantaged backgrounds gaining entry to universities and hence to the professions is not likely to increase until the proportion from advantaged backgrounds reaches a saturation level. It is only when virtually the entire population of particular age groups from higher status backgrounds enter universities can we expect to find the proportion from disadvantaged backgrounds rising (Blossfeld and Shavit 1993).

It seems clear that, for the foreseeable future, the professions will recruit new members from the same relatively advantaged position in the social structure they themselves are occupying.

*The Value of University Education for Professional Practice*

One of the hallmarks of a profession is an extended period of formal training. Historically professional training occurred in the workplace but the variability of the work performed resulted in the different professions establishing guidelines and credentials for training. The evolution of this process resulted in the establishment of professional training schools within universities. This process occurred at different historical points for the different professions in the move toward formal qualifications. The *Professions in Australia* study has consistently asked a number of questions about the relevance and importance of formal education and training for professional work.

The training provided by universities has often come under criticism—too specialised, not specialised enough, is not practical enough, does not provide practitioners with management skills or people skills, and so on. Figure 3.1 shows, however, that only a minority of professionals believe that training for the profession could be carried out better by a professional institute, and this opinion has changed little over time with the proportion holding this view on entering their university course in 1965–1967 remaining fairly stable over the course of their university training and into work. There are, however, differences between the professions. Medical practitioners are most likely to support the view that professional training would be best located in a specialised professional institute and engineers the least likely. This may reflect the realities of the workplace. Doctors perhaps can obtain virtually all their training within the confines of a single institution—the hospital—although this is changing with the growth in public health and the increasing specialisation of general practice. Engineers, on the other hand, require very different work environments depending on their specialisation.

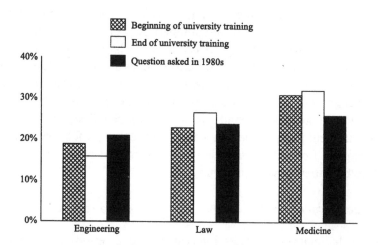

**Figure 3.1    Percentage of respondents who agreed that training for their profession could be carried out better by an institute controlled by their profession than by a university**

More specific questions on the importance of training were asked in 1982 and again in 1998. One question asked all respondents to rate the importance of different educational experiences for their current professional activities. The experiences concerned first degree studies, subsequent formal studies, in-service or on-the-job training and self-education and actual experience. The proportion rating each of these learning experiences as 'very important' is shown in Figure 3.2.

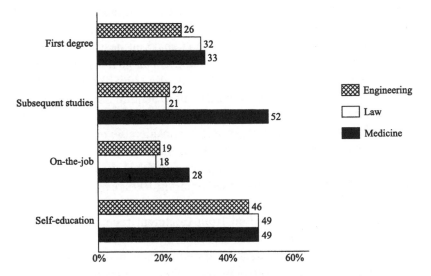

**Figure 3.2   Percentage of respondents rating different learning situations as very important for work in the 1990s**

Skills acquired by self-education and actual experience received the highest ratings with almost 50 per cent of each group indicating that these skills are very important for their present professional activities. Equally significant perhaps is the extent to which skills acquired in first degree studies have continued to be seen as important over time. These skills were acquired more than 25 years ago, yet they are judged by between one-quarter and one-third of each of the groups as still being very important for their current professional activities.

The doctors tend to rank learning experiences more highly than do the other two groups. Over half (52 per cent) report the skills acquired in subsequent formal studies are very important for their present work whereas no more than 20 per cent of the other two groups make a similar claim. Skills acquired in in-service and on-the-job training are reported as very important by 28 per cent of doctors and again by less than 20 per cent of the other two groups.

*Professional Misconduct*

Professional misconduct is an area increasingly coming to the attention of both the public and professional bodies. Rates of litigation against doctors provide the best empirical evidence we have of this phenomenon among medical professionals, but this evidence is shaky at best; for every article that claims a crisis in medical litigation, another claims it is merely a beat-up (Drury 1996; Dunn 1996; Keaney 1996; Nisselle 1996; Trebilcock, Dewees and Duff 1990). Reliable figures are difficult to acquire but the Final Report of the Review of Professional Indemnity Arrangement for Health Care Professionals, published in 1995, provides considerable evidence that there is simply *no* explosion of medical negligence (Henderson 1996). Nevertheless, reports of medical negligence and malpractice often make it into the general media. For instance, a widely discussed report in 1998 revealed that errors of omission were found to have been the major cause of the 18,000 deaths and 50,000 disabilities which resulted from treatment received in Australian hospitals the previous year (Eccleston 1999a).

But what of crime, rather than mere malpractice, by professionals? The so-called 'MRI scam' which broke in late 1999 was a case of medical insider trading committed by one-quarter of Australia's radiologists. A report by the Health Insurance Commission (1998) alleges that radiologists backdated orders for MRI machines, or used revokable contracts, in order to profit illegally from the budget decision to introduce Medicare rebates. The medical profession's response was most interesting. It sought both to keep the radiologists' names confidential (AAP 1999) and warned that too many convictions could lead to a shortage of radiologists in Australia (Eccleston 1999b). Interestingly, it is significantly more difficult to find comparable evidence or media coverage of malpractice or crime within the legal profession.

While professional misconduct was not an area of central concern to the *Professions in Australia* study, we did address certain matters relating to it.

The following question was asked in the first week or two of university and then on several further occasions, culminating in the final questionnaire completed in 1998.

If a doctor/engineer/lawyer has reason to believe that a colleague is seriously incompetent in their work, the doctor/engineer/lawyer should:

1. Attempt to demonstrate the colleague's shortcomings to them.
2. Alert the public to the fact so that the profession should not come into disrepute.
3. Take little or no action since variation in competence among the members of any profession is one of the features of professional life.
4. Attempt to handle the matter through the professional association so the public does not learn of the state of affairs.
5. Take little or no action since independence of action is one of the factors of professional life.

On each occasion the respondents were asked to indicate the answer which came closest to their view as to the appropriate course of action. We collapsed categories 3 and 5, calling them 'no action'. We called category 1 'a personal alternative', category 2, 'the public oriented alternative' and category 4, 'the professional oriented alternative'.

These categories are really self-explanatory. 'No action' implies simply ignoring the situation, 'personal' implies acting individually in attempting to change a colleague's behaviour, 'public oriented' means exposing the defaulter to the community at large while 'professional oriented' means endeavouring to handle the matter 'in club' so that the public does not become aware of the situation but attempts at reform are put in place.

For lawyers and doctors, data are available from responses provided when the groups commenced university, when they graduated, at mid career and when commencing the home run. For engineers, data are available for the first, third and fourth time-points. Figure 3.3 presents a summary of the data. It is clear that while almost no one at any point in time has advocated responding to the situation by going public, there are differences in both the way the groups believe the problem should be handled and the way in which these views have changed over time.

If we look first at the doctors, we can see that over the period 1967 to 1983, there was a slight increase in those preferring a personal strategy, up from 58 per cent in 1967 to 60 per cent in 1983, but then a sudden drop to 47 per cent in 1998. Accompanying this trend was a substantial increase in those opting for a professional response, rising from around 18 per cent in 1983 to 50 per cent in 1998. Clearly trying to demonstrate a colleague's shortcomings to him or her is going out of favour while calling on a professional body, the AMA perhaps or a specialist college, to discipline a wayward colleague appears more attractive.

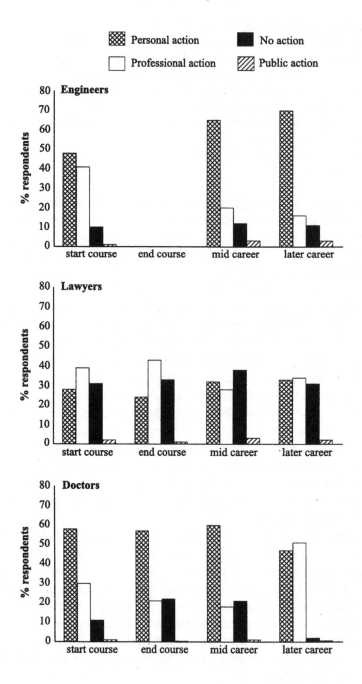

**Figure 3.3   Changing views on dealing with incompetent colleagues**

The engineers see things quite differently. At the beginning of their course about half of them (49 per cent) were advocating a personal response. This had risen to 67 per cent by 1983 and 70 per cent by 1998. Clearly the engineers have more confidence than do the doctors in their ability to personally rectify the situation. Overall, the lawyers show very little change. At the beginning of their course around one-third believed no action was the appropriate response, one-third saw the personal response as appropriate and one-third a professional response. By the time they had completed their course the professional response had increased in popularity but not greatly so. By 1983 the personal response had dropped to where it was in 1965 and by 1998 it has not changed much from this position. The other two response categories had also stayed quite similar.

Of course these aggregate trends may hide patterns of change that are occurring within the groups. For example, the relative constant response patterns for lawyers may come about because some lawyers are changing from a personal to a professional orientation while others are changing from 'professional' to 'personal'. The aggregate response patterns hide these internal changes. We will look briefly then at these patterns of change, starting with the doctors.

We have already observed a significant overall shift among the doctors to a professional response to matters of incompetence, whereby concerns over the actions of a colleague are referred to a professional body to handle. This shift appears to have been most marked between 1983 and 1998. The data reveal that this has come about largely by a shift from responses characterised by 'no action' or 'personal' to responses described as 'professional'. Of the 102 individuals indicating a 'professional' response in 1998, a little over one-quarter (27 per cent) had moved from 'no action' in 1983. A further 50 per cent had moved from a 'personal' orientation while the remaining 20 per cent had remained constant with a 'professional' orientation. This latter group comprises over half of the 34 respondents who had indicated a 'professional' orientation in 1983.

It is very clear that in dealing with matters of professional incompetence at the present time, this group of doctors far prefer an institutional response. This preference has emerged over the last ten to 15 years. It is perhaps no accident that this period of time saw the emergence of Medicare and certainly a greater perception on the part of the medical profession of government interference in medical practice. It would perhaps be not too outrageous to suggest that recourse to professional bodies is seen as an important antidote to increasing pressures from government authority.

The explanations for the patterns exhibited by the other two groups are somewhat more problematic. Among the engineers there is simply a shift to a greater reliance on personal action to counter the incompetent behaviour of colleagues. Perhaps the engineers see it as appropriate to take matters into their own hands, because they have been under relatively less pressure than the medical profession and therefore have not needed to rely on their professional bodies to the same extent?

The lawyers are a particularly interesting case. Despite reviews by the Trade Practices Commission in the early 1990s which concluded that the 'Australian legal profession [was] heavily over-regulated and in urgent need of comprehensive reform' (Trade Practices Commission 1994, p. 3), there is no pattern to the views held by the legal profession, and to 'take no action' is seen as a viable alternative for lawyers in a way it apparently is not for the engineers or the doctors.

A related matter only considered in 1998 concerned the determination of negligence and the standards of professional conduct to be used in that determination. The question was posed in the following way:

> The standard of professional conduct used in legal proceedings to determine engineers'/lawyers'/doctors' negligence should be ascertained primarily by considering the views of:
> 1. other lawyers with similar qualifications to those of the individual in question;
> 2. a judge hearing a case in a court of law;
> 3. members of the lay public.

For each of those three alternatives the respondents were provided with a four-point scale ranging from 'strongly agree' through to 'strongly disagree'. Their answers would indicate the extent of their agreement that other lawyers, judges or members of the lay public should have a say in the determination of what should be regarded as negligence.

Figure 3.4 shows us that the results are clear-cut. Judgements about negligence should be based on the views of one's professional peers. In addition, lawyers are also open to the views of a judge hearing a case in a court of law in a way that engineers and doctors are not. The views of the lay public, however, are not acceptable to any of the professions, but it may not surprise you to learn that the lay public have different ideas. For instance, in New South Wales, when asked, 'who do you believe should deal with complaints against lawyers?', nearly 80 per cent of people surveyed wanted regulation by a public authority *independent* of the legal profession (Law Reform Commission 1993).

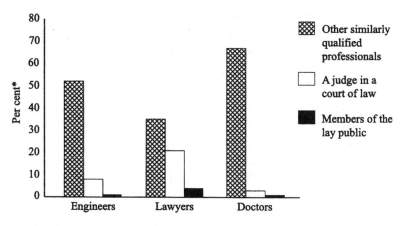

* indicated 'strongly agree'

**Figure 3.4   Who should ascertain the standard of professional conduct used in legal proceedings to determine an engineer's, a lawyer's or a doctor's negligence?**

The strengths of professional cultures are highlighted by this pattern of responses. Professions are very much 'closed shops' and despite encouragement from the Hilmer Report and reviews by the Australian Competition and Consumer Commission, members of the professions appear to be very strongly of the view that they should set the standards of professional activity and also police those standards.

**Conclusion**

This chapter has reviewed our progressive understanding of the professions from the time they were first systematically investigated early in the twentieth century until the pronouncements of the ACCC almost 100 years later. We saw that the three key characteristics of the professions were autonomy, exclusive competence and the right to monopolistic control of a field of endeavour. The insistence of the professions on maintaining the integrity of these three characteristics has brought them into conflict with the microeconomic reform agenda of successive Australian governments since the early 1990s.

The chapter then moved to a consideration of the *Professions in Australia* project; a unique 30-year longitudinal study that has significantly increased our understanding of the characteristics and complexities of the professions. We saw that recruits to the profession some 30 years ago came from relatively advantaged positions in the social structure, a situation which shows little change today. One of the hallmarks of a profession is an extended period of formal training usually based at a university. Our data support this contention but also indicate that self-education is seen as even more important in maintaining a level of professional competency.

Professional misconduct is an area increasingly coming to the attention of the public and professional bodies. Our respondents differed in how this should be handled. The doctors called on their professional bodies, the engineers preferred the personal touch, while the lawyers were undecided about the most appropriate strategy, although 30 per cent of them preferred to take no action. We then considered who should determine the negligence of a professional in legal proceedings. Overwhelmingly the three groups believed they should be judged by their peers and comprehensively rejected assessment by the lay public who, as a separate study revealed, held somewhat different views.

A number of related issues were also considered in the last wave of data collection, all of which bear in one way or another on the changing nature of the cultural authority of the professions over the last 20 years or so, and will be discussed in a forthcoming book which hopefully will put the study to rest. The relationship of the professions to society is clearly changing and while the professions are likely to remain relatively privileged occupational niches into the future, external accountability is on the rise and is likely to continue to be so.

## Note

1   The *Professions in Australia* project began under the direction of Don Anderson in the 1960s at Melbourne University and John Western, then at the Australian National University. It recruited Trevor Williams in the late 1970s when he was at the Australian National University (ANU). By that time Don Anderson had moved to the ANU and John Western had moved to the University of Queensland. Toni Makkai completed her PhD on the engineers' sample and has been instrumental in progressing the project to the final stage. Julie McMillan completed an honours thesis on the lawyers' sample, thought better of it for her PhD and is now a research fellow at the Australian Council for Educational Research. Kathryn Dwan has had a continuing interest in the medical profession and, against her better judgment, has agreed to be involved in this project.

# PART II
# THE NATURE AND EXTENT OF
# CRIME IN THE PROFESSIONS

Chapter 4

# Crime and Misconduct in the Accounting Profession

Andrew Williams

## Introduction

Despite the generally accepted view in the community that accountants are
highly regarded, those who are involved in the daily administration of
professional disciplinary matters involving accounting professionals are aware
of the fact that dishonest and criminal acts are not at all uncommon within
the accounting profession and that, indeed, they represent a cause of great
concern. The usual profile of the criminal accountant is recognised as being
a sole practitioner with little or no accountability to other partners or directors.

Data relating to dishonesty within the accounting profession are limited
in the public domain, the sources being restricted to published disciplinary
cases within professional journals, and court cases covered by the media
where the magnitude of the losses, or the circumstances and personalities
involved, are regarded as newsworthy. The present chapter draws on the
author's experience as a divisional director of Aon Professional Services
(Aon), one of the two largest insurance brokers in the world which arranges
risk transfer and risk management in the professions.

## Types of Dishonesty in the Accounting Profession

From an insurance broking perspective, a range of dishonest acts affecting a
range of individuals have been observed, which fall broadly within the
following four areas. Criminal conduct relating to each of these can have a
dramatic effect on both a professional practice and the lives of the victims.

*Dishonesty of Proprietor or Principal(s)*

Where criminal acts are perpetrated by the principal(s) of a professional practice, the window of opportunity is very wide and the preventative mechanisms very weak. This is due to the inherent power of the perpetrator within the firm, and the absence of any real barriers or challenges to his or her actions prior to detection and/or discovery of the conduct.

*Dishonesty of Staff Employed by the Practice*

There also exists a broad range of opportunities for staff dishonesty which range from theft of property belonging to the employer through to theft of client's property and funds by abuse of a position of trust. Internal controls and supervision by the principal(s) of the firm are the sole preventative measure in the absence of an external auditor.

*Dishonesty of Clients Embroiling Accounting Firms*

Again there exist a range of scenarios in which a 'bad' client can involve a professional firm. These extend from the client seeking a stamp of respectability by attributing support or approval by the firm, through to involving the partners of the firm in a fraudulent arrangement by virtue of their being directors or shareholders in the business vehicle.

*Dishonesty of Third-Party Professionals Involving Accounting Firms*

Finally, firms can inadvertently be drawn into dishonesty by the activities of joint venturers or other professional firms involved in a project. In such cases the perception may be given that the fraudulent conduct of one entity erroneously reflects upon the other 'innocent' parties.

## The Consequences of Dishonesty

Once an act of dishonesty has been perpetrated, a number of consequences ensue. An initial problem is that although firms will be aware of crimes which have been discovered, the great unknown and fear of all enterprises are losses arising out of criminal acts that have not yet been discovered, especially in cases where electronic funds transfers have been used to move funds quickly and without notice.

The other consequence of discovering criminality is the need to recover assets that have been misappropriated, either by direct recovery, if the assets both exist and can be located, or indirectly through insurance policies held by the enterprise. In addition, action may need to be taken against third parties, such as external auditors and financial institutions, which have acted as avenues of conversion and which responsibly should have detected or have been alerted to the fraudulent activity.

Part of the recovery process inevitably involves individuals, firms or companies looking to their liability insurance programmes to shield them from loss or to defend a claim for compensation. In a number of cases, however, insurance is not available or will not cover certain losses which have been sustained.

A number of difficulties arise when insuring in the areas of fraud and dishonesty. Losses which arise from the dishonesty of individuals other than the firms' principals will usually be covered by professional indemnity insurance or a crime or fidelity insurance policy. In cases where one of the proprietors or partners has acted dishonestly, insurance will only protect the innocent partners, while in cases where the perpetrator is a sole practitioner, ultimately there will be no cover at all. As a result, cases involving a dishonest sole practitioner are hardly ever referred to an insurance company other than via a third party, and most often are not reported at all, as the offender has well and truly fled the scene.

Finally, crimes of dishonesty by accountants may result in investigation by professional bodies and law enforcement agencies and inevitably finish with the application of justice in the courts.

## The Motivations behind Accountancy Crime

On the basis of cases recently dealt with by Aon, it appears that the proximate causes of criminal acts within the accounting profession fall into a number of closely linked categories.

### Greed

The first involves greed mixed with a betrayal of trust where funds are either misappropriated from trust accounts without the client's knowledge, or solicited directly for some grandiose investment scheme with the objective of benefiting the perpetrator. In the case of misappropriated funds, often there is an element of arrogance whereby the initial objective is to 'borrow' the capital, use it in a speculative venture, hopefully make a substantial profit, and repay the capital without anyone being the wiser. When the enterprise fails, the illegal nature of the activities then becomes apparent. In such cases, the prime objective has always been personal gain for the perpetrator.

## Incompetence

Secondly, incompetence may lead to illegal behaviour taking place. Often, for example, an initial error of judgment is sought to be patched up by using other clients' funds. This leads progressively to a worsening situation which can involve a large proportion of the client base who may have funds held in trust by the practitioner concerned. Although the proximate motivation for the crime in this case is not personal gain for the perpetrator, the problem arises where the perpetrator tries to buy time in which to rectify the situation with the unauthorised use of other people's money.

## Lifestyle

An accountant's lifestyle may also provide a recipe for quick and substantial losses, often with overworked professionals chasing fast leisure to recharge their batteries but becoming more involved than they originally anticipated. Easy access to other people's funds can lead to substantial problems. Often the funds are squandered on lifestyle with little or no residual capital benefit with which to reimburse anybody. The easy availability of credit and loan facilities also provides an environment in which accountants, like others in the community, are able to live beyond their means. In order to relieve financial pressures, the temptation then arises to abuse professional trust and misuse client funds.

## Risk Management Factors

The central question from a prevention or risk management point of view is how peers, clients and professional bodies are able to avoid problems of fraud and dishonesty and minimise the damage which follows from it.

One positive initiative in recent times which has been used to prevent investment-related fraud is the requirement, policed by the Australian Securities and Investments Commission (ASIC), for all investment opportunities to be accompanied by a registered prospectus. Although there are certain exceptions to this rule within the new Corporate Law Economic

Reform Programme (CLERP) legislation, the prospectus provisions appear to have reduced, although not removed, instances in which individuals have been tricked into investing in barren schemes promoted by professional people.

However, in a low-interest environment, greed often appears to be inflamed rather than suppressed in some individuals who are happy to invest in schemes which offer returns of between five and ten percentage points above the standard moderate interest return—regardless of their security.

An example of the greed and gullibility of some people is demonstrated in the campaign recently conducted by ASIC to raise public awareness of the risks associated with some investments. The Commission intentionally created and advertised in the press a number of totally implausible investment opportunities promising unbelievable capital growth and high revenue returns in order to gauge public reaction. To its surprise, ASIC was deluged with interested responses from a wide cross-section of the population who were seemingly happy to invest in such schemes without undertaking any proper inquiries.

ASIC regularly publicises the need for caution in taking up investment opportunities. During 1999, for example, it was conservatively estimated that Queenslanders lost more than $62 million in illegal fundraising schemes which were said to have increased sharply in that state. Many such schemes were based overseas and promised outrageously high profits in the absence of a registered prospectus (*Australian Financial Review*, 24 January 2000).

ASIC specifically warns of so-called High Yield Promotional Enterprises (HYPES) with any of the following features:

- education packages offered at seminars as the first stage of investment opportunities;
- suggestions that government institutions, regulators and lawyers are not useful or should be avoided;
- promises of unbelievably high returns;
- offshore tax havens where there is little or no regulation;
- bank debentures or government guarantees allegedly offered by the Reserve Bank;
- having to sign a confidentiality agreement such as by promising not to talk to regulators (*NIBA Gazette*, February 2000).

Such advice, although readily available, is, however, often ignored by members of the public, some of whom demonstrate a complete disregard for their financial wellbeing in dealing with their money. Protective legislation and the efforts of regulators can, in the end, only do so much to prevent economic crime.

A notable feature of 'white collar' or corporate crime is the fact that despite checks and balances and, in some cases, mandatory audit, most crimes in the financial world are discovered purely by accident. Often they become apparent when the perpetrator is on sick leave or vacation, or as a result of an internal mail mix up. One of the key risk management factors relating to internal control is to check the accrued leave register to identify which employees—particularly those in positions of trust—never take holidays. Failing to take leave may simply indicate that the individual has 'no life' outside the job, but it may also indicate more sinister reasons for always being at the office. Unfortunately, such indicators of fraud are often not examined prior to an offence taking place, following which the unusual patterns of work and lifestyle become all too readily apparent.

Other problems arise where the boundary between ethical and unethical conduct is perceived to be unclear. Daily practice may, for example, require accountants to witness the signature of documents when one or some of the parties are not present, be economical with the truth by failing to provide sufficient information when asked about a given course of action, or being party to the dishonest actions of others. In some cases the professional person may observe or be faced with situations in which a client knowingly commits criminal acts and the professional has either to work with or to ignore such behaviour. This clearly creates ethical dilemmas for an individual who wishes to comply with professional codes of practice but nonetheless wants to retain an important client. The accountant may then be placed in the position of a priest in a confessional but perhaps without the same immunity.

Consider the hypothetical example of an accountant's client who has a history of starting a business, employing staff, deducting tax instalments, superannuation instalments, sales tax and so on, but never registering or remitting these payments to any of the revenue-gathering bodies. The client then closes the business, possibly with trade debts, and walks away.

Such conduct on the part of the client is almost certainly illegal in that it represents a deliberate attempt to defraud the Australian Taxation Office, state revenue offices, employees and trade creditors rather than being a case of total incompetence leading to business failure.

The question that arises, however, is whether or not the accountant is an accomplice when acting for such a client. When should the accountant abandon the professional relationship and when should the matter be referred to the authorities? It is well known, however, for whistleblowers worldwide not to have a record of being positively rewarded for the actions they take. Unless it is likely that the professional would become personally liable or implicated in the criminal activities of the client, there may be no incentive to draw attention to such antisocial or criminal behaviour. The fact of being implicated, itself, may also result in a reluctance to take action on the part of the professional.

## Some Recent Criminal Cases

Although insurance brokers see only a very small number of matters arising from criminal activities, the following cases in the public domain illustrate the range of problems which may affect the accounting profession.

### Share Registry Activities

In one case, an accounting practice operated a share registry which handled a corporate rights issue in which cheques were misappropriated by registry employees. There was evidence of collusion between a number of employees of the registry who were able to bank cheques into accounts which had been opened by other employees in similar sounding names to the company having the rights issue.

The crime was discovered when the perpetrators fell out over shareholders' requests for documentation being unable to be dealt with in a consistent way, thus leading to shareholders' suspicions being raised. Hundreds of thousands of dollars in funds were misappropriated, with only part being recovered from the perpetrators, as well as from banks, building societies and the accounting practice which operated the registry.

### Investment Advice

Another area of illegality relates to misappropriation of funds which have been placed for investment on behalf of clients who have sought financial planning services from firms of accountants.

Recent data collated by Aon Risk Services Australia Ltd relating to its financial planners indemnity insurance facility, indicates that claims involving 'misappropriation of funds' made up only seven per cent of the number of reported claims, but 37 per cent of the dollar value of all claims made. If the value of claims attributed to quasi-dishonest behaviour such as 'conflict of interest' and 'misleading statements' are added, the total claims arising from this broad description of dishonesty rise to approximately 50 per cent of the dollar value of all claims made against financial planners—not all of whom are accountants.

## Trust Account Embezzlement

In another case, a partner in a two-partner accounting practice had misappropriated trust account funds, transferring them to overseas destinations, prior to 'disappearing' without trace. The case was discovered when clients became concerned after being unable to obtain access to their funds, despite repeated requests having been made to the accountant.

Losses amounted to millions of dollars, with recoveries being made from the accounting practice and the remaining partner, along with some contribution from the banks involved in the conversion of the funds.

## Dishonest Clients and Possible Collusion

In the case of the investment bank Nugan Hand, funds were obtained from unwary investors, ostensibly for worthy investments in the Indo-China region, some decades ago. One of the principals of the firm disappeared along with the funds while another committed suicide.

Notwithstanding the public image of the bank as being at 'the big end of town', the audit firm used by the bank was neither an international firm nor even a middle-tier firm, but a two-principal practice in which over 40 per cent of the fee income was earned from the bank appointment alone. Consequently, the partners of the firm were extremely reliant on this one client for their livelihood, creating the situation in which the compliant relationship between the auditor and the client was able to avoid highlighting the true situation.

## Unloading an Unprofitable Company on a Client

In another case, the principals of an accounting practice operated a computer bureau business as a side interest to the practice, although the business did not trade very successfully. A client of the accounting firm expressed an interest in buying a good operating business with his superannuation payout, and the accounting firm sold its computer business, suitably dressed up, to their client.

Once the artificial support of the accounting firm had been removed, the business traded poorly and failed within six months of the sale, the client losing his life savings. A successful common law action was brought against the partners of the accounting practice, who personally made good the loss. The case raises questions of breach of trust as well as misrepresentation and fraud, but also demonstrates a lack of care taken by some clients in investing their funds.

## Examples of Professional Disciplinary Responses

*Fraudulent Conversion of Cheques*

In South Australia, the Disciplinary Committee of the Institute of Chartered Accountants in Australia dealt with an accountant after he had pleaded guilty to, and been convicted of, two charges of fraudulent conversion of cheques payable to a client totalling $160,464. The individual concerned was expelled from membership of the Institute, and the appropriate professional bodies and regulatory authorities were notified of the case (Institute of Chartered Accountants in Australia 1999).

*Abuse of Position as Treasurer and Secretary Manager of Registered Club*

In New South Wales, the Australian Society of Certified Practising Accountants found a member guilty of conduct derogatory to the profession, and failing to observe a proper standard of care, skill and competence in relation to the following matters:

- allowing regular unrecorded cash advances in excess of $215,000 to be made to members and employees, including cash advances to himself of $36,000 and cash advances to former staff/office holders of $118,000. Irregularities involved in these transactions included altering records, failing to countersign cash advances, in certain instances permitting the recipient of the cash advance to authorise the advance, and failing to issue receipts for repayments;
- allowing cash payments of $26,000 to be made without supporting documentation and without approval or authority of the Board of Directors;
- allowing wages totalling $12,000 to be recorded as 'out of pocket expenses';

- failing to deduct income tax from payments made to himself, or to identify the recipient, resulting in non-payment of appropriate payroll tax and workers compensation contributions;
- miscoding the safe balance sheet to omit $42,000 from the club's annual accounts;
- manipulating cash at bank to disguise shortfalls in poker machine takings;
- using the petty cash system for payments for services rendered, but coding them incorrectly and using incorrect payees' names; and
- failing to maintain proper records of the sale of real estate property and the movement of same into the club's accounts.

Membership of the Society was forfeited and the individual was required to contribute to the Society's costs relating to the investigation and determination of the matter (Australian Society of Certified Practising Accountants 1998).

*Theft from Trust Accounts*

In Victoria, an accountant was sentenced in the Melbourne County Court to 18 months' imprisonment with a 14-month suspended sentence after pleading guilty to ten counts of theft of clients' funds from the firm's trust account (Australian Society of Certified Practising Accountants 1999).

## The Victims of Accountancy Crime

The victims of crime committed by accountants come from all sectors of the community and include both small and large-scale investors. Because investment invariably entails risk, many of those who are defrauded simply walk away from the loss treating it as one of the accepted pitfalls of investment.

Often the victims are small investors who look to professionals as trustworthy experts. They are understandably shattered when that trust is broken, and they are left feeling vulnerable in a corporate world which they perceive to be acting in collusion against them.

Where the victims are very wealthy individuals, they are often willing to take risks in order to gain high returns on their investments. Such investors invariably blame their professional advisers when difficulties arise, despite the fact that they may have been aware of the level of risk involved in the transactions.

Many 'get rich quick' schemes equate to gambling rather than investment, but people need to be protected from themselves and the flow-on effect to others. Bodies such as ASIC have an important role to play in both creating and policing legislation which seeks to reduce and to control corporate impropriety.

The Corporate Law Economic Reform Program (CLERP) legislation which will relax some of the rules for raising capital that relate to so-called 'sophisticated investors' has been criticised as watering down the protections which should govern investments. Sophisticated investors are defined as individuals who have averaged income of $250,000 over the last two years, who have assets greater than $2 million, or who have been declared 'sophisticated investors' by an accredited financial adviser. Under the new rules, such individuals will not have to be provided with a prospectus, merely a brief summary of the opportunity. Although it is impossible to remove risk from any capitalist system, concern has been expressed that more people may be victimised by unscrupulous promoters under the amended framework of CLERP.

## Conclusion

The accounting profession provides a representative sample of the business community in that it is basically sound and populated by people of great skill and integrity, with isolated instances of fraud and impropriety being committed by a small minority of the profession driven by a mixture of greed and incompetence assisted by the presence of an environment in which inside knowledge is available of the client's business affairs.

Experience indicates that the risk is highest with sole practitioners due to lack of accountability and peer 'supervision', but again experience indicates that fraud and dishonesty can also be perpetrated in partnership situations where lack of proper controls can enable strong personalities or deviant personalities (sometimes one and the same) to abuse the system.

Only the future will tell whether the approaching golden age of a single world economy, a falling birth rate and greater use of technology will result in less or more criminal behaviour amongst the accounting and the other professions.

Chapter 5

# Crime and Misconduct in the Medical Profession

Andrew Dix

## Introduction

Crimes committed by members of the professions have always been the subject of great fascination, possibly tinged with a degree of gloating, for the public at large. Perceived as having set themselves aside as superior to the mass of ordinary people engaged in trade, industry or other non-professional occupations, any fall from grace is viewed with a certain amount of relish.

In the spectrum of salacious interest, from the perspective of the public, crime on the part of medical practitioners probably vies with the misdeeds of the priesthood as the most fascinating and outrageous. From Shakespeare to lawyer jokes, we seem to have always had low expectations of the legal profession, so that the odd crime perpetrated by a lawyer (possibly excepting the judiciary) is not viewed with great surprise. The felonies of accountants similarly seem to fail to fire the imagination.

What is it about medical crime, or the medical profession itself, that gives it this edge? Are there some types of criminal activity that are the special province of doctors, and do we have a particular attitude towards them that makes their crimes more unacceptable? What sort of crimes do doctors commit?

This chapter briefly attempts to address these questions and then focuses on how medical boards (in particular the New South Wales Medical Board) handle doctors accused or convicted of the commission of crimes.

## The Types of Crime in the Medical Profession

The special relationship of doctor to patient, involving trust and both physical and mental intimacy, creates the opportunity for certain types of crime, while it may be the same special relationship that makes the doctor's crime so repugnant and fascinating.

As far as general crime is concerned, there is no evidence that doctors are better or worse than the rest of us. The vast majority are law abiding, while a very small minority (presumably commensurate with their socioeconomic peers) engage in criminal activity.

It is possible to classify criminal activity engaged in by doctors into two groups, namely: 'everyday' crimes, which are available to anyone; and 'medical' crimes, where the crime is made possible or at least facilitated by the doctor's professional status.

In the first group is included the entire spectrum of criminal activities. Cases considered by the NSW Medical Board in recent years have included resisting arrest, fraud, manslaughter, attempted murder, drink-driving, assault and drug trafficking. All these have occurred in non-medical contexts—that is, the fact that the crime has been committed by a medical practitioner has been incidental and immaterial.

Sometimes criminal conduct occurring outside the context of medical practice may attract additional opprobrium because of the perpetrator's status as a medical practitioner. A practitioner gaoled for his involvement in a plan to import five tonnes of cannabis resin and a conspiracy to supply Indian hemp was struck off by the NSW Medical Tribunal, which made the following comments:

> Importation of drugs for illegal use is a disgraceful involvement in a crime by a person with a degree in medicine, who should know the terrible ravages arising from the use of drugs, both to the user and often to those associated with him. It is criminal conduct which is incompatible with a right to practise medicine (*Re Paltos* Unreported decision of the NSW Medical Tribunal, 17 December 1986).

The second group involves crimes whose commission occurs in or as a result of the professional doctor–patient relationship. While most transactions with professionals involve a significant element of trust, patients grant to members of the medical profession the authority to engage in legitimised assault and intimacy. The nature of the relationship permits a situation to be created where, in the absence of proper professional standards, consent to these acts may be vitiated, and the examination or consultation changes its fundamental nature. Abuse of the professional responsibility/obligation that this permission creates provides the opportunity for particular kinds of criminal activity, involving, in particular, sexual assault.

The NSW Court of Appeal put this issue as follows:

All patients are entitled to approach their medical practitioners secure in the belief that their ills will be treated to the best of the skill and ability of their medical practitioners and without any interference of an improper kind with their persons or in relation to their affairs. Respecting the vulnerability of those who attend upon them when in need is fundamental to the practice of medicine (*Richter v. Walton* Unreported decision of the NSW Court of Appeal, 15 July 1993, p. 2, *per* Kirby, P. and O'Keefe, A. J. A).

Other types of criminal activity which are usually associated with doctors or which are made possible by the fact of registration as a medical practitioner include offences under the *Health Insurance Act 1973* (Cth), offences against poisons legislation, illegal termination of pregnancy, assisting surrogacy arrangements and euthanasia. At the far end of the spectrum is the doctor who uses his or her clinical knowledge or position to murder patients. The cases of Dr Shipman in the United Kingdom (Carter, H. 2000) and Dr Swango in the United States (Stewart 1999) are the most recent in an unhappily long tradition.

A third group can also be identified, consisting of medical practitioners who have engaged in, or have been complicit in, activities which may be lawful and, indeed, sponsored by the state, but which may be viewed in a broader context as criminal or in breach of international law (see British Medical Association 1992). These include the involvement of some doctors in experimentation and murder in Nazi Germany (Annas and Grodin 1992; Hoedeman 1991; Lifton 1986), doctors administering torture, surgical removal of the hands and feet of thieves in Iraq, and the participation of doctors in capital punishment (Editorial 1994; Sharp 1994), including putting convicts to death by way of exsanguination and collection of their blood, as has occurred in China.

## The Incidence of Crime in the Medical Profession

Having sketched an outline of the scope for crime in the medical profession, this chapter now considers how much of it actually occurs and what regulatory bodies do about it.

There appears to be no systematic means of recording the incidence of crime committed by medical practitioners in Australia. In New South Wales, section 71 of the *Medical Practice Act 1992* provides as follows:

> Referral of matters by courts
> 71. (1) A court in New South Wales before which a person is convicted of an offence (other than an offence prescribed by the regulations) is to cause a certificate of conviction in respect of the person to be sent to the Registrar if the court has reasonable grounds to believe the person is or was, at the time the offence was committed, a registered medical practitioner.

Similar provisions exist in New Zealand (*Medical Practitioners Act 1995* (NZ), section 85), but not in other Australian jurisdictions. Offences excluded from this obligation by regulation relate to parking or minor traffic offences (*Medical Practice Regulation 1998* (NSW), clause 6).

The number of notifications of convictions received by the NSW Medical Board as a result of this mechanism is remarkably small, suggesting either that doctors are not prone to conviction or that the obligation to report is not well known or understood in NSW courts. Most of the five or six notifications received annually relate to drink-driving offences and it is New South Wales Medical Board policy to treat these initially as matters of possible impairment rather than misconduct. It is the Board's experience that one-off drunkenness leading to a conviction is a very rare thing and the majority of the doctors brought to the Board's attention in this way have become participants in the Board's impaired registrants program.

In the context of mandatory notification, a problematic issue is raised by the status of a finding by a court of guilty, accompanied by the exercise of . discretion in favour of the defendant doctor so that a conviction is not recorded (for example, *Crimes Act 1900* (NSW), section 556A). The words of section 71 of the *Medical Practice Act 1992* are quite clear, and such a decision is not reportable, but, given the essentially protective nature of the jurisdiction of medical boards, it may well be that it is in the public interest for the finding to be considered by the Board. The New South Wales Medical Board has been made aware of this issue when the lawyer defending the doctor on, for example, a drink-driving charge has approached it for a letter outlining the serious consequences for the doctor if a conviction is recorded and the Board notified. Assuming those consequences are not capricious, it would seem that the Board should be able to consider whether the offence that has been proved warrants action on its part. Proposed amendment of section 71 will see the notification requirement extended to cover the situation where a charge has been proved but no conviction recorded (New South Wales, Health Department 1998, Recommendation 9).

In addition to notification from the courts, complaints received from the public or any other source by the New South Wales Medical Board or the New South Wales Health Care Complaints Commission may also be categorised as possibly involving criminal activity, although the matter will usually have been the subject of criminal proceedings. Statistics kept by the Board and the Commission do not include a specific category for criminal activity but complaints alleging fraud, improper prescribing and sexual misconduct could well involve elements of criminality. Approximately 15–20 per cent of the 1,000 complaints received each year relate to conduct that could involve criminality. A similarly approximate analysis suggests about 50 per cent of over 230 cases considered by the NSW Medical Tribunal in the past 20 years have involved elements of criminal conduct, although only a relatively small percentage have had an actual criminal conviction as the basis for the proceedings.

Several recommendations of the 1998 Review of the New South Wales Medical Practice Act will have a significant impact upon the Board's ability to deal with criminal behaviour by medical practitioners in New South Wales. It is proposed that the Act be amended to impose a positive obligation on practitioners to notify the Board if they are convicted of an offence (irrespective of whether it is recorded or not) unless it is a prescribed offence that is not required to be reported. A further recommendation would oblige a medical practitioner to notify the Board within seven days if charged with a 'serious sexual violence offence' where the allegations relate to conduct occurring in the course of practice. A 'serious sexual violence offence' means an offence involving sexual activity, acts of indecency, physical violence or the threat of physical violence that would be punishable by imprisonment for 12 months or more (ibid.).

## The Effect of Conviction on Registration

In most Australian jurisdictions, when applying for medical registration, applicants are required to disclose criminal convictions. As the majority of applicants are recent graduates, disclosures tend to relate to undergraduate indiscretions and are usually dealt with in New South Wales by way of an interview and a warning. However, more serious matters may result in an enquiry under Schedule 1 of the *Medical Practice Act 1992* to determine whether the Board is able to satisfy itself that the applicant is both competent to practise medicine and is of good character. Convictions involving drug or alcohol offences where there is evidence of ongoing abuse may result in conditional registration with regular monitoring.

Convictions which may reflect on character are more difficult to deal with. An applicant who declared in his registration application that as a student he had been convicted of forging a cheque for a substantial amount and threatening a shopkeeper with a knife when challenged in relation to the cheque, was considered to be psychologically impaired. Following a Schedule 1 inquiry, he was granted registration but subject to stringent monitoring regarding his psychiatric condition. An applicant for registration who had been convicted while a student of offences relating to TEAS under the Commonwealth *Crimes Act 1914* and had subsequently been convicted of failing to disclose this conviction when applying for medical registration in South Australia was rejected as being unable to satisfy the Board regarding her character. This decision was upheld by the Medical Tribunal (*Re Neill* Unreported decision of the NSW Medical Tribunal, 9 December 1988). Another applicant had been found guilty of manslaughter after fatally shooting his partner several times while under the influence of drugs and alcohol. This had, in fact, occurred while he was a registered practitioner but his registration lapsed through non-payment of the roll fee pending the trial, and so the relevant court was not required to notify the Board under section 71. The matter first came to the Board's attention when relatives of the deceased's partner wrote concerning his imminent release from custody. The Board twice rejected his application for registration on the grounds that it was not satisfied as to his good character, but on appeal the NSW Medical Tribunal restored his name to the Register subject to conditions.

This case raises the issue of whether there can be some defects of character (or mental capacity) manifested in the commission of particular crimes by a doctor which are so fundamentally antithetical to the practice of medicine that they would preclude registration forever. In considering this, the decision stated (*Re Sliwinski* Unreported decision of the NSW Court of Appeal, 31 May 1994, p. 28):

> Should this Tribunal, in the exercise of its discretion, reject the appeal because, having regard to the nature of the offence and the circumstances in which it was committed, it is of the opinion that the conviction renders the person unfit in the public interest to practise medicine?

In considering this question, this Tribunal is bound to consider the public interest.

Nonetheless, manslaughter is a crime which involves the taking of a life and it is clear in the public interest that a person who has wilfully taken a person's life should not be allowed to practise medicine. The appellant's crime lacked such wilfulness.

In deciding whether registration as a medical practitioner should be refused under Section 15 of the Medical Practice Act, it is not possible to lay down any general rules. Each case must be looked at in the light of its own circumstances.

A different approach was taken in another case where the Tribunal, in a one-page decision, simply stated (*Re Andronicus* Unreported decision of the NSW Medical Tribunal, 21 May 1990):

> Since that date (of registration) he has been convicted of serious criminal offences and as such it would be inappropriate for him to remain registered as a medical practitioner.

The nature of the offences were not referred to and the practitioner consented to the order removing his name.

The fact that the offence may have occurred and the conviction recorded at a time when the practitioner was not registered does not pose a significant problem as the issue being considered is whether the offence demonstrates a defect in character which precludes registration or at least requires limitations on registration. The passage of time since the conviction and claims of reformation of character will be factors in determining how the conviction is viewed. Spent conviction legislation reinforces this, though the low threshold for erasure would mean that crimes of sufficient gravity to warrant disciplinary consideration would not generally be erased.

Guidance as to how seriously crime is viewed, and the redemptive effects of time and character reformation comes from cases involving applications for restoration to the Register by previously struck-off doctors.

The case law regarding restoration to the Register in New South Wales is firmly based on the notions of repentance and reformation (*Ex parte Tziniolis* (1967) 1 NSWR 357). The applicant who can acknowledge the wrongdoing that led to the original order for removal and demonstrate an appropriate level of remorse, a resolve not to reoffend and a suitable degree of involvement in continuing medical education is usually readmitted after a suitable effluxion of time. With the other considerations met, the gravity of the original offence is probably the most significant prediction of the appropriate period of deregistration. In contrast to professional disciplinary hearings for lawyers where stains on character appear to be more indelible, reformation leading to restoration is more the norm for doctors. This is so even in cases of conduct which could be seen to go to the root of the relationship of trust, such as sexual assault on patients, sometimes including minors. In the United Kingdom, between 1980 and 1990, 58 per cent of those who applied for restoration of their names to the Register had their applications refused (Smith 1994, p. 206). Recent proposals put forward by the General Medical Council calling for a tougher approach to restoration applications reflects concern within medical regulatory circles at this situation (General Medical Council 1999, pp. 1, 3).

A certificate of conviction will generally be taken to constitute a complaint (for example, *Medical Practice Act 1992* (NSW) s. 71(3)) and its receipt provides the medical board with the trigger to set in train its complaint-handling process. In the absence of a certificate (through lack of notification provisions or oversight), a board may receive a complaint or, as occurs not infrequently, it may become aware of a conviction through the media, and act as nominal complainant.

Once it is in receipt of notice of a conviction, how a board handles a matter will depend upon the legislation. In all states other than Queensland, misconduct is defined to include conviction for a criminal offence, or it constitutes grounds for a complaint. Not all convictions will lead to disciplinary action; for example, as noted earlier, drink-driving offences will more usually be considered to be suggestive of impairment.

Some offences may not be considered to be of sufficient gravity or relevance to medical practice to warrant action. Connection with medical practice is not a prerequisite (for example, murder in a non-medical context, or conviction for fraud) where the gravity of the offence reflects upon the character or suitability of a person to practise medicine. An offence which is considered to be relatively minor and not related to medical practice may not lead to disciplinary action. Some difficult value judgments may be involved here (for example, the medical practitioner convicted of assaulting a spouse, or involved in tax avoidance). In the absence of judicial guidance, these cases will be decided on an individual basis by individual boards, and possibly with quite divergent outcomes.

Several complexities arise due to differences between the criminal and disciplinary jurisdictions. As the medical board's jurisdiction is primarily protective, provision is made for proceeding with complaints under section

56 of the *Medical Practice Act 1992* (NSW) notwithstanding the fact that other civil or criminal proceedings are currently on foot or proposed. Rather than wait several years for the outcome of a criminal trial, the board may deal with a complaint founded on particulars which will possibly also be the basis for a criminal charge. The reported statements of the General Medical Council in the Shipman case that disciplinary action was not commenced until after his conviction contrasts with this provision, though in practice in New South Wales, evidentiary and other considerations may mean that disciplinary proceedings are stood over until the conclusion of the criminal matter.

The standard of proof required in disciplinary proceedings is that described in the case of *Briginshaw v. Briginshaw* ((1938) 60 CLR 336). Evidence led in the Medical Tribunal could well satisfy this standard while falling short of the criminal standard of beyond reasonable doubt. This creates the potential for conflicting decisions, with a positive finding of professional misconduct and an acquittal on essentially the same evidence. However, the fact of the different standards, the different conduct of proceedings and the different natures of the jurisdictions means that such an outcome may be anomalous, but it is not fundamentally unsound.

This issue was considered in some detail by the New South Wales Court of Appeal in the case of *HCCC v. Litchfield* (Unreported decision of the NSW Court of Appeal, 8 August 1997) which stated:

> Disciplinary proceedings consequent upon a conviction in criminal proceedings are not barred by *autre fois convict* or any wider principle of double jeopardy...The converse is also true and adverse disciplinary action does not bar later criminal proceedings arising out of the same facts...
>
> The proposition that an acquittal does not inhibit disciplinary proceedings arising out of the same facts is well established in other common law jurisdictions...It is also sound in principle because both the onus and proof and the purpose and focus of the proceedings are different.

## Crimes Involving Sexual Abuse

Of the types of crime open to doctors by virtue of their position, those involving sexual misconduct are perhaps the most troubling as their commission is generally facilitated by the very fact that the perpetrator is a doctor who has created and then abused a relationship of trust. There is a broad spectrum of transgression involved, from the apparently genuine 'falling in love' category to outright sexual assault. Many of the 'love' relationships will be shown to have substantial elements of inequality and commonly the doctors involved have a remarkable propensity for falling in love on a serial basis. While the patient's capacity to make a fully informed decision about the relationship may be in question, there is rarely any suggestion of criminal behaviour in this kind of relationship. The NSW Medical Board policy on Medical Practitioners and Sexual Misconduct presumes that there is a relative inequality, and states that any sexual relationship between doctor and patient is *prima facie* misconduct.

From the hapless lovers and the loving predators, we move to the next group who seek sexual gratification through inappropriate sexual behaviour, generally masked as clinical care. This group includes the doctor who asks unnecessary and intrusive questions about the patient's appearance or sex life (or makes comments about his or her own) and the doctor who conducts unnecessary examinations or who renders necessary examinations improper by the method of execution.

Much of this behaviour could be described as sexual assault. At the far end of the spectrum is simple sexual assault, for example drugging a patient and then engaging in sexual acts or forcing sexual acts on a patient without any pretence of medical treatment (*Re Hare* Unreported decision of the NSW Medical Tribunal, 14 December 1990).

An area of particular sensitivity in NSW since the Wood Royal Commission has been sexual offences in relation to minors. It is difficult to imagine that the 1987 case of *Kleiner v. Secretary of the Department of Health* (Unreported decision of the NSW Court of Appeal, 20 October 1987), in which the court overturned a deregistration order in relation to a doctor who had pleaded guilty to an offence of indecency towards a four-year-old child, would receive the same treatment today. In this case, the defence had argued that it was an isolated incident occurring at a time when the practitioner was under great stress and expert evidence was tendered that there was virtually no likelihood of repetition.

Guidelines developed by the NSW Department of Health now require all employees or candidates for employment by the Department of Public Health instrumentalities to be subjected to a criminal record check. The checks relate to sexual offences, serious offences involving a threat or injury to another person, and other serious offences where they are directly relevant to the duties of the position (for example, embezzlement or larceny for financial positions). The policy goes on to state:

> Whilst each matter is to be determined on a case-by-case basis, as a general rule NSW Health policy is that persons convicted of sexual offences against children and other vulnerable people will not be employed/appointed (New South Wales, Health Department 1997).

### Crimes Arising from the Prescription of Drugs

Conduct involving improper use or handling of prescription drugs is dealt with more frequently in New South Wales through professional disciplinary procedures than by way of prosecutions under the *Poisons and Therapeutic Goods Act 1966* (NSW). This approach reflects the impairment paradigm in relation to self administration, while it reflects the practical realities of jurisdictional preferences and effectiveness in relation to improper prescribing for patients or third parties. Many practitioners, when confronted with evidence of breach of their statutory obligations, are prepared to voluntarily surrender their prescribing rights. Depending on the seriousness of the breach, different levels of disciplinary proceedings may follow and in extreme cases a criminal prosecution may also be instigated.

While conditions reinforcing the removal of prescribing rights and monitoring drug intake through urinalysis will apply to the less serious cases, the Medical Tribunal in the case of *Re Katelaris* (Unreported decision of the NSW Court of Appeal, 13 April 1991) observed:

> Ordinarily a finding of professional misconduct arising from continued self-administration of drugs of addiction and the deliberate flouting of the law or proper authority concerning the prescription of drugs of addiction will lead to an order that the medical practitioner be removed from the Register.

### Crimes of Dishonesty

Fraud in relation to the payment of benefits under the *Health Insurance Act 1973* (Cth) is a fertile field for medical practitioners with an interest in crime. Unsatisfactory professional conduct is defined in section 36 of the *Medical Practice Act 1992* (NSW) to include conviction for offences under sections 128A, 128B, 129, 129AA and 129AAA of the *Health Insurance Act 1973* (Cth).

## Crimes Involving Reproductive Interventions

Judicial interpretations and changes in social attitudes have meant that the prosecution of medical practitioners for unlawfully terminating pregnancy has become a rarity. The outcome of the most recent attempt to enforce anti-abortion law in Western Australia was the passage of the *Acts Amendment (Abortion) Act 1998* (WA) which, in effect, legalised abortion in that State. While unlawful termination of pregnancy remains an offence in other jurisdictions, interpretation of the term 'unlawful' has meant that prosecutions and consequential medical disciplinary hearings in relation to practitioners performing abortions have effectively ceased.

Changing social views have also lead to increased debate about issues such as surrogacy, euthanasia and a wide range of reproductive technologies. While medical practitioners have been substantially involved in these activities, both at the theoretical and practical level, with the potential for involvement in offences, there have been few attempts to instigate criminal proceedings which could become the subject of disciplinary processes.

## Conclusion

In conclusion, medical practitioners do not appear to be more criminally inclined than other professionals or their peers in society at large. The fact of being a registered medical practitioner does put the doctor in an advantageous position to perpetrate a number of crimes such as sexual assault, illegal prescribing of drugs, euthanasia, abortion and medicare fraud. Some of these crimes go to the heart of being a professional, as they abuse the trust that is a key element of the professional relationship. Professional consequences of criminal activity are generally serious, but the means of bringing crimes to the attention of the regulatory authorities are somewhat haphazard. Faith in the power of repentance means that in most situations, practitioners who have been sanctioned by the disciplinary authority following a criminal conviction will be able to return to the profession, even if their crime involved a breach of what could be viewed as the fundamental underpinnings of their professionalism.

Chapter 6

# Crime in the Nursing Profession:
# A Nurse Regulatory Authority Perspective

Leanne Raven

## Introduction

Nurses hold positions of trust within the community and are generally well thought of by the public. Therefore, the concept of crime is somewhat antithetical to professional nursing practice, as it is not conceptually consistent with either the purpose or the philosophy of contemporary nursing practice. As a result, a natural tension exists between the two concepts because the essence of nursing practice predominantly lies within a therapeutic care model and not a criminal justice model. This tension was mentioned in Bryant's (1999) delivery of the Joan Durdin Oration in Adelaide. Her inquiry into culpability raised many pertinent questions that are worthy of more rigorous examination.

Rather than focusing on this tension, however, the present chapter examines the notion of crime within the profession from the experiences of a nurse regulatory authority. An attempt will be made to present the reality of what is seen and how that reality is managed—bearing in mind that this reality is limited as it relies on what comes to the attention of nurse regulatory authorities. The approach will include broad comment on the nature and extent of crime within the Australian nursing profession. This will be followed by an impression of the general view of crime by nurse regulatory authorities and an indication of the nature and extent of unprofessional conduct by nurses. Some thoughts on preventative action being undertaken by nurse regulatory authorities will be discussed and areas of concern for the future will be raised. Examples will mainly be drawn from the nurse regulatory environment within the state of Victoria, however reference to national directions will also be made.

## The Nature and Extent of Crime

The full range of criminal offences can and have been committed by individuals within the nursing profession. Fortunately, the nursing profession in Australia has had very little to do with what could be described as heinous crimes such as murder and rape, although there have been a small number of cases in which nurses have been charged with such crimes. Over the last five years in Victoria, for example, there have been two such cases. In one, the charges of murder, then manslaughter were not proved, and in another the nurse committed suicide before the charge of rape could be heard by the court.

Given that the majority of convictions for nurses relate to crimes of theft, fraud and drug-related offences, one could be lead to believe that the nature and extent of crime within the nursing profession is inconsequential. However, the true nature and extent of the nursing profession's involvement in behaviour which is of a lesser standard than the public and the profession would reasonably expect, is revealed through cases of unprofessional conduct. These cases are considered in most states and territories of Australia by the nurse regulatory authorities.

One area where national data has been collected is that of child molestation. In a recent report published on child abuse, Johnstone (1999) conducted a survey of Australian nurse regulatory authorities. She found for the period from 1993 to 1998 that a total of 14 nurses were reported for misconduct that related to the maltreatment of children. Twelve of these cases related to sexual abuse of children and two involved physical abuse. Eight of the cases involved child molestation committed outside of a professional capacity and two involved sexual assaults occurring while the nurse was practising. While these figures would not be statistically significant when considered in relation to the total substantiation rates within Australia—which were 89,159 between 1993 and 1997 (Johnstone 1999, p. 6)—or to the total number of registered and enrolled nurses within Australia—which ranged from 281,453 in 1993 to 264,819 in 1998 (Australian Institute of Health and Welfare (AIHW) 1999, p. 3)—Johnstone (1999, p. 236) quite rightly argues that they are of significance in other ways. First, they are of personal significance for those directly affected by the behaviour—the children and their families. Secondly, they are professionally significant for the broader nursing profession and for nurse regulatory authorities.

## Nurse Regulatory Authority View of Crime

In the legal profession, considerable discussion has taken place concerning the definition of crime (Murugason and McNamara 1997). However, Murugason and McNamara (1997, p. 1) suggest that the following definition by Lord Atkin in *Proprietary Articles Trade Association v. Attorney-General (Canberra)* [1931] AC 310 at p. 324 has stood the test of time:

> The criminal quality of an act cannot be discerned by intuition: nor can it be discovered by reference to any standard but one: is the act prohibited with penal consequences?

Murugason and McNamara (1997, p. 1) go on to cite a more contemporary definition by Glanville Williams (1983, p. 27) which expresses a similar view: 'A crime (or offence) is a legal wrong that can be followed by criminal proceedings which may result in punishment.'

From a nurse regulatory perspective, these definitions raise the question as to whether penal consequences are different from Williams' reference to punishment. If punishment means the same thing as penal consequences— where one interpretation would be to equate punishment with 'time in prison'—then crime is something that is outside the realm of a nurse regulatory authority, as such authorities do not have the power to sentence nurses to imprisonment. However, they do have the ability to punish nurses by imposing penalties that could range from mere cautions to cancellation of registration. Cancellation of registration disallows individuals from practising their chosen profession and, as such, represents a severe punishment which can have direct bearing on the person's livelihood.

Generally, nurse regulatory authorities tend to take the view that if nurses are thought to have committed criminal acts then they should first be dealt with by the police and criminal courts in the same way as any person within the community at large. Usually when serious charges have been laid against a nurse by the police then any investigation by the regulatory authority into professional conduct is postponed until the outcome of the criminal investigation is known and any hearing into the matter has been completed. In cases where serious charges are alleged and there is a potential for further harm to be caused to the public, the regulatory authority may suspend registration pending the final hearing of the matter.

Notwithstanding this, some statutory definitions of unprofessional conduct/ misconduct in Nurses Acts or codes referred to in the legislation, include reference to criminal convictions or the non-compliance with statutes or criminal laws. In Victoria, for example, a finding of guilt of an indictable offence or an offence where the nurse's ability to continue to practise as a registered nurse is likely to be affected as a result of that finding, is automatically considered to be unprofessional conduct. The seriousness of such conduct and the way it should be dealt with is usually left to the discretion of the authority or tribunal. However, sometimes Nurses Acts give direction as to how particular kinds of conduct should be dealt with. For example, the *Nurses Act 1991* (NSW) differentiates between 'professional misconduct' and 'unsatisfactory professional conduct'. Professional misconduct is defined as 'unsatisfactory professional conduct of a sufficiently serious nature to justify the removal of the nurse's name from the Register or the Roll'. The Victorian legislation also differentiates between serious and less serious forms of conduct and provides a different range of sanctions for each.

The mode of trial for offences that come to the attention of nurse regulatory authorities is often a distinguishing factor as well—that is, whether they are summary or indictable offences. Indictable offences are more serious in nature and must be heard before a judge and jury, whereas summary offences tend to be less serious than indictable offences and usually involve trial by a judicial officer alone. In some cases, legislation permits an offender charged with an indictable offence to elect to be tried by a judge alone (Murugason and McNamara 1997, p. 16). Individual nurse regulatory authorities form their own view as to the seriousness of cases brought before them with each case being considered individually within the relevant jurisdiction of the authority established under the particular state or territory law. Some distinctions are, however, clear. A cannabis conviction, for example, would generally be viewed as far less serious than a conviction of child molestation.

If one takes the view that crime only extends to that which has been dealt with by the courts then there are many grey areas between crime and unprofessional conduct of nurses. Of course the different standards of proof which apply to the courts and nurse regulatory authorities have some bearing on this and often the evidence gained during an investigation will be enlightening as to whether a case involves a crime or unprofessional conduct. The seriousness of the matter and the type of behaviour are also influential. However, there are some areas, such as the abuse of older people, that have generated considerable discussion as to whether society should consider amending criminal codes to include such behaviour (Kinnear and Graycar 1999). These debates have particular relevance for nurse regulatory authorities that frequently inquire into these types of cases.

## Nature and Extent of Unprofessional Conduct by Nurses

Most annual reports of Australian nurse regulatory authorities indicate the number and nature of complaints of unprofessional conduct with which they deal. However, to date there is no national framework for this reporting and therefore only limited comparisons between the states and territories can be made, if at all.

The Australian Nursing Council Incorporated (ANCI) is currently working on a project to develop a national data collection framework. All of the state and territory nurse regulatory authorities have agreed on the importance of such an endeavour and the ANCI has prioritised the project accordingly. The work within this project is premised on the fact that all of the authorities have agreed upon a set of principles for dealing with professional conduct issues (ANCI 1996). These principles relate to: protection of the public interest; accountability; adherence to the principles of natural justice; relevance to contemporary societal values and beliefs; and equity in dealing with the rights and responsibilities of stakeholders (Fletcher 1998, pp. 77–8). The purpose of these principles was to promote a consistent approach amongst nurse regulatory authorities when dealing with professional conduct matters.

At best it is only possible to give a general indication of the nature and extent of unprofessional conduct by nurses as reported by nurse regulatory authorities in their annual reports.

In the annual report of the Nurses Board of Victoria (1999, p. 19 and 36), data on the types of complaint over the preceding five years are presented along with data on the practice area for each complaint over the last two years. The total number of complaints ranges from 55 to 74 cases per year over the five-year period. The data show that physical/verbal abuse of the elderly (9 to 20) consistently remains the highest area of complaint, with alcohol and drug-related complaints (4 to 21) a little less but still high. Incompetent practice combined with incompetence in drug administration is, on average, at the same level (5 to 23). Sexual misconduct has steadily increased (2 to 6) since the first case appeared in 1997, and the physical/verbal abuse of psychiatric clients (3) emerged as a separate category for the first time in 1999. In relation to the number of complaints by practice area, it can be seen that acute health (6 to 17) and gerontology (15 to 16) are the practice areas with the highest number of complaints. Others include psychiatric, community, palliative care, midwifery and intellectual disabilities.

The South Australian data also suggest that acute care and aged care settings are the practice areas in which most reports arose in 1998–99—14 and 28 respectively (Nurses Board of South Australia 1999, p.10). In New South Wales for 1999, out of a total number of 173 complaints, drug-related offences (43) were the highest type of complaint followed by complaints involving nurse incompetence (32). Impairment (24) was high, with breach of confidentiality (12) and patient assault (12) at the next level (Nurses Registration Board New South Wales 1999, p.6). Queensland, with a total of 70 complaints for 1999, reported that sexual misconduct constituted ten per cent of all types of complaints. Aged care and general nursing were also the practice areas in which most complaints arose (42) (Queensland Nurses Council 1999, p. 50).

The annual reports of both the Victorian and Tasmanian authorities present a sample of case studies each year, from which one conduct-type case and one health-type case have been selected as illustrative of how such matters are dealt with.

## Case 1

Nurse A was alleged to have engaged in unprofessional conduct of a serious nature in that while employed at a mental health service, he physically assaulted a client. Although the nurse did not appear at the formal hearing, he admitted at interview with the Board staff to striking the patient. He said he thought his action was not excessive and claimed he had struck the client in self-defence in order to resist an attack by the client. At the time of the assault, the nurse was described as being determined and red in the face. Several staff members were also restraining the client. The panel noted that the client's behaviour was provoked by the inappropriate behaviour of the nurse. The blow was a deliberate attack on a restrained client, and not an instinctive response by the nurse. The staff who witnessed the attack said the action was an unnecessarily excessive response. The panel recognised that the nurse worked in a stressful environment and that he was not offered, nor did he seek, any counselling regarding the incident. The panel found the nurse had engaged in unprofessional conduct of a serious nature and determined that the nurse's registration be suspended for six months. He was also required to undergo monthly counselling and consultations with a psychiatrist, and enrol in and satisfactorily complete a postgraduate subject in professional issues and psychiatric nursing (Nurses Board of Victoria 1999, p. 19).

*Case 2*

Nurse B, registered as a nurse, responded to the following allegation: that in the performance of her duties as a registered nurse, Nurse B took narcotic substances, namely pethidine, the property of her employer, for her personal use. Nurse B was employed as a clinical nurse in an acute care facility. Over the course of a single evening shift, Nurse B misappropriated, through fraudulent entries in the narcotics register a total of 725mg of pethidine hydrochloride. The matter was discovered by nurses on the following shift and referred by the management of the facility to the police the next day. The Board found the matter substantiated. They noted difficult personal circumstances pleaded in mitigation by the nurse, however, the Board did not consider those circumstances legitimised Nurse B's conduct. The Board was of the view that as a registered nurse, she had both the knowledge and the availability to seek appropriate medical assistance for any health problem she had. Further, the Board considered that she had a responsibility to conduct herself in a manner that provided both the community and her fellow colleagues with a role model. The Board clearly enunciated the professional requirement of honesty, opining that 'dishonesty will destroy professional relationships regardless of the level of knowledge, skill and competence that the nurse possesses…Misappropriating any level of property in general, and in particular drugs, is a serious matter and cannot be tolerated by either the profession or the Board'. The Board determined that they would accept an undertaking from the nurse:

1. to be of good behaviour for a period of one year in that Nurse B comply with the *Poisons Act 1971* (Tas.), the *Poisons Regulations 1975* (Tas.), the *Nursing Act 1995* (Tas.) and the Board's by-laws as proclaimed pursuant to section 11 of the *Nursing Act 1995* (Tas.) from time to time;
2. to complete a Substance Abuse Rehabilitation Program in accordance with the Nursing Board of Tasmania's policy—Substance Abuse Rehabilitation Programs for Nurses; and
3. that, until (2) above has been complied to the Board's satisfaction, she place conditions upon her annual practising certificate to exclude her from possessing, supplying or administering Schedule 8 substances unless they are prescribed for her personal use by a medical practitioner or dental practitioner (Nursing Board of Tasmania 1999, p. 25).

Numbers of complaints made to nurse regulatory authorities are, however, a poor indicator of the extent of unprofessional conduct within the profession.

The collective number of complaints in Australia is so small in comparison with the number of registered and enrolled nurses that it is not possible to draw conclusions of statistical significance. For example, Fletcher (1998, p. 79) claimed that in 1995–96 there were approximately 600 to 620 nurses reported to regulatory authorities throughout Australia and that there were approximately 265,000 nurses on the register in that year. This proportion of complaints to total numbers of nurses (0.2 per cent) remains substantially unchanged. In Victoria for 1999, the 110 complaints considered represented 0.16 per cent of the total population of registered nurses in that state (70,000). However, the trends that emerge within this area are of significance to the nursing profession and broad social policy. It is for this reason that the work of the nurse regulatory authorities and the ANCI on developing a nationally consistent framework is ever so important.

**Preventative Action by Nurse Regulatory Authorities**

The types of preventative measures being currently undertaken by nurse regulatory authorities focus on the areas of nurse competence and professional education.

Over the last decade within Australia there has been extensive work undertaken in relation to nurse competence and the measurement of this phenomenon. The adoption of national competencies for beginning practice, the development of a national code of ethics and a national code of professional conduct are testament to this (see Fletcher 1998). These professional tools are subject to continual revision by the ANCI and the Royal College of Nursing Australia in consultation with the profession generally. However, a significant development recently occurred in this context when the ANCI agreed that two principles would underpin any process for determining the continuing competence of nurses in any jurisdiction within Australia (ANCI 1999). These principles are:

1. that a process of self-assessment be the basis for determining continuing competence of an individual practitioner; and
2. that a process of self-assessment be implemented within a quality and improvement framework.

Each of the nurse regulatory authorities will implement these principles in a way that suits their local jurisdiction. In Victoria, every registered nurse is currently required to declare in their application for annual renewal of registration to practice that they have maintained a satisfactory level of competence. Guidelines are given to assist nurses in forming a personal view as to their level of competence. These guidelines require nurses to make a decision about their competence based on a self-assessment of their nursing practice over the last five years. They state that self-assessment may include consideration of the four following areas:

1. continually assessing your knowledge, skills and professional judgement and, where necessary, taking action to improve the quality of your practice;
2. undertaking professional development activities in the last 12 months that were aimed at enhancing your nursing practice;
3. reflecting on recent workplace performance appraisals to confirm your competence to practice; and
4. promoting a positive image of nursing by your practice.

They also make reference to the array of tools mentioned above and in particular the ANCI national competency standards which come with an assessment method. As a result of the successful outcomes from this approach, a number of nurses have approached the Board in Victoria to discuss the ways in which they can achieve the required level. In the future, the Board will be looking at ways to strengthen the self-assessment process and confirm the validity of this process. Some states, particularly Tasmania and Queensland, have introduced an auditing system which they have recently evaluated with quite positive results in relation to validity.

With respect to education of the profession concerning the types of situations which give rise to unprofessional conduct, the nurse regulatory authorities work very closely with academics to ensure that nursing courses address this area. Some authorities have moved towards providing information to the profession in the form of case studies published in annual reports or newsletters. This has been an important step forward for the profession. Unless the members of the profession become aware of the nature of the matters which come before the regulatory authorities and the outcomes of these cases, they will not be afforded the opportunity to reflect on these matters in relation to their own practice and ultimately learn from these situations. The movement away from the approach where everything was considered to be 'in confidence' to one of transparency in communicating with the nursing profession, represents an important step forward in regulating the nursing profession. In Victoria, the Board has begun publishing a series of articles in its newsletter entitled 'Learning from unprofessional conduct'. The first in the series on abuse of patients, clients and residents presented an outline of five cases that had been considered over the preceding two years. It also discussed what could be learnt from these scenarios and provided direction as to how these incidents could have been better managed and thus avoided.

## Areas of Concern for the Future

There are many changes occurring within the nursing profession and the health care system which affect the environment in which nurses practice. The health care system is dealing with the complexity of quality versus cost at all levels. All health practitioners are faced with uncertainties which these changes create and have to deal with the moral dilemmas which confront them daily.

At present, the majority of nurses are employees within the health care system and are required to practise within such an environment. Should there be some movement towards more nurses becoming self-employed then their practice environment will change considerably. As a result, nurse regulatory authorities could expect to see a change in the nature of complaints dealt with. For example, complaints involving payment of fees for service and medicare fraud could become more frequent.

As the members of the nursing profession are affected by general population health trends, the growth in mental health problems and substance abuse will continue to be problematic. Changes in the role of nurses, such as the authorisation of nurse practitioners to prescribe medications applicable to the context of their practice, will also present interesting challenges for the profession and nurse regulatory authorities. Finally, as discussed in chapter 15 (Smith), the electronic delivery of services will certainly have an impact on professional conduct issues in nursing as the regulatory environment of telehealth develops.

## Conclusion

Crime has a presence in nursing practice even though it is conceptually inconsistent with the purpose and philosophy of nursing. The number of nurses convicted of crimes or found to have engaged in unprofessional conduct is small, particularly when compared with the total number of nurses within Australia. Although statistically insignificant, professional crime and misconduct in nursing does have significance in two areas. It is significant for those people and their families who are directly affected, and it is also of significance for the nursing profession at large.

The nurse regulatory authorities have the mandate to protect the public and they are supportive of the need to develop a national framework for the collection of complaint data. It is hoped that such a framework would assist in our understanding of the trends and inform preventative action by these authorities and the ANCI. It would also place these authorities and the profession in a better position for dealing with future areas of concern.

For the last six years the Australia-wide Morgan Poll has shown that the nursing profession rates best of all the professions for maintaining high standards of honesty and ethics (Roy Morgan Research Centre 1999). If the nursing profession is to maintain this standard and its good relationship with the public, there is much work to be done and much to be learnt in the regulatory and practice areas.

# PART III
# DEALING WITH CRIME IN
# THE PROFESSIONS

Chapter 7

# The Role of Codes of Ethics in Preventing Professional Crime

Margaret M. Coady

## Introduction

There is a danger that either too much or too little will be expected from codes of ethics in the professions. On the one hand they may be seen as the solution to both the criminal and ethical transgressions which in recent years have so concerned both the clients of professions and the general public. On the other hand codes of ethics can be dismissed as ineffective by those who are more cynical about the ability of groups to regulate themselves or about the very possibility of ethical behaviour. They can also be scorned by those who are aware of the many misuses of codes of ethics in the past to cover up malpractice, for example, or to control dissident members of the professions. This chapter, while admitting misuses of codes, argues that there is a role for codes of ethics as one element in decreasing crime in the professions. However, they will not be a miracle cure. They will not, at least not by themselves, do away with greed and other motivations for crime, including what seems to be the motivation in much computer crime, namely the desire to match wits with the security devisers.

There are several reasons why we may be cautious about seeing codes of ethics as solutions. One of these lies with the motivations which groups have had for constructing codes of professional ethics. In some cases the motivation seems to have more to do with establishing status than with producing more ethical behaviour. While this accusation of the self-serving drive for professional status has been made of the new or aspiring professions (Condren 1995), there is also historical evidence (Kultgen 1995; Siggins 1996) of the medical profession in several countries using professional organisation and self-regulation through codes to establish hegemony over the healing occupation. Medical professionals could attract high monetary and other rewards by creating an elite and keeping the numbers of qualified small.

## Failure to Enforce Codes of Ethics

History has other lessons to teach us about codes. One of the most worrying of these is how infrequently codes of ethics are enforced in the professions. This may sometimes be because the codes are expressed in such vague and lofty terms that they are unenforceable (Kultgen 1988). Many of the professional codes mention 'integrity', 'service to mankind', 'best interests of the client' and similar broad terms. And unlike the situation in the justice system, there is no case history of established courts which may give a clearer meaning to these exalted terms. It has even been suggested that this vagueness of expression is a calculated machination to present a highly ethical appearance, while avoiding accountability (Kultgen 1988, 1995).

But there are other plausible explanations of the lack of specificity which present professionals in a more agreeable light. These explanations involve pointing out that perhaps it is not always a bad thing if codes express aspirations rather than the 'lowest common denominator' behaviour of the acceptable professional. When codes are in full or in part expressions of aspirations, it would be unfair to use sanctions against those who do not always live up to these descriptions of the ideal professional. Why should a professional group not express what it aspires to, rather than simply describe the ground beneath which a professional must not sink if he or she is to continue to practice. Having ideals to strive for, even if they are rarely achieved, must improve the practice of any professional. If these aspirations are to be at all meaningful, however, one would expect that particular instantiations of the ideals in the profession would be referred to, reflected on and pursued.

All the same, most failures of enforcement cannot be explained in the above ways and many failures of enforcement seem reprehensible. As we have also seen in earlier chapters, professionals even fail to take action against their fellow professionals who are lacking minimal competence (May 1980; Rodwin 1993). Kultgen (1995, p. 189) claims that while many individual professionals may be dedicated to serve the public, 'much of the effort of their professional organisations is devoted to improving the occupation's position in society and its ability to serve those who pay the freight—patrons, clients and employers—rather than the nebulous cause of "public welfare"'. Evidence about the disciplinary actions of professional bodies is quite difficult to obtain, at least in the United States, since many professions are not keen to publish information about, for example, the number of licences revoked (Rodwin 1993, p. 43). This is possibly because of a persistent but debatable view about bringing a profession into disrepute; it seems doubtful which brings more disrepute to a profession—disciplining offenders or ignoring transgressions and pretending there are no bad apples in the barrel.

Mystification about the nature of professionals' moral responsibilities has also contributed to this lack of openness about the failings of professionals. There is a common belief that the particular ethical nature of the professions requires applying higher moral standards to professionals (Jennings, Callahan and Wolf 1987; Coady 1997). There is some disagreement in legal decisions in Australia and elsewhere (Freckelton 1996) about the reach of the term 'professional misconduct'. But, as Freckelton points out, there is a certain elitism about the idea that a particular category of people must conform to exemplary standards in every facet of life in order to protect the reputation of the profession.

> Lawyers who 'borrow' money from their trust accounts because of cash flow crises or because of pathological gambling problems are little different in terms of principle from persons in disadvantaged neighborhoods who are unable to manage their social security benefits efficiently or those who suffer from another form of addiction (Freckelton 1996, p. 152).

Yet the gap between the myth of professionals' exemplary behaviour and the reality of their yielding to temptation seems to lead to a kind of group psychological denial.

Other explanations of non-enforcement lie not with the individual psyche and conscience of the professional, but with the structure and organisation of a profession. Many professional groups simply do not link enforcement procedures to their codes of ethics. Professions, at least in theory, can impose a range of penalties on those professionals who breach the code of ethics, ranging from a private rebuke from the ethics committee, through publication of the facts of the breach, to suspension of the right to practice. Of course all this must be done while respecting the principles of natural justice. The breach must be properly investigated, the 'miscreant' informed clearly of the charge and be given a genuine opportunity to defend himself. Those who sit in judgment must be unbiased, and the miscreant's right to appeal against any penalty recognised. In other words most aspects of the police and courts are necessary in a disciplinary hearing and sentence. All of this is expensive in both time and money, and the less powerful professions do not have the wherewithal to support the process. Bird (1998) points out the time-consuming and expensive nature of these investigations, and argues that establishing the exact nature of the act of misconduct in terms of the intentions of the wrongdoer is often very difficult. However she does cite the view of the President of the American Psychological Association, Norman Abeles (1998), that '...each scientific society must decide for itself the price it is willing to pay for the enforcement of scientific ethics. But the real question that must be asked is what is the price for not enforcing ethical standards?' These difficulties of enforcing codes of ethics do not in the end seem insuperable. In the United States, a much more litigious society than most, several models have been put forward which maintain procedural fairness while taking seriously the need to act against those guilty of professional misconduct (Mishkin 1995), and the chapters of the present volume indicate the attempts by professional associations to come to terms with these problems.

## Can Codes of Ethics Change Behaviour?

There are several theoretical reasons why one may expect codes of professional ethics to change the behaviour of professionals. One of these is the psychological pressure of the public statement of expected behaviour by those with whom the professional presumably identifies. Most professional societies have at least the means to express their disapproval of a professional's conduct, if not to put the professional out of business.

Another reason why codes may change behaviour is that codes of ethics can in one sense provide knowledge in that they can point out the temptations to be found in particular professions which may not be apparent. For example, the codes for the Royal Australian and New Zealand College of Psychiatry and for the National Tertiary Education Union, like the codes of several other professions and organisations, contain provisions which relate to sexual relations between professionals and clients. It is possible that the abuses of power involved in such relations may not be realised by the neophyte or naïve or obtuse professional, and that the code of ethics can inform them of this, or at least move them to query their own assumptions about such relations.

A more credible example of the way in which a code can provide knowledge of which the professional is ignorant occurs at the interface between university research and big business. Many research professionals are innocent of the ways of business, and are willing to sign clauses in contracts with sponsors which give sponsors control over publication, not realising that corporate sponsors may refuse to publish results which, though accurate and important, go against the interests of the sponsor (Rennie 1997). Many university research codes now contain clauses forbidding researchers to sign agreements which give the rights to publish to the sponsor.

An interesting account of how codes of ethics can influence behaviour even without the threat of sanctions comes from coordination theory (Lichtenberg 1996). Coordination theory points to two relevant principles which can affect a person's motivation to act. The first is the *Contribution Principle* according to which a person is more likely to act in a given way the greater the contribution to a collective good purpose achieved by that act. The second is the *Sacrifice Principle* according to which the lower the sacrifice involved for an individual in acting collectively, the more likely the action. An example which shows how these principles can apply to a code of ethics is the provision in the Code of Ethics of the Society of Professional Journalists which states that 'only an overriding public need can justify intrusion into anyone's privacy' (Code of Ethics of the Society of Professional Journalists in Gorlin 1999). An individual journalist may be able to secure a titillating scoop by invading the privacy of grieving parents whose young daughter has just committed suicide. But the journalist will, at least according to coordination theory, hesitate because she believes that her fellow journalist on a rival newspaper will also have qualms about breaching the privacy provision in the code. She will not have to sacrifice much since the rival journalist will forgo the scoop also, and together they will be contributing to the good of protecting the privacy of the parents' grief, a protection which would not have occurred if only one journalist had determined to respect that privacy. Derisive laughter is often the response when a lay audience consider the journalists' commitment to respect for privacy, but the present writer can vouch for the occurrence on at least one occasion of the decision-making described above.

This anecdotal evidence may not be of much consolation to those who are expecting more of codes. Other empirical studies in the area do not provide any firmer ground for making claims about codes of ethics. Empirical studies on the efficacy of such codes, while tending to dismiss their effectiveness, are generally flawed, and empirical work in the area is fraught with difficulties. Cleek and Leonard (1998) surveyed business students, giving half of them a specific code of ethics and simply telling the other half that their hypothetical employer had a code of ethics. The students were all then given descriptions of ethically problematic situations and asked for a response. Since there was 'no difference in decision-making' (the details of the meaning of this are not given in the article) between the group which had the code in front of them and the group which merely knew of the existence of a code, the unwarranted conclusion is drawn that there is no relationship between having a code and ethical decision-making. Apart from its other problems, this study shows a lack of understanding of what a code of ethics might do; in its conclusion it seems to assume that a previously unsighted and undiscussed code, in effect just a piece of paper with a list of affirmations and prohibitions, can provide immediate answers to how the professional should act.

A more interesting and informed, though earlier, experiment which reaches a similar conclusion is what the authors call a 'natural experiment' looking at the impact of codes of ethics on journalists' decisions (Pritchard and Morgan 1989). In this case the researchers compared the decisions about hypothetical situations of journalists from two newspapers. The newspapers were comparable in that they belonged to the same company and espoused similar political stances; in addition the journalists from the two newspapers had similar education and age profiles. Both newspapers had codes of ethics, but they differed in content and in how they had been developed. The code of the *News* was developed in consultation with the journalists themselves, but it focused entirely on conflicts of interest. The *Star's* rank and file journalists had no input to their code, and its content was much broader, giving extensive coverage to issues of fairness, compassion and sensitivity.

Three of the hypotheticals put to the journalists of the *Star* and the *News* raised issues to do with conflict of interest, while three raised issues of fairness, sensitivity or compassion. On the conflict of interest hypotheticals there was no meaningful difference between the two sets of journalists. In only one of the other three hypotheticals was there a statistically significant difference. This hypothetical asked journalists what they would write about a prominent local person who had escaped uninjured from a fire at a Key West hotel which was described in the wire service as a well-known rendezvous of gays. The celebrity requested the newspapers to keep his name out of the story, threatening to commit suicide if it appeared. Responding to this hypothetical, 48 per cent of the *News* journalists were prepared to run the full story in spite of the threat, while only 20 per cent of the *Star* journalists would. On the next hypothetical which involved unauthorised taping of a just-nominated presidential candidate's discussion with party officials, the *News* staff were more ethical, while on the third, involving respecting the privacy of the families of just-returned hostages, there was no difference between the two groups. The researchers therefore conclude that their study gives no support to the idea that codes of ethics directly influence the behaviour of journalists.

This empirical evidence may seem disappointing to supporters of codes of ethics, and doubly disappointing to those who argue that for codes of ethics to be effective they must be drawn up by those to whom they apply. However this disappointment is a sign of too great an expectation of the effectiveness of the single device. Later in the chapter it will be argued that an ethical environment requires the coincidence of a large number of factors. As Pritchard and Morgan (1989) put it, 'formal norms are only one ingredient in a rich stew'.

## Ethics is Different from Law

Another approach to this question of the relation of professional codes of ethics and crime is to argue that it involves a category mistake, since codes of ethics have to do with ethics and not with the law; and crime, by definition, has to do with breaches of the law. Let laws deal with crime and let codes of ethics deal with ethics, it may be said. However to make a sharp dichotomy between law and ethics is too simple. It is true that some of the provisions in typical codes of ethics of professions are of an essentially ethical nature and could not be legislated. The statement in the *Code of Ethics of the Royal Australian and New Zealand College of Psychiatry* that psychiatrists should respect the essential humanity and dignity of each patient is one such example. Other provisions, however, while essentially ethical, can have legal consequences in civil proceedings, if, for example, a person sues for damages which have been caused as a result of a breach of a professional's code of ethics. The matter of crime arises when a professional breach is a serious offence against the community. Examples are: fraudulently claiming qualifications that one does not have; fraud through over-servicing; and theft of intellectual and other property through misuse of computers. These activities are clearly both criminal and unethical.

One philosopher, John Ladd (1992), goes so far as to argue that imposing codes of ethics on other people 'in the guise of ethics contradicts the notion of ethics itself, which presumes that persons are autonomous moral agents'. There are many responses and comments which could be made about Ladd's argument. One response is that his argument would have some validity if espousing a code of ethics involved handing one's autonomy over to others. But in fact a code of ethics is a statement of the values which are involved in the practice of the profession, and the individual professional is free to decide whether or not to follow it in particular circumstances.

Ladd's analysis also raises the question of who should decide on the content of the code of ethics. One view at least about business codes is that the owners of the company should decide. Elaine Sternberg (2000, p. 244) argues:

contrary to popular belief, employee consultation is not necessary for legitimising a moral code...If a code of conduct is meant to express a company's fundamental aims and values, then it is for the company's owners, not its employees, to stipulate what those aims and values are.

It is likely that there are some fundamental differences between the purposes of codes of ethics for businesses and those for professions, though even here it seems *a priori* more likely that people will more willingly obey those rules which they have been involved in compiling. But if Sternberg is right about whose values should be enshrined in codes of ethics, then Ladd's argument has more relevance, since codes of ethics just seem another way of controlling the behaviour of the uncooperative employee.

On some occasions the most ethical action involves breaking the law, and indeed professional codes of ethics can play a role in professional opposition to or non-compliance with the law. The case of the library, the art thieves and the FBI (Vocino and Tyler 1996) is only one of many examples which could be used to illustrate this point. In this case the FBI believed that by gaining access to confidential circulation records of art books in a library they could get valuable information about a series of art thefts, during one of which an elderly woman was bashed and left with severe head injuries. The inexperienced librarian, in charge of the library over a weekend, yielded to the pressure of the FBI, pressure which included vivid descriptions of the woman's injuries, and hectoring about the hesitancy caused by the librarian's realisation that he was being asked to act in a professionally unethical manner. To the librarian's initial response that he was not 'comfortable' with giving them confidential information, one agent responded:

> We all need to do things we don't want to do, and frankly, pal, we can't wait until you get the OK from your boss. You're the man in charge. Let us see the records so we both can get about our business. You're making more of this than need be (Vocino and Tyler 1996, p. 51).

In this event the code was breached, but rather than showing that codes are useless, this example suggests that codes should be strengthened, in particular by being combined with ethics education, including specific training in ethical dilemmas which are likely to arise and protocols for handling them. Presumably if the code had not existed the librarian would not have thought twice about handing over the information to the authorities.

In other more extreme cases of unethical laws, the professional may decide not merely to refuse to cooperate with the law enforcers, but to disobey the law itself. In Nazi Germany some teachers and librarians refused to obey the edict to remove from their domains all books which showed Jews in a good light (Kamenetsky 1984; Coady 1996). These cases also raise issues about the nature of 'professional deviance'. On the one hand the term can mean deviation from the important values embodied in the professions. On the other it could be argued that all professionals are in a sense deviant in that while cooperation with the law is generally a good thing, the particular role of a professional may involve non-compliance with the law. In the librarian case, the code of ethics, used properly, at least in the eyes of the professionals and probably most ethicists, may have stood in the way of solving crime and therefore possibly of deterring it in the future. Looked at in this way, codes of ethics are certainly not a key to crime minimisation, and the cooption of professional regulators into crime prevention or detection is problematic.

**Professional Values**

Within the literature on codes of ethics there is a debate about whether codes should be profession-wide or organisation-wide (Sinclair 1996). The two journalists' codes considered above are organisation-based, whereas the librarian's code is that of the American Library Association based on the profession. The argument for having codes based on the local organisation is that loyalties tend to be local. There is, it is argued, a greater chance of compliance at this level, particularly given the changing nature of professional employment, where professionals are often no longer employed by their fellow professionals, but in complex multidisciplinary organisations. But it is this very fact which leads to the counterargument, which is that codes of ethics have a new importance where many professionals are in fact employed by individuals or by groups who do not share the same professional background. The idea of protecting the values of the profession, not simply the wellbeing of the professionals themselves, has become increasingly significant.

An example from Michael Davis (1991) illustrates this. Davis argues that proper attention to the engineers' code of ethics could have averted the 'Challenger disaster' in the United States. The engineers in the firm which manufactured the space shuttle recommended against the launch on the particular day because extreme weather conditions were a threat to safety. But the head of the company, not himself an engineer and under extreme economic and political pressure since the State of the Union message to be given next day was to include acclaim for the launch, asked the chief of the engineers to 'think like a manager, not like an engineer'. The result of the chief engineer's overturning the recently expressed professional judgment of his professional group was the dramatic failure of the shuttle and the deaths of all those on board.

This example, while somewhat sensational, demonstrates the role a code of ethics could and should have played in a complex, multidisciplinary, politically sensitive contemporary organisation. Seen in this light, an important function of a code of ethics is the statement by the profession to outsiders of the values of the profession. Such a statement is necessary, not to promote the profession itself, but to give a warning to those outside the profession that the compliance of the professional cannot be taken for granted if such compliance involves compromising professional values. This role of codes of ethics is a protective role though not, as earlier professional codes of ethics often were, protective of the individual professionals or of the profession itself, but protective of the values inherent in the activities of the profession. In this particular case of the engineers this was the value of designing safe and effective shuttles.

Engineers are not the only professional group whose exercise of professional judgement is threatened by pressures from outside the profession. The librarian needed protection against pressures from the FBI, journalists may need protection against pressures from corporate owners, and researchers may need protection against pressure from sponsors. Doctors, teachers, accountants, computer professionals and in fact all professionals can face such pressures. The values that these professionals stand for, caring for the ill, ensuring safe structures, teaching, searching for knowledge and so on are all values which can be included in the relevant professional codes. They are all values which are important for the community but which can be threatened by organisations which are myopically pursuing profit and power, or which simply do not recognise the threat to these values, or which lack the knowledge of how to protect these values.

This argument about the fragility of professional values can look rather like the argument for professional self-regulation, an argument which has fallen into some justified disrepute because of past failures by the professions themselves to regulate. But there are ways of learning from the unhappy history of codes of ethics, while maintaining some place for such codes in an ethical professional culture.

In this ethical culture it will be necessary to maintain some kind of autonomy for professionals in the sense that their expertise in their particular area needs to be recognised. Only an engineer can determine whether the O-rings on the Shuttle will be safe. Only a kidney surgeon can determine the best way to operate on a diseased kidney. While it would be a mistake to overemphasise the exclusivity of professionals' knowledge, it is equally mistaken to ignore it. Neither the courts nor the person in the street can take the place of the expertise learned not just through theory, but through practice in a community of fellow professionals. And there is a danger that this expertise will be discounted when pressures from other sources, insurance companies, governments, international corporations and so on, come into play. Codes of ethics should provide ways of protecting the values involved in the practice of this expertise while at the same time holding the professional accountable.

## Professional Power and Professional Temptation

Nevertheless it needs to be acknowledged that professions, apart from being custodians of important community values, can also be, like other organisations, sources of corruption for the individual members (Coady 1996). The writer C.S. Lewis describes the insidiously corrupting process in one of his novels where he refers to the 'chatter of laughter between fellow professionals which of all earthly powers is strongest to make men do very bad things before they are yet, individually, very bad men' (Lewis 1965, p. 130).

This is precisely the kind of group corruption which Darley (1996) describes so graphically in his case studies of several organisations notorious for their involvement in corruption. Like Lewis, Darley holds that it would be a mistake, at least in the initial stages of the corruption, to explain the harm by reference to the decisions of evil individuals. In the initial stages of a process which leads to disastrous harm there is often no clear victim and no individual who decides to commit an evil act, but a number of factors which in hindsight can be seen to have contributed. These include, in Darley's analysis, the existence within the organisation of certain fears, the fear of losing profits and the fear of losing jobs. Other factors relate to management by objectives where these objectives are defined solely in terms of profit, and incentive, bonus and promotion schemes where these are judged also simply in terms of economic profit to the organisation. Unreasonable pressure of time is also often a factor, and later in the process misuse of confidentiality to cover up mistakes.

An important danger sign is the existence in the organisation of ethically dubious practices which are already well established. Darley gives the Saloman Brothers case as an example. In this case the stockbroker firm moved off poor-quality bonds to their least sophisticated customers, and gave larger bonuses and promotion to those salespeople who successfully 'got rid of' the useless bonds to clients whose interests the company was meant to be serving. The unethical actions of the stockbrokers resulted in a loss of life savings for many elderly customers. Though the person who initiated this practice left the company, the practice grew and spread to other companies. It became part of the culture of several stockbroking firms and new members were socialised into it. The same scenario can occur within other professions and organisations. A powerful influence on a professional's practice seems to be the early socialisation by other professionals in the workplace, and it is here that ethically unsound practices can easily be perpetuated.

While group corruption has a long history, the last decade has seen an increase in the temptations faced by many businesses and professions. Downsizing has been a fashionable way of increasing the appearance of productivity, and the loss of jobs which follows from this downsizing has led to the kinds of fear which Darley (1996) notes as a factor in evildoing. In the academic world positions are becoming scarcer, leading to increased and often desperate competition, with the attendant risks of plagiarism and fraudulent production of results. In addition, academic research is increasingly dependent on sponsors for supporting research which can lead to dangerous compromise of academic values (Rennie 1997). With changes in employment practices, increasing use of expensive equipment and greater rewards to be gained from new treatments, the practice of medicine has become more involved with business, and the possibilities of fraud have increased. Rosenberg (1996) noted the increasing use of secrecy in medical research, a secrecy which is not equivalent to the kind of confidentiality aimed at the clients' interest, but a secrecy motivated by market forces. With such changes, the kinds of professional corruption noted in earlier times by writers from Paracelsus, through George Bernard Shaw (1925, Preface, p. xxii, who in 1906 described all professions as 'conspiracies against the laity') and C.S. Lewis, to contemporary commentators is likely to flourish.

**Professions and Business**

Rodwin (1993, p. 11) described the great changes which have overtaken the medical profession in the United States since the Second World War. 'Medicine, once a quasi-eleemosynary institution, has become an expensive article of commerce.' The eleemosynary aura of medicine has helped to reinforce another continuing myth about professionals which is that they are ethically superior to those who earn their living through businesses. After all, so the myth goes, professionals have a vocation; unlike those who go into business, professionals' motivations in undertaking their occupations is not primarily to make money, but to serve the public. Professor Western discussed this claimed characteristic of professions in chapter 3 earlier in this book. What is not so often admitted is that most professionals are either small businesses themselves or employed in bigger businesses, so that not only professional ethics but business ethics is relevant to them.

The myth of ethical superiority of professions to business may have been one of the factors which have led professionals to downplay business ethics in their codes and education. It is true that some codes of ethics have contained reference to what might be seen as business ethics. But Rodwin (1993) documents the ambivalent attitude that the American Medical Association has had towards fee-splitting and other business aspects of practicing medicine. While many codes of ethics have in the past had provisions regulating the relations between fellow professionals, including such matters as not undercutting the price of services offered by fellow professionals, few, with the exception of codes for the legal profession, have had provisions which protect the client, such as those which deal with conflict of interest. Mention of 'fair dealing' occurs in some codes, but what this means in practice needs to be discussed by each professional group, and in particular what are the temptations which occur in particular professions which may lead to a failure to deal fairly.

Another aspect of the business/profession interface is that many professionals, and not only in Australia, now gain a good deal of their monetary rewards from taxation monies, or at least their incomes are extensively affected by taxation and other government policies. Yet the ethical challenges in this area are largely unexamined either in codes of ethics or reports of ethical discussions in the professions. References occur in some codes of ethics to the fact that the professional should obey the law, and this may at first sight seem aimed at preventing the kind of corruption involved in fraud cases, including taxation fraud. However, as an element in a code of ethics, this injunction to obey the law seems redundant. Professionals are under no greater compunction to obey the law than others and, as argued earlier in this chapter, they may on occasions have a professional duty not to cooperate with the forces of law.

Rather than simplistically telling their members to obey the law, professions should look more carefully at the ethos and practice of their professions, and ensure that their particular code delineates the complex relationship of the profession and the law. Freckelton (1996, p. 144) claims that:

> Certain kinds of ethical misconduct, such as filing dishonest tax returns, have long been tolerated among professionals...because they apparently did not offend against the predominant ethos of professional practice.

If this is true, the widely reported case of the alleged scam by Australian radiologists (Zinn 2000) should have come as no surprise.

## Some Modest Proposals

Proposals on this matter need to be modest because knowledge is limited. The motivations of professionals who commit crime is probably as varied and as unascertained as the criminal motivations in the population at large. However from examination of codes and the ethos of professions and an analysis of corruption in groups, both business and professional, we can get some clues for reform. While governments should ensure prosecution of fraud cases, regardless of the lofty positions of those who commit them, and they should avoid trying to deal with scandal by legislating in ways which overlook the need for professional judgment on many matters, the main arena for reform is probably the professional associations themselves.

It is important that there be an updating and continuing review of the code of ethics of each profession. This updating and review should be carried out by the broad membership of the profession who are willing to be committed to these values. But the involvement of an outside viewpoint is also important in this process. The point of involving outsiders is not so much to have consumer or taxpayer representatives, as to provide a different perspective from that accepted as the norm by those socialised into the existing professional ethos. The process should be informed by past criticisms of the code of ethics both by outsiders and by the members of the profession. It should also take into account both the values of the particular profession, for example healing in the case of medicine, safety in the case of engineers and so on, and the temptations faced by the particular profession.

In spite of its unfashionable theological overtones, I have used the word 'temptation' in preference to 'dilemma'. 'Dilemma' can imply that an interesting conflict of principle is involved. Such dilemmas are often intellectually challenging and possibly for that reason regularly form the basis of academic classes in professional ethics. But in real life the nature of the ethical action can frequently be determinatively settled; the question that needs to be looked at is what are the forces which lead the professional from that path. Again the combination of some people with an outside perspective with practitioners of the specific profession will be needed to identify these temptations, since what is apparent to an outsider is sometimes clouded in the process of socialisation into the assumptions and practices of a profession. Some of the temptations will involve the business aspects of the practice of the profession and these should be fully acknowledged and discussed.

A professional body should also ensure that the codes of ethics of the profession with which it is concerned is widely known and understood, not only by the particular profession and its clients, but by employers, managers, chief executive officers and government officials whose decisions impact on professional practice. On a very practical level there need to be regular meetings between the chief executive officers of an organisation and representatives of the different professions employed within that organisation. The point of these would be to ensure that any discrepancy between the code of ethics of the organisation and the professional codes can be remedied. This sharing of information and views may go some way toward remedying the ethical problems which have arisen as a result of the changed nature of the employment of many professionals.

Analysis of the code of ethics should be part of the initial training of each professional, but the profession should provide continuing ethics education through the life of practice since, as practice continues, ethical challenges will be better understood and these challenges will change over time. Codes of ethics are also used in conducting the rather vogueish 'ethics audits'. One reason for this terminology in businesses is to put ethics on at least the same level of importance as the financial details. In the professions this can also be important because it suggests both the attention to ethical detail and the involvement of outsiders. Properly conducted, these audits can reveal any tensions between the stated values of the profession and the general ethos of the profession.

A final point may seem at first to run somewhat counter to earlier arguments about greater enforcement. It is important that professionals get the opportunity to deliberate on their ethical responsibilities (Coady 1996). This will require time, space and at least a temporary lessening of pressures, including the pressure to appear always totally competent. Some hospitals (Gawande 1999) have already set up forums where doctors can discuss mistakes and near-misses without fear of reprisals, with a view to finding out from deliberation with their peers better ways of performing procedures. It seems possible and desirable to do the same with regard to ethical mistakes and challenges. A forum of a rather similar kind has been operating at St Vincent's Hospital, Melbourne, among a group of psychiatrists. Such opportunities for unpressured ethical reflection may lessen the kinds of fears and resulting cover-ups described by Darley (1996) in relation to those aspects of organisations which led to evildoing and often disaster. They should also bring before the conscious minds of the professionals any tensions between their code of ethics and the reality of practice. However the membership of these forums is of crucial importance. Apart from the professional membership, there should be at least one outsider since a forum in which one can admit mistakes and temptations without fear may otherwise easily become a forum for group-bonding through reassurance and rationalisation. 'He would have died anyway', or 'we all have to take risks', or 'the elderly live too well anyway on unearned income' are rationalisations less likely to be comfortingly sought in the presence of an outsider.

This chapter has been in part a plea for realism. It has argued that the myth of the high moral vocation of professionals is dangerous. This myth has led to a culture of denial which has been a barrier to the investigating of wrongdoing in the professions. But equally dangerous would be a backlash cynicism which refused to recognise the very important values embodied in the professions, and it is here that the professional codes of ethics have a vital role.

Chapter 8

# Fraud Control in the Australian Defence Organisation

Carla Day[1]

## Introduction

As in many other public sector institutions in Australia, the Australian Defence Organisation has had responsibility for fraud control, prevention and detection since the late 1980s. More specific policy guidance was afforded public sector agencies in 1994 with the development of interim guidelines on the fraud control policy of the Commonwealth. The Commonwealth Law Enforcement Board (CLEB) develops and reviews policy and practices on a regular basis. Each Commonwealth agency has an annual reporting requirement to CLEB on fraud and fraud control measures. This enables CLEB to identify common trends in fraud statistics across the Commonwealth, while ensuring that the quality of investigations and reporting satisfy standards set for the conduct of investigations and preparation of briefs of evidence for the Director of Public Prosecutions.

In recent years, and in the light of the development of a revised Fraud Control Policy of the Commonwealth, more responsibility for the management and control of fraud is being devolved to individual agencies. This has occurred in a climate of decreased government spending and concomitant focus on the accountability of agency heads to deliver timely outcomes. Increasing public interest in the use and management of public moneys has also focused managers' attention on the need for competency and transparency in their business arrangements. These factors impact on the way an agency approaches its program delivery. Beginning with the commercialisation of many support services in Defence in the late 1980s, the agency has learned to address fraud and misappropriation from a 'system' or procedural perspective as well as from a personnel perspective. This chapter briefly explores both perspectives and comments on the overall experience of fraud control in Defence.

## System Approach

A system approach entails an identification and assessment of Defence functions likely to be at risk of fraudulent exploitation. Functions identified as 'at risk' are those which carry high to extremely high residual risk and require some form of remedial action. Residual risk is assessed by determining a function's exposure to fraud less the degree to which controls are effectively in place. Functional examples include financial systems, such as pay and allowances, major capital equipment projects and information systems, that is, those areas where there are attractive and accessible resources. Strong control measures need to be in place to minimise (or mitigate) the risk of losses from fraud, waste or abuse.

Fraud risk assessment has been a part of the fraud control process since the early 1990s but it was in 1996 that a major study of more than 400 Defence units was conducted to measure risk in a quantifiable way across the Defence organisation. This was a significant and resource intensive undertaking devised to draw the common threads of fraud risk across an agency that is geographically and structurally complex. With the assistance of the Australian Bureau of Statistics, a methodology was developed to assess fraud risk on a continuum. Results of this assessment were used to develop a corporate level fraud control plan which was to act as the departmental guide for Defence Groups to develop their own Group plan and sub-Group plans in accordance with the risk priorities identified in the corporate plan.

The strength of this approach is that a uniform classification of functions and their associated risks could be devised for the development of a benchmark against which future measures could be contrasted. By treating the 'extremely high', 'high' and 'medium' level risks identified through the fraud risk assessment, we believed that the majority of risk in common areas could be mitigated. At-risk Commonwealth resources not only include cash and consumables but also time, property and information.

Once a quantified measure of risk was determined for each high to very high-risk function, a fraud control plan could be developed to mitigate risks in a manner that enabled comparison of common and shared risk factors within a heterogeneous workplace such as Defence. Fraud control plans have a dynamic life. In Defence's case, under legislation a new risk assessment and plan should be completed every four years. An important component of the fraud control planning cycle is evaluation and reporting on the implementation of fraud control. This enables the organisation as a whole to identify common obstacles in implementing fraud control and provides important lessons on future fraud management strategies. Adequate controls, however, are only one aspect of the fraud control and prevention process. Fraud control can really only be successful if there is a clear understanding and commitment by personnel towards reducing risk.

## Personnel Approach

There are four main areas under which personnel issues in fraud control are addressed: policy, training and awareness, culture and management support.

### Policy

*Compliance and guidance*  It is a mandatory legislative requirement for all Australian Public Service agencies to develop and to implement a fraud control plan. Because of the size, complexity and the structure of Defence, planning is hierarchical beginning with a corporate-wide plan. The process of planning Defence-wide then takes on a matrix-type structural arrangement, with each Defence Group required to develop plans that address their specific risks as well as those identified corporately. Responsibility is devolved within each Group for unit-level planning. The issue for Defence personnel is in the efficient communication of fraud control guidelines out to the unit level. It has been found that while some news can travel particularly quickly, providing sufficient guidance on fraud control planning (for example) requires high levels of interaction between the policy developers and the planners. It is important that every effort is put into communicating clearly in the early stages because plans completed in this way are usually well supported by those who are required to implement them.

*Detection and recovery*  While this chapter concentrates on preventative measures in fraud control, it is worthwhile mentioning that Defence has a firm action policy in relation to the investigation and prosecution of fraud cases, as well as the recovery of losses from fraud. An important policy element of fraud investigation is the policy guidelines for reporting perceived wrongdoing (Defence Whistleblower Scheme). This policy provides guidance for individual members who wish to come forward to report a perceived fraud, or who have observed waste or abuse of Commonwealth resources. The policy offers appropriate protection to individuals who come forward with allegations of this nature.

*Training and Awareness*

In exploring ways to communicate fraud control in Defence, two separate factors arise. First, through research, it has been found that one of the most important contributing factors to the reduction of risk is job training for personnel. Training, in this sense, refers to developing job skills and competencies. It should be relevant, continuous and evaluated. A skilled person is a valuable asset in the protection of public resources.

*Fraud and ethics awareness seminars and presentations* The second factor is the challenge of providing sufficient, relevant information to a large and complex organisation such as Defence. Our efforts to raise awareness on fraud and ethical issues have provided Defence personnel with relevant guidance and advice for almost a decade. Our program consists of ethics presentations and discussions with Defence personnel from all regions in Australia, and includes those staff occupying or about to take up overseas postings. Presentations are augmented with videos, and ethics- and fraud-awareness printed and electronic material. Awareness seminars begin on induction and continue throughout the individual's career. The ethics program pays particular attention to providing awareness seminars for commanders and managers responsible for resource management. Changes or additions to Defence policy are promulgated widely by printed and electronic means. As mentioned above, the challenge lies in ensuring that information is available to all members.

Recently, Defence, in consultation with industry, developed an ethics statement that has been well accepted by members of industry and Defence personnel. The statement provides a basis for industry associations and individual suppliers to adopt standards of ethical behaviour that meet the requirements of government procurement; particularly Defence procurement. Mutual cooperation and reciprocal obligation are important elements in developing this type of relationship.

*Culture*

Defence has undergone considerable change over the past decade, structurally and in the way business is done. The positive results of change can be seen in the freeing up of prescriptive rules together with a leadership focus on the use of values and ethical standards in resource management. This enables management discretion in how it manages resources within an identified organisational ethical framework.

Change also brings uncertainty and new ways of performing work. Some personnel have struggled to relinquish outdated and entrenched practices. Part of this struggle involves a perceptual shift in the way risk is managed. Time to adjust to change, timely, relevant training, and specific information and experience are necessary to assist staff make the transition from a culture of risk avoidance to one of risk management. A perceived ability to control how change occurs in the workplace is an important psychological element in maintaining staff morale, as is the level of support provided to personnel during periods of change.

## Support

While there are many avenues for assistance for staff within their work areas, three support areas have significant impact at the corporate level of an organisation.

The first is ethical leadership. Defence leaders have emphasised the importance of ethical leadership particularly since the mid-1990s. This is not a new concept to Australian Defence Force personnel as traditionally, values and ethical standards were (and still are) important inclusions in all military training. The emphasis for leaders now, however, is on personnel developing a sound understanding of probity in Defence contracting and resource management since more Australian Defence Force members are required to work closely with contractors and private firms.

The second factor is generating and maintaining interest in, and promotion of fraud control throughout the organisation. While the ethics program broadly explains fraud risk assessment and fraud control, it has been found that the best method for promoting fraud control is in staff developing and/or implementing their own fraud control plans. A 'by-product' of fraud risk assessment and planning is the enhanced understanding that comes from doing a detailed assessment of our work functions. In this situation, on-the-job training is quite enlightening.

The third area of support is in providing avenues for advice to personnel who are tasked with implementing fraud control. Advice can take the form of presentations to representatives of different Defence Groups, one-to-one assistance with planners and, in particular, clearly developed Group plans that enable all members of the Group to interpret and implement.

## Evaluation Process

A program implementation is incomplete without an evaluation process. Such a process should be designed specifically to obtain information about the success or otherwise of goals and expected outcomes of the program. Evaluation of fraud prevention and control measures takes several forms in Defence. In evaluating fraud control planning and implementation, there is a formal reporting requirement to a Defence senior committee on the progress and difficulties experienced in implementing fraud control. Lessons learned through this reporting mechanism allow the organisation as a whole to address common weaknesses and pass on innovative ideas to other areas with similar functions.

Evaluation of the fraud and ethics awareness program is based on written feedback from participants, organisers and managers who have been exposed to the program. Information may also be obtained through informal discussions with staff and through regular telephone and email contact. A useful outcome of evaluation are case studies developed as a result of using information gathered from audit and other evaluation reports.

## Future Challenges

To conclude, the implementation of fraud control in a complex organisation such as Defence has shown that clearly written guidance and concentrated efforts to communicate that guidance to all areas of the organisation are essential to the successful implementation of preventative fraud control measures. At a time when many activities compete for priority, there is concern that insufficient attention will be given to a program as important as fraud control. An ethically aware culture, which encourages each staff member to be personally responsible for how he or she uses and manages public resources, will enhance the success of compliance programs such as fraud control.

## Note

1　The views expressed in this chapter are solely those of the author and do not necessarily reflect the official policies or views of the Australian Defence Organisation.

# Chapter 9

# Protecting Consumers of Financial Services

Tim Phillipps

## Introduction

This chapter examines the problem of crime in the professions from the perspective of those who are affected by unprofessional and criminal conduct—namely, the consumers of professional services. Previous chapters have documented the nature and extent of a range of crimes committed by accountants, doctors and nurses—and clearly there are other professionals who act in illegal and unprofessional ways. There are also, of course, other non-professionals in the community who break the law.

Crime perpetrated by professionals can take a myriad of forms which range from inadvertent misconduct to serious demonstrations of deceitful and harmful behaviour. Almost all have one common element—a victim, who may be a consumer or investor, who has lost his or her life savings because he or she has unquestioningly trusted a professional adviser, has been unmercifully manipulated, or, perhaps, has just been 'plain stupid'!

The Australian Securities and Investments Commission (ASIC) has estimated that over the past ten years over 100,000 Australians have lost their life savings as a consequence of scams, swindles or professional misconduct (Brown 1998). In just a few such major matters which include the collapse of the Estate Mortgage Group, Bond Corporation and Security Directors, approximately 60,000 Australian consumers lost some $2 billion.

Although the arrogance and staggering value of losses involved in cases such as the Bond Corporation have not re-emerged, the consistency and rate with which smaller value losses inflicted by corporate professionals appear, is very disturbing. Unfortunately, this type of misconduct has been appearing on the Australian corporate landscape consistently for the past decade and a half.

## More Government Regulation, Professional Ethics or Common Sense?

The dilemma for organisations such as ASIC, the Australian Competition and Consumer Commission (ACCC), Departments of Fair Trading, law enforcement agencies and professional conduct review organisations, is how to strike a balance between regulation, setting acceptable standards of business conduct and persuading consumers to exercise common sense when conducting financial transactions.

Calls for greater levels of government intervention, regulation and higher standards of professional conduct and review are regularly made, but rarely is a comparable public call made for higher levels of common sense to be exercised by consumers. This chapter will address each of these issues and then consider the impact of technology upon them.

### 'It's about time the government did something about it!'

A Commissioner of the Federal Trade Commission in the United States—with the unlikely name of Orson Swindle—has quoted the following observation about the role which government should play in consumer protection, of former President Ronald Reagan:

> When government decides to solve something, we have learned to be wary. The cure may not always be worse than the disease—but it usually is bigger and costs more (Swindle 1999).

Swindle has also suggested that governments should adopt a consumer-focused Hippocratic oath along the lines of '…do no harm'. To this we might add a business principle which would advise that 'good ethics equals good business', and a principle for consumers to follow: 'take care of yourself'!

In the context of the financial services sector in Australia, ASIC and the ACCC play significant roles. The ACCC has a focus on competition issues in business and ASIC is the consumer regulator for superannuation, banking, life and general insurance and the securities markets. Requiring that the government 'take action' in these circumstances is problematic. On the one hand, significant regulation might impose an unsatisfactory burden on business which would have an impact on its cost and efficiency, while, on the other hand, too little regulatory intervention might well lead to an unacceptably low standard of protection for consumers.

ASIC has adopted a multi-tiered approach to this issue which entails: reviewing and defining standards of compliance; promoting disclosure and consumer knowledge; supporting self regulation (including through the use of codes of conduct); enforcing breaches of consumer protection laws; and educating consumers.

One of the most significant results that ASIC has achieved to date in this regard was its acceptance of an enforceable undertaking from Westpac which required the development of a compliance adviser training program and improved consumer disclosures (ASIC 1999). The issue arose in the context of the professional conduct of Westpac's network of financial advisers. Westpac offered retail investment advisory services to its customers through a network of advisers who received financial incentives based upon the products and services which they recommended. Advisers who recommended Westpac's financial product rather than those offered by others, were rewarded with higher levels of remuneration. ASIC took the view, however, that there was insufficient disclosure of this arrangement to consumers.

Although arguably not criminal, Westpac's actions clearly placed consumers at risk of being advised to invest in products that might not be in their best interests and potentially suffer financial loss as a result, due to individual advisers possibly being motivated by the financial incentives that were offered.

## Ethical Standards in Business Have Never Been Better?

In late August 1988, Alan Bond described the takeover of Bell Resources by the Bond Corporation as a 'great day' for the shareholders of the cash-rich Robert Holmes-a-Court flagship. Holmes-a-Court had decided to sell his substantial personal stake after liquidating the majority of the assets of Bell Resources and holding in excess of $1.2 billion in cash deposits around the world.

Bond's description of the marriage of the two great Australian companies neglected to mention that Bond Corporation was desperately short of cash and needed an immediate injection of funds in order to survive. On the very first day of the combined new company, 26 August 1988, $25 million dollars was transferred from Bell Resources to the Bond Corporation through an intermediary established by the Bond Corporation for the purpose. By the end of 1988, almost all of the shareholder funds previously held by Bell Resources ($1.2 billion) had been consumed by the Bond Corporation through highly suspect and illegal back-to-back transactions conducted conspiratorially by a number of key executives from within the corporation.

Current experience suggests, however, that while the size and arrogance of this type of activity has abated somewhat, the ethical standards of some business entrepreneurs and ventures has not necessarily improved.

In the past two years a number of significant and illegal fundraising schemes have been discovered in Australia. One Queensland venture raised in excess of $130 million, capturing innocent victims from across Australia— including members of various police services. The venture—essentially a Ponzi[1] scheme—offered annual interest rates of 50 per cent and had only one real product, namely, to raise more money and meet its obligation to pay interest to previous investors, as well as paying exorbitant 'management' fees to the promoters of the scheme. Investors numbered more than 3,000 who were expected to receive little or no return.

The effort to remain competitive and profitable in business today continues to challenge the ethical standards of many business executives. Recent media reports have described a number of instances of unconscionable, although not necessarily illegal conduct, which have taken place in the retail and entertainment sectors.

The first involved a shopping centre development. Planning approval had been withdrawn following active local community concern which had been expressed to the planning authorities about a range of issues to do with the development. Further enquires provided evidence that the local 'action' group was, in fact, a representative group established by a major competitor seeking to protect local dominance in the marketplace (*Sunday Program*, Channel 9, Television Broadcast, 13 February 2000).

Similarly, a tactic employed in the entertainment industry involves staff and friends causing disruption to business competitor's telephone call centres during peak load periods.

In the emerging technology sector, concern has been created by the use of high-level executive option schemes as an alternative to the payment of high salaries. For example, the recent spectacular rise of the Publishing and Broadcasting Limited subsidiary *e-corp* saw its share price move from an initial listing price of $1.20 to in excess of $8.00 in just nine months. That made the 17 million options of its Chairman and CEO each worth approximately $130 million. The key question here concerns the incentive itself. Does such an arrangement encourage the CEO to lift revenues and earnings for *e-corp* (which was losing about $10 million per year) and therefore the profits for the shareholder? Or could it also be construed (in less ethical circumstances) as an incentive to get the share price up as high as possible, irrespective of the base upon which the business is built, in order to improve the exercisable option price? For that matter, do the shareholders of technology stocks, many of whom purchase stock for its speculative value rather than its true earnings value, really care anyway?

### 'If it sounds too good to be true it probably is!'

Protecting consumers in the financial services market is a task not only carried out by government regulatory agencies. Clearly a balance needs to be struck between the responsibility of business professionals to act honestly and consumers not to act irresponsibly and without regard for their own wellbeing. In the words of the Chairman of the Securities and Exchange Commission in the United States, Arthur Levitt, who recently warned investors about complacency in years of good returns on investments: 'no government agency can protect you from your own foolishness!' (Levitt 2000).

In Australia, a number of government agencies and professions have taken major steps to educate consumers as to their personal responsibility for protecting themselves in the financial market. One of the most significant industry/government examples of recent times can be seen with the effort by ASIC and the Financial Planners Association (1999) to educate investors regarding their choice of professional adviser. Their joint publication *Don't Kiss Your Money Goodbye* made use of lessons from past instances of misconduct and guided prospective investors through key questions to help them avoid being misadvised or defrauded.

There remains, of course, the need for a useful legal framework to be combined with competent enforcement, as well as targeted education, in order to limit the impact of professional dishonesty in this area. Consumers need to exercise increasing degrees of common sense when dealing with investments. The past ten years have seen a long line of frauds perpetrated by business executives and professional advisers, many of whom achieved their criminal success by exploiting the gullibility and trust of many consumers.

The man described as 'the biggest investment cheat in Australian history' (Brown 1998), David John Gibson, established his investment advisory practice over many years in Brighton, Victoria. As time went by his wealth and success became more apparent to clients, demonstrated by expensive cars, luxurious and stately homes, wine collections, North Queensland property investments and first-class overseas holidays.

The legend of David Gibson grew in direct proportion to his client base and the funds invested with him. His rates of return were almost double those of any other adviser which his dedicated followers attributed to his unique ability to identify successful investment opportunities. Unfortunately, his great wealth was really a sign of his great success as a fraudster. When Security Directors collapsed in 1990, 700 investors had lost over $43 million. David Gibson was sentenced to 12 years imprisonment with a minimum of nine years on fraud and dishonesty charges (Brown 1998).

Greed played a role in this case, as did blind trust on the part of investors. Is it reasonable to expect that Gibson's investors should have known what was happening by relying upon simple investment rules such as insisting on regular statements, questioning why interest payments came in the form of cash or personal cheques, and questioning how the interest rate could be as high as it was.

A more recent instance of 'consumer gullibility' was highlighted last year by ASIC. As part of ASIC's annual 'April fools day campaign' to educate investors, ASIC set up a web site in the name of Swiss Millennium Bug Insurance which purported to offer a Y2K investment able to return no less than 300 per cent over 12 months. Over $4 million dollars was promised by investors entirely on the basis of a well constructed web site which contained very little information at all (<http://www.asic.gov.au/consumer/index.htm> visited 27 March 2000).

## Will New Technologies Result in Higher Levels of Crime in the Professions?

The Internet revolution has already changed the balance between consumers and business. Investors are more prepared than ever to speculate by placing enormous trust in those who manage their affairs that their shareholding will be applied to the development of their business. In many cases, speculative investors themselves are not specifically concerned about how funds are placed and the underlying value of the business—rather their interest lies only in the steady increase in the share price.

The Internet is rich in information, consumer choices and investor opportunities. It has provided consumers with access to increased sources of information and many more intermediaries with which to conduct business (for example, buying insurance policies through the Internet, <http://www.quicken.com/insurance/> visited 27 March 2000). Unfortunately, the

Internet is also fertile ground for those who prey on consumers with scams, swindles and other fraudulent practices.

The opportunity for crime to be committed by professionals and businesses will continue to exist in the new technological age. Technology itself, however, does not change the fundamental landscape of crime in the professions—it only changes the ease of accessibility and the reach—and of course the opportunities for who might be described as ethically challenged.

## Conclusion

The challenges for government, business and consumers are never ending—history, particularly relating to business ethics and consumer protection, will continue to repeat itself.

It is without reservation that the present author is able to predict that Australia will in the future see further examples of government being overly enthusiastic with unnecessary or excessive regulation in this area, dramatic examples of business arrogance and unethical conduct having an impact on investors and consumers, and, just as predicatably, consumers demonstrating less than adequate standards of common sense.

Without doubt the real challenge ahead lies in finding a balance between encouraging business to take responsibility for building consumer confidence by fulfilling ethical obligations, and government being more supportive by taking a less interventionist position. That leaves us finally with the consumer—who must take responsibility for becoming informed, exercising caution and better judgment, and occasionally standing in front of the mirror and repeating 'don't be an idiot'.

## Note

1   Italian-born Charles Ponzi, after whom the crime was named, became famous in the United States in the 1920s by persuading people to invest funds with him for a high return. Interest returns were, however, paid from the investment capital of new investors. In the summer of 1920 he defrauded thousands of people out of US$20 million.

# Chapter 10

# Health Providers, Complaints and Unprofessional Behaviour in a Changing Environment

Beth Wilson

## Introduction

Health disputes may be settled as a result of litigation or they may be resolved by conciliation carried out by independent, accessible complaints commissioners (Wilson, Jackson and Punshon 1998, p. 59). Commissioners work with the relevant professional registration boards in ensuring that allegations of professional misconduct, unprofessional conduct or unsatisfactory conduct are dealt with (Breen, Plueckhahn and Cordner 1997). This chapter describes the overlap and interaction between the various 'watchdog' agencies which receive complaints about the conduct of health service providers, explores some gaps in the system and questions whether our existing practices are capable of meeting the new challenges offered by the changing health service environment. In particular, the following questions will be explored: should registered practitioners be able to 'de-register' themselves and therefore avoid professional disciplinary hearings; when should registered practitioners facing disciplinary proceedings be named; should mandatory reporting of unprofessional conduct by peers be introduced in Australia; and what special problems arise when a non-registered practitioner is accused of professional misconduct?

## The Health Complaints Commissioners

There are now health complaints commissioners in each state and territory of Australia. In Victoria the Health Services Commissioner was established by the *Health Services (Conciliation and Review) Act 1987* (Vic.). A similar model has been followed and improved upon in Western Australia (Office of Health Review), Queensland (Health Rights Commission), Northern Territory (Health and Community Services Complaints Commission), Australian Capital Territory (Health Complaints Commission) and Tasmania (Health Complaints Commissioner). All of these bodies have jurisdiction over practitioners in both the private and the public sectors. In South Australia, however, an Ombudsman deals with health complaints and the jurisdiction is confined to the public system. This is a significant anomaly as there is no reason why consumers of health services in South Australia should not have access to an independent complaints resolution service dealing with private as well as public providers as is the case in all other states and territories (Wilson 1999, p. 180). In Tasmania and the Northern Territory the health complaints commissions are included within the office of the Ombudsman.

In 1984, a Health Complaints Unit was established in New South Wales within the Health Department. It was replaced, in 1994, by an independent Health Care Complaints Commission which has similar functions to the other Commissions, except that the New South Wales model requires the Commissioner to prosecute registered providers charged with professional misconduct before the relevant registration boards. In New Zealand the *Health and Disability Act 1994* established a Health and Disability Commissioner. The Commissioner is empowered to promote and protect the rights of consumers of health and disability services, and has developed a code of rights to apply to all types of health and disability services.

## The Relationship between Health Complaints Commissioners and Professional Registration Boards

In Australia registered health professionals are regulated by professional boards established in each of the states and territories. As was discussed in chapter 1 of this book, mutual recognition legislation allows health practitioners registered in one state or territory to be registered and to practice elsewhere in Australia. There are, however, important differences between the legislation applicable in different states and in different professions (see the discussion below).

Each of the legislative schemes provides for registration, education and procedures for dealing with professional conduct issues (see Fletcher 1998). In Victoria, for example, there are registration boards with jurisdiction respectively over doctors, dentists, nurses, chiropractors and osteopaths, physiotherapists, psychologists, podiatrists and chiropodists, pharmacists, optometrists and radiographers. Competition policy now discourages the registration or regulation of other health providers (Carlton 1998, p. 83).

In all states and territories a process exists of 'sharing' health complaints between the health complaints commissioners and the relevant professional registration boards. Aggrieved health consumers may lodge complaints with either the registration boards or with the complaints commissioners. The various legislative schemes provide for consultation and exchange of complaints so they may be dealt with by the appropriate body. In Victoria, for example, subsection 6 of section 19 of the *Health Services (Conciliation and Review) Act 1987* makes it clear that where the Commissioner receives a complaint about a registered provider, the Commissioner must refer the complaint to the relevant registration board if, after consultation with the board, the Commissioner considers that the board has power to resolve or deal with the matter and it is not suitable for conciliation. There are corresponding provisions in the legislation which establishes the relevant registration boards (for example, section 23, *Medical Practice Act 1994* (Vic.)). Matters taken into account in determining that a complaint is unsuitable for conciliation include the degree of risk to the public, the aspirations of the complainant (for example whether compensation is sought) and the nature of the complaint. It would be an extremely rare case in which a complaint about sexual misconduct was deemed suitable for conciliation.

The commissioners also have jurisdiction over non-registered health service providers such as counsellors, social workers, naturopaths and many more. In dealing with this group of providers, the commissioners have fewer sanctions because referral to a registration board is not available. Problems arise where a complaint involves allegations of unethical behaviour which does not amount to a breach of the criminal law (see discussion below).

The current relationship between the health complaints commissioners and the professional registration boards is one of cooperation. The commissioners and the boards provide advice to health service users on making complaints and on the appropriate body to deal with a complaint. The legislation makes it clear that the responsibility for adjudicating about a registered practitioner's conduct in terms of whether it has been unprofessional or not is the province of the registration boards (Breen et al. 1997, p. 101). Where allegations of professional misconduct or unsatisfactory conduct are made about registered health practitioners an array of sanctions exists. A registered practitioner who is reported to a registration board could be counselled or may be required to appear before a formal hearing. If found guilty of unprofessional conduct, he or she could be struck off the register or may be required to undergo training or restrictions may be placed on practice (Breen et al. 1997, p. 62).

The role of the commissioners is to receive and resolve complaints from users of health services with a view to improving the overall quality of health services. In all states other than New South Wales, the commissioners provide confidential and privileged conciliation services which are an alternative to litigation and which are able to deal with a wider range of complaints than does the common law. In New South Wales, conciliation is available but is administered separately from the office of the complaints commissioner.

An important difference between New South Wales and the other jurisdictions is that the New South Wales legislation requires the Commissioner to prosecute cases before the registration boards. This is also done in the Australian Capital Territory, but at the request of the relevant board rather than as a legislative requirement. In other jurisdictions the commissioners may assist the registration boards if requested to do so. They may also, with the consent of the board or with the approval of the Minister, be represented at any proceedings before a registration board and cross-examine or call and examine witnesses and make submissions (s. 10(i), *Health Services (Conciliation and Review) Act 1987* (Vic.) and see Wilson 1999, p. 184).

## Medical Misconduct and Crime

In exploring what he described as the criminalisation 'solution' to medical misconduct, Freckelton (1998, p. 26) noted:

> A variety of responses exist to deal with misconduct by medical and other health practitioners. At one end of the spectrum, criminal sanctions can be imposed. This has the advantage of being highly public, enabling imposition of harsh sanctions and broadcasting in a very clear way a message to the general community as to standards of professional behaviour which will not be tolerated. It is a flagship in upholding the rights of victims. However, it is dependant upon proof of criminality beyond reasonable doubt.

He went on to consider whether the sanctions available within the disciplinary context are preferable to the sentencing dispositions available upon proof of criminal offences by professionals beyond reasonable doubt, and concluded that:

the rationales for the imposition of disciplinary sanctions bear many features in common with those in the criminal milieu, and ultimately in most circumstances are as effective in terms of protecting the general community and in punishing the malefactor (ibid.).

While additional criminalisation of medical misconduct would be unhelpful, there are problems with the current system which, in some jurisdictions, inhibit the abilities of complaints commissioners and registration boards to discipline health providers and thereby protect the public. The problem with using the criminal law in these cases is that proof beyond reasonable doubt is difficult to establish, and also the criminal law covers only criminal conduct whereas most complaints are about unethical conduct or failures to meet consumer expectations. Some cases are complex and may require action by the commissioner, the relevant registration boards, criminal proceedings and claims for compensation. In these, it is essential that legislative arrangements exist to allow full cooperation between all the relevant agencies. In some parts of the United States of America any sexual contact between doctor and patient has been made a criminal offence.

**The Changing Environment**

In Australia a complicated set of structures exists to promote quality health care. Health complaints commissioners respond to consumer complaints and have an overall review function designed to promote quality services. Registration boards concentrate on professional standards. Hospitals and other health institutions have their own quality assurance arrangements and activities, while professional colleges and associations are involved in standards of clinical care and educational and accreditation processes. Consumers are involved in limited ways on registration boards and on the boards of hospital quality committees as lay representatives, they make complaints as individuals, and organised consumer groups lobby for change and greater involvement in the health care decision-making process.

As Bryant (1999, p. 8) explains, many of our disciplinary and legal structures have failed to take account of the changing health care work environment. She argues that concentration on disciplining individual practitioners by using the 'bad apple' approach alone does not recognise the changing and complex environment within which health service providers work. In Australia, for example, nursing remains a predominantly female profession with, in Victoria, the vast majority of nurses being employees. In

1998, only one per cent of Victoria's nurses were self-employed (Bryant 1999, p. 18). Many doctors and nurses now work in practices that are not owned by registered practitioners but by companies. The traditional partnership structure that doctors relied upon has given way to associations and other business arrangements. This has brought with it pressures to save on costs and has led to complaints being made by consumers that examinations have been too hasty resulting in wrong or missed diagnoses (Lupton 1996, p. 158). It is not uncommon now for patients to be asked questions like, 'Are you a ten-minute or a twenty-minute patient?'

Registered providers remain individually responsible for their own professional behaviour but tensions exist between the business imperatives and professional standards. In recent years we have seen the emergence of 'super clinics' with doctors and other health providers working in practices which employ dozens of providers offering multiple services. Competition policy has also influenced service delivery with the removal of regulations on, for example, advertising. Although it is not suggested that individual professional responsibility should be abandoned, these changes must be recognised and the question debated as to whether or not further sanctions are required in order for the owners of practices to be obliged to take public interest issues into account when managing their business affairs.

Legal responsibility for medical negligence has focused primarily on doctors, although increasingly the conduct of nurses is being questioned in the law courts (*Elliot v. Bickerstaff* New South Wales Court of Appeal, 7 March 2000, Australian Health and Medical Reporter, p. 66). In 1999, two nurses were found to be negligent in caring for a patient who had suffered injuries through falling whilst under their care (*John James Memorial Hospital Ltd v. Keys* Federal Court of Australia, 21 May 1999). More recently in the case of *Elliot v. Bickerstaff* (ibid.), the New South Wales Court of Appeal held unanimously that a surgeon was not responsible for injury to his patient caused when a surgical sponge was left in the patient's abdominal cavity following hysterectomy. The Court found that the surgeon undertook the provision of his own surgical services as one team member, the others being the anaesthetist and hospital staff. The Court recognised that, in the operating theatre, there is divided responsibility. The surgeon was responsible for his own conduct but is reliant on other team members for the due discharge of their duties. The surgeon was not personally negligent but it could be inferred that there had been a miscount or error by the theatre sister or a nurse subservient to her.

Further complications arise where state governments and the Commonwealth share responsibility for health services. In 1997, the

Commonwealth set up its own complaints resolution scheme for nursing homes consisting of a Complaints Resolution Unit within the Department of Aged Care and an external Accreditation and Standards Agency. A complaint about a nursing home might allege that residents had been injured because the proprietors had been driven by economic considerations rather than patient care and that, as a result, there were too few trained nurses, resources were tight and poor practices were allowed to occur. Such a complaint might well involve several agencies. The Commonwealth Complaints Unit could be asked to investigate and if it found there to be some substance to the complaint, it must refer it to the Accreditation and Standards Agency. The Commonwealth also has power to withdraw funding which is a 'big stick' approach and one that can be detrimental to residents and their families. This was graphically portrayed in the extensive media coverage in March 2000 of residents being removed from the Riverside Nursing Home in Victoria following allegations that residents had been subjected to kerosene in baths for the 'treatment' of scabies.

A complaint may also involve questions about the standards of practice of registered nurses that would need to be examined by the state-based nurses registration board. The complaints commissioner may be involved as well if compensation is sought for injury. The successful resolution of these issues depends upon close cooperation and communication between the various agencies, but the Commonwealth legislation does not allow the Commonwealth Complaints Unit to provide information to the other bodies involved except on a case by case basis with the express permission of the Secretary of the Commonwealth Department of Aged Care on public interest grounds (see Commonwealth Department of Aged Care 1997, and division 86, *Aged Care Act 1997* (Cth)). This can cause unnecessary delay and, arguably, requires amendment to ensure that state agencies can exercise their responsibilities in cooperation with the Commonwealth.

Some of the confidentiality provisions of the commissioners' legislation also require examination. For example, if the Health Services Commissioner in Victoria refers a matter to a registration board the legislation makes it clear that information can be provided by the Commissioner to the board and to all parties in the interest of natural justice. If, however, the Commissioner decides not to refer the matter to the board, the complainant may choose to do so on his or her own initiative. In these circumstances the legislation makes no provision to allow the Commissioner to provide information to the board. Similarly, if a complaint is made to the Commissioner of sexual assault and the complainant refers the matter to the police, the Commissioner can only give evidence to the police or in court with the express permission of the Minister (s. 32(4) (b), *Health Services (Conciliation and Review) Act*).

## A Recent Case of Sexual Misconduct

In September 1999, the Medical Practitioners Board of Victoria conducted a formal hearing pursuant to the *Medical Practice Act 1994* (Vic.) into the professional conduct of Dr Michael Yardney. The Board found that, pursuant to subsection 1(a) of section 50 of the Act, Dr Yardney had engaged in unprofessional conduct of a serious nature. It also found that Dr Yardney had engaged in unprofessional conduct because he was found guilty of indictable offences at the Magistrates Court at Frankston on 13 October 1997, and at the County Court at Melbourne at 29 April 1999. He was also found to have engaged in further unprofessional conduct within the meaning of section 3 of the *Medical Practice Act 1994* (Vic.) in that he had misled the panel of the Medical Practitioners Board of Victoria at an earlier formal hearing. Finally, he was found to have engaged in 'infamous conduct in a professional respect' and 'professional misconduct'. The Board cancelled the registration of Dr Yardney and published reasons for its determination.

The Board considered the reasons for its decision would make a contribution to the ongoing education of the medical profession and the general community in regard to the total unacceptability of Dr Yardney's conduct and of sexual misconduct generally. The Board acknowledged that the experiences of the victims in this case emphasised how difficult it was for victims of doctors to feel sufficiently confident and empowered to tell anyone about their concerns. The Board emphasised its own duty to find ways to ensure that all patients know ahead of time that such behaviour is wrong, unprofessional, harmful and must be reported, observing: 'We need to find ways of working with you, so that some greater benefit for our whole community might be gained from your intolerable experiences.'

One of the reasons for the Board's inquiry into the conduct of Dr Yardney was that he had told the Board previously he had engaged in sexual conduct which was inappropriate and/or unnecessary with between 25 and 30 women, but he later admitted the number of patients with whom he had engaged in sexual misconduct was double this number.

Dr Yardney had been found guilty of unprofessional conduct of a serious nature in 1996 and his registration was suspended for two years. Following that hearing, a number of additional former patients came forward to lodge complaints about his conduct with them and he subsequently faced two sets of criminal proceedings. He was convicted of indecent assault and given a suspended sentence of nine months' imprisonment by the Frankston Magistrates Court. In October 1998 he pleaded guilty at a committal hearing in respect of charges relating to a further eight women. He pleaded guilty to charges of indecent assault in respect of six of the eight women and was sentenced to 12 months' imprisonment, nine months of which was suspended. The 12-month sentence represented the concurrent sentencing of six months for two counts and 12 months for the other six representative counts.

The Yardney case, because of the seriousness of the matters dealt with, provides an appropriate context in which to examine the questions explored in this chapter.

### Should Registered Providers be able to De-Register Themselves?

Not all registration boards have the same view of their role and jurisdiction and there are also important variations in the legislation that governs each board. In Victoria a registered dental practitioner was charged with unprofessional conduct in that he (among other things) rectally administered ozone for the relief of dental pain (*Dr Noel Rodney Campbell v. The Dental Board of Victoria* 14 December 1999). The matter was to be determined in November 1999 at a hearing of the Dental Practitioners Board of Victoria. Prior to the hearing the dentist's counsel argued that his client had withdrawn his registration, was no longer a registered dentist and therefore the Board had no jurisdiction over him as the legislation only gave it power to deal with registered dentists. The Dental Board accepted this argument with the result that the allegations of unprofessional conduct were not heard.

By comparison, in *Dr Wartski v. The Medical Board of Victoria,* a case involving allegations of sexual misconduct against a doctor were due to be heard on Monday 31 January 2000. Prior to the panel hearing the doctor requested the Board to remove his name from the register and argued that the panel had no jurisdiction. The panel referred the matter back to the Board. Unlike the Dental Practitioners Board, the Medical Practitioners Board decided that it did have jurisdiction to hear the matter and the doctor could not remove himself from the register to avoid disciplinary proceedings. The legislation governing the two Boards is not dissimilar. It was open to the Dental Practitioners Board to take jurisdiction and, if there was objection to this, the dentist could exercise his right of appeal to the Supreme Court. If registered practitioners are able to remove their names from the register in order to avoid disciplinary proceedings there are serious issues of concern to the public. A practitioner in the situation of Dr Yardney, for example, who was facing unprofessional conduct charges could have avoided a hearing and then re-applied for registration some years later. A registration board considering the application for restoration would have only allegations to consider rather than the benefit of the findings of a full board hearing. It is also generally much more difficult to uncover evidence of complaints when they are many years old. Moreover, constant challenges to the jurisdiction of the Boards by practitioners seeking to avoid disciplinary hearings is expensive and protracted.

In the Yardney case the Medical Practitioner's Board stated:

> This 'reasons' document will be of interest to all those present, and will outline the gross abuse of trust displayed by Dr Yardney over more than ten years as a busy general practitioner. Whilst the panel cannot imagine any circumstances under which Dr Yardney might establish that he can ever be entrusted again with the serious responsibilities of medical practice, the 'reasons' document will be relevant should he ever apply to be restored to the medical register (Formal Hearing of the Medical Practitioners Board of Victoria, 8 September 1999).

Interestingly, in the United Kingdom, a committee of the General Medical Council, the Registration Committee, considers all applications which are made for voluntary erasure from the register and is able to refuse such applications where there is a possibility that disciplinary proceedings might be taken against the practitioner (Smith 1994, p. 16). This question was discussed by the English Court of Appeal many years ago in the case of *R v. General Council of Medical Education and Registration of the United Kingdom* ([1930] 1 KB 562, 569) in the following terms:

> It is idle to suppose that a registered medical practitioner who has been charged with infamous conduct in a professional respect may avoid all enquiry into his conduct by the simple means of a request to have his name taken off the register. To allow this escape would defeat the object of section 29.

A related issue concerns the question of whether or not a registration board has jurisdiction to deal with a matter if the practitioner is no longer registered, although was registered at the time the alleged misconduct took place. Practitioners are registered for a specified time period, usually a year. Problems have arisen in those jurisdictions in which the legislation does not make it clear that the board has jurisdiction over a practitioner who, at the time of the alleged misconduct was registered, but is no longer registered. In such circumstances some boards have been obliged to act very quickly where registration of a person charged with misconduct was about to expire. This is clearly unsatisfactory. Legislative intervention is required to make it clear that every registration board in Australia has jurisdiction to hear complaints made about conduct at the time the practitioner was registered even if the registration has subsequently lapsed. This is already the case in some states but only for some boards. In Queensland, for example, the medical board now has power to hear cases even where the doctor is no longer registered, and in Victoria the Minister for Health is about to introduce similar changes in Victoria to the *Medical Practice Act 1994* and the *Nurses Act 1993*. These reforms need to be extended to cover all boards that have jurisdiction over registered practitioners, not just those that deal with doctors and nurses and harmonisation of the legislation throughout Australia would also be useful.

## When Should Practitioners Facing Disciplinary Proceedings be Named?

The obligation of registration boards is first and foremost to protect the public. Too often professional associations act to protect their profession rather than the public. The ability to self-regulate should be seen for what it is—a privilege, and the price of this privilege is a demonstrated ability to put the public interest ahead of the interests of the profession. If a board fails to do this then other forms of intervention are justified. In examining the role of disciplinary regulation of doctors, Dix (1998, p. 55) has noted:

> Changes in philosophy and direction of disciplinary regulation have in the past tended to be driven by factors internal to the medical profession, and the pace of change has been leisurely and to a certain extent determined by the regulatory bodies. In contrast, the future of professional disciplinary regulation appears uncertain, with changes to the nature of health delivery that will have profound effects on the way in which medicine is practised, and the relationship between those they seek to regulate.

Disciplinary proceedings are now usually open to the public and practitioners accused of unprofessional conduct are identified unless suppression orders are granted. Proponents of naming argue that any publicity would assist other victims to come forward (as was the case with Dr Yardney). Others say that boards must have discretion to suppress names to avoid injustices. The Yardney case took many years and raises questions about the ability of boards to protect the public while ensuring procedural fairness to accused practitioners.

Members of the public can contact registration boards to find out if complaints have been made about the conduct of a practitioner, however this is not widely publicised and most patients would have no idea that they can do so. Questions now being raised by some consumer groups are whether this information should be more widely available, whether it should be on the Internet as it is in some parts of the United States, and at what stage of proceedings should practitioners be named. Is it fair, for example, to name a practitioner accused of unprofessional conduct prior to a formal hearing as is currently done in criminal cases?

In its *Review of the Nurses Act 1993 and the Medical Practice Act 1994* conducted in 1999, the Victorian Government sought submissions on whether there should be powers for formal hearing panels to order suppression of the identity of a registered practitioner against whom a complaint has been made but a determination not yet made. The Medical Practitioners Board of Victoria and the Nurses Board argued that they should have discretion to determine whether suppression orders should be granted until unprofessional conduct charges have been proved. The Health Services Commissioner agreed.

While the available evidence indicates that sexual and other misconduct is under-reported, any complaint system must be accessible and fair to all the parties. Allegations of misconduct can cause extreme damage to the reputations of accused parties, whether in criminal or in disciplinary contexts. The media has shown great interest in reporting allegations, particularly of sexual misconduct, but takes very little interest in reporting acquittals. Fairness would indicate that boards should continue to have a discretion to suppress names on a case-by-case basis but once a health practitioner has been found guilty of professional misconduct then this information should be freely available to all, including via the Internet.

## Should Mandatory Reporting of Unprofessional Conduct by Peers be Introduced in Australia?

It is unfortunately the case that many practitioners have been reluctant to report their colleagues. United States research indicates that doctors are very reluctant to report colleagues (Walton 1998, p. 118). Some of the reasons for this include a fear of reprisal as well as bad press for the profession as a whole (ibid., pp. 122–3; see also Schoner, Milgram and Gonsiorek 1989).

On 14 July 2000, *The Age* (Melbourne) newspaper reported the new President of the Medical Practitioners Board of Victoria, Dr Joanna Flynn, as acknowledging the under-reporting of sexual misconduct. Dr Flynn was also reported as saying this is a serious issue facing the medical profession and doctors were sometimes reluctant to report sexual misconduct because of the 'misguided belief that they would be exposed to defamation action'. Dr Flynn also said doctors were often unaware they could report these, and other complaints, to the Board without the patient needing to be involved. The Health Services Commissioner, on the other hand, requires the complaint to come from the patient unless the patient is unable to do so. However, if a patient is unwilling to be involved in a complaint to either body, there are obvious problems of proof. On the subject of mandatory reporting Dr Flynn was reported as being undecided and said there would be extensive consultation with the profession and the public on this issue.

During a seminar organised by the Medical Practitioners Board of Victoria in March 2000, Dr Garry Johnson of the College of Physicians and Surgeons of Ontario described and analysed mandatory reporting of sexual misconduct by peers in Ontario. Mandatory reporting was introduced there in 1994 as a statutory requirement under the *Regulated Health Professions Act 1994*. Ontario is the only province in Canada that has mandatory reporting. Walton (1998, p. 133) has argued that if mandatory reporting were to be introduced in Australia, it should be done nationally rather than on a state-by-state basis. She has also argued that mandatory reporting would only be necessary if the professions failed to accept their ethical responsibilities to patients and clients (ibid.).

Dr Garry Johnson acknowledged that, in Ontario, the profession had 'dithered' on the issue of sexual misconduct by doctors. This was a primary motivating factor for the introduction of mandatory reporting in that jurisdiction. In Ontario, a high rate of approval by medical practitioners for mandatory reporting of sexual offences has been found probably because it provides some protection from reprisals (College of Physicians and Surgeons of Ontario 1993). Similar research is, arguably, needed in Australia to determine the attitudes of the public and of professional groups to this issue. It is also important to evaluate the success or otherwise of mandatory reporting in those few jurisdictions in the world which have introduced such requirements.

In the nursing profession, the *Code of Professional Conduct for Nurses in Australia* developed by the Australian Nursing Council Inc. is used by the nurses' registration boards as a yardstick when determining whether or not a nurse has breached professional standards (Bryant 1999, p. 15). As well as offering guidance on nurses' responsibilities for the provision of safe and appropriate care, the Code also provides some direction for nurses who face various professional dilemmas. For example, it requires nurses to report concerns that nursing standards have been compromised to 'the appropriate person or authority', and if that concern is not resolved and continues, the matter must be reported to a relevant professional body. The *Code of Practice for Midwives* in Victoria goes even further:

> Each midwife has a professional responsibility to identify policies, procedures or practices that are restrictive and/or may be detrimental to the standard of midwifery practice and woman-centred care (Nurses Board of Victoria 1999; see also Bryant 1999, p. 16).

These provisions have their foundation in protecting the public interest, but they do pose difficulties for individual nurses who may find themselves obliged to criticise their employers or other members of the health team.

## Non-Registered Practitioners

Health care complaints commissioners have jurisdiction over all health service providers including those not registered by a statutory authority. While sexual misconduct by a registered provider may be dealt with by a registration board, this sanction is not available in the case of a non-registered provider, such as a counsellor or some psychotherapists. Commissioners are able to investigate complaints involving non-registered providers but have fewer sanctions than for registered providers.

Commissioners often enlist the support of professional associations such as the Australian Association of Social Workers but not all non-registered providers belong to a professional association. Such associations also have limited powers over their members and do not have statutory powers to compel answers, conduct formal investigations or discipline members. A provider who has transgressed ethical rules of an association may be denied membership of the association but this primarily operates to protect the profession rather than the public. In some cases loss of membership of an association means loss of a provider number which prevents clients from claiming expenses on their private health insurance. A registered provider who has been de-registered for sexual misconduct can continue to practise as a non-registered provider, provided that he or she does not claim to be registered. The ethical basis for a taboo on sexual behaviour between unregistered providers and their patients is the same as for registered providers; namely, that the relationship is based on trust and that patients seeking the professional services of providers are extremely vulnerable and need to be protected from unprofessional behaviour.

The question thus arises as to how the public can best be protected from the unprofessional conduct of non-registered providers. In Victoria, this question is currently being addressed by the Department of Human Services in a discussion paper for public consultation. The inquiry attempted to ascertain the extent of the problem, which at present is not known. Few complaints of sexual misconduct by unregistered providers are received, although there are good reasons to believe that such matters are greatly under-reported, as is also the case with registered providers. Potential complainants may be too embarrassed to come forward or they may be unaware that they have a right to complain. Sometimes complaints are received from parents whose young adult children have entered 'cults' or are having a sexual relationship with an unregistered counsellor. If the patient does not want to complain then little can be achieved.

Complaints sometimes allege conduct of a criminal nature. In most jurisdictions in Australia sexual contact with a mentally impaired person is specifically proscribed as an offence by the criminal law. Such cases are, however, difficult to prove and there is often a reluctance on the part of the prosecuting authorities to take them up. Ironically, the laws are designed to protect people with a mental impairment but it may be difficult to gain a conviction on the uncorroborated evidence of a person with a mental impairment. The experience of the Commissioner in Victoria is that many complainants simply do not wish to pursue criminal proceedings. If the provider is registered, complainants usually prefer that the matter be heard by the relevant registration board. If their complaint is acted upon and substantiated they feel vindicated.

## Conclusions

Health services are now provided in a rapidly changing environment. The regulation of professional health providers through registration and disciplinary proceedings operates in complex employment structures where economic imperatives often place strain on professional values. The 'health market' includes registered and non-registered practitioners and consumers are increasingly choosing alternative or complementary healing. Interestingly, the health complaints commissioners continue to receive far more complaints against registered practitioners than they do about other providers, and doctors continue to be the most complained about profession.

The primary goal of regulation must be to protect the community by acting in the public interest, not in the interest of a particular profession. The experience of the complaints commissioner in Victoria is that the system is working but continued vigilance remains necessary to meet the challenges of changing times and attitudes. Most importantly we need harmonisation of legislation throughout Australia to make it clear that registered practitioners are not able to 'de-register' themselves to avoid disciplinary proceedings. We also require further research on the role of health service providers who are not registered to determine if there is a risk to the public and, if so, how to deal with this. Cooperation between the various agencies and boards which deal with complaints is vital and should be strengthened. Finally, a recognition that the 'bad apple' approach has its limitations and that most health providers work in teams must be taken into account when framing legislation and developing policies.

Chapter 11

# The Professions and Whistleblower Protections

Sitesh Bhojani

## Introduction

Those who report crime in the public interest come within a group in society colloquially known as 'whistleblowers'. The Macquarie dictionary defines 'whistleblowing' as '...the activity of blowing the whistle on or exposing the corrupt practices of others' and 'whistleblower' as '...someone who alerts the public to some scandalous practice or evidence of corruption on the part of someone else'. For the purposes of the present chapter 'whistleblowing' will be regarded as a reference to disclosure of conduct which amounts or could amount to a breach of the civil law as well as to conduct which could amount to a criminal offence in the strict sense.

Whilst the need to be vigilant regarding the maintenance of the role of the rule of law in our society may be perennial, it is also true to say that the rule of law is a crucial foundation that characterises our society. The community regards law and order, and hence observance of the law, as a fundamental matter of concern to it. Compliance with the law is a matter of significant public interest. This arguably extends well beyond just the criminal law. For example, it certainly extends to compliance with Australia's competition and consumer protection laws. This can be readily seen from the object of the *Trade Practices Act 1974* (Cth) ('the Act') which is to enhance the welfare of Australians through the promotion of competition and fair trading and provision for consumer protection (see section 2 of the Act). This view is further supported by the significant consequences for contravention of Part IV of the Act (or the equivalent Competition Codes of the States and Territories). For example, civil pecuniary penalties of up to $10 million *per* contravention for corporations and up to $500,000 *per* contravention for individuals are provided for in the Act.

139

Although there may not be a universally accepted definition of 'a profession', as we have seen in earlier chapters, the following definition provided by the Australian Council of Professions[1] encompasses its most important characteristics (see Southwick 1997, p. 36):

> A disciplined group of individuals who adhere to high ethical standards and uphold themselves to, and are accepted by, the public as possessing special knowledge and skills in a widely recognised, organised body of learning derived from education and training at a high level, and who are prepared to exercise this knowledge and these skills in the interests of others; and inherent in this definition is the concept that the responsibility for the welfare, health and safety of the community shall take precedence over other considerations.

## Reporting Breaches of the Trade Practices Act

In Australia, the Act expressly deals with the issue of protection of a person who provides information or documents to the Australian Competition and Consumer Commission (ACCC) or to the Australian Competition Tribunal. The relevant provision is section 162A which provides as follows:

> Intimidation etc.
> A person who:
> (a) threatens, intimidates or coerces another person; or
> (b) causes or procures damage, loss or disadvantage to another person;
> for or on account of that other person proposing to furnish or having furnished information, or proposing to produce or having produced documents, to the Commission or to the Tribunal or for or on account of the other person proposing to appear or having appeared as a witness before the Tribunal is guilty of an offence punishable on conviction;
> (c) in the case of a person not being a body corporate—by a fine not exceeding $2,000 or imprisonment for 12 months; and
> (d) in the case of a person being a body corporate—by a fine not exceeding $10,000.

Although the Act does not specifically focus on whistleblowers as such, it in effect protects them through the creation of the above criminal offence. This provision has not, as yet, been tested before the courts.

## The ACCC's Approach

In its enforcement of competition and consumer protection laws, the Commission is certainly concerned to ensure that an environment that supports and protects people who come forward with information regarding possible contraventions, is created and maintained. That is, an environment that encourages genuine complaints and provides some confidence to complainants through a practice of preserving confidentiality and a leniency or indemnity policy, that disclosure of their identity and/or information they have provided will be preserved on a confidential basis—until, of course, disclosure becomes necessary for the proper performance of the Commission's duties or functions.

The Commission endeavours to encourage people who may have engaged in conduct that amounts to a contravention of the Act or who may be an accessory to such conduct, to come forward and disclose the conduct to the Commission. On numerous occasions the Commission has granted an indemnity from legal proceedings to people who have agreed to provide full and frank disclosure to the Commission (see, for example, *TPC v. CC (NSW) Pty Ltd & Ors* (1994) ATPR 41-352). Even after proceedings have been instituted against an individual, the Commission has been prepared to offer support where an individual has assisted the Commission in enforcing the Act, such as by providing evidence—which might not otherwise have been available—that has allowed the Commission to join other key parties. This approach has had judicial support such as in the case of *ACCC v. Alice Car & Truck Rentals Pty Ltd & Others* ((1997) ATPR 41-582) where the Commission took proceedings against a number of car rental companies and their individual managers for price fixing in contravention of the Act. The following extract from the judgment of Mr Justice Mansfield sets out what happened in respect of one of those managers.

> In the case of Mr Hunter, I should note the following. In May 1997 after the trial date had been set, Mr Hunter approached the Commission and admitted being knowingly concerned in making the arrangement and putting it into effect. He then had a number of lengthy meetings with the Commission, during which he fully and frankly detailed his role in the contravening conduct and that of the other respondents to his knowledge. I accept that his evidence was then the basis upon which the Commission subsequently joined the eighth and ninth respondents to the proceedings. They have each subsequently admitted that conduct. Accordingly since May 1997 he has fully cooperated with and assisted the Commission and its legal advisers in relation to these proceedings and it was proposed that he would give evidence for the Commission at any trial. The Commission's view is that his information and his assistance and cooperation

were substantial factors in the decisions of all the other respondents not to contest these proceedings and to admit the contraventions set out in the further amended statement of claim. I accept the view put by the Commission, with the support of Mr Hunter, that there is a considerable public benefit in recognising and encouraging persons with relevant information to approach and assist the applicant in enforcing the Act. Mr Hunter's actions are properly so characterised.

The joint submission of the Commission and Mr Hunter proposes that no penalty be imposed on him. It will not be common for the Court to be satisfied that that is an appropriate order but in the particular circumstances and for the reasons identified in the joint submission which I accept, and which I have briefly referred to above, I am prepared to so conclude in this instance. In particular in my view there is considerable public benefit in persons with relevant information concerning breaches of the Act to provide that information to the Commission. I have also had regard to Mr Hunter's personal circumstances in reaching that view (ibid. at p. 44-051).

The Commission currently deals with the issue of leniency and indemnity for individuals or corporations on a case-by-case basis. It has published flexible guidelines on the issue[2] because the policy continues to evolve in the light of Commission experience and marketplace changes.

## The Nature of the Professional Relationship

The traditional role, perception and standing of the learned professions can be gleaned from the following comments of Dr John Southwick, President of the Australian Council of Professions:

> The elevated position of professionals in the community did not occur by accident. It was because of the function of individual professionals in banding together and agreeing amongst themselves to adopt high standards of entry and to observe high standards of performance that the community came to respect and trust persons providing those services.
>
> Self-regulation and autonomy were an integral part of the development of those standards and it was in the interest of the members of the professions that those standards be maintained. From the point of view of the community it helped to ensure the quality of the services being provided.
>
> The public interest in maintaining the highest standards in the provision of professional services and in the behaviour of those professionals was given effect to by statutes empowering professional associations, or in some cases licensing boards consisting mainly of the professionals, to set criteria for entry, to control conduct of members and, where appropriate, to exclude from professional practices those whose standards fall below acceptable levels (Southwick 1997, p. 36).

The question also arises as to the nature of the relationship between a professional and client, and whether this may be characterised as fiduciary. In Australia there are certain relationships that the law recognises as fiduciary relationships—these are relationships of trustee and beneficiary; agent and principal; solicitor and client; employee and employer; director and company; and partners (see *Hospital Products Ltd v. United States Surgical Corporation* (1984) 156 CLR 41 at 96; *Breen v. Williams* (1996) 186 CLR 71 at 92 and 107).

However, it cannot properly be said that a relationship between any professional and his or her client is a 'fiduciary relationship'. As was pointed out in a recent decision of the High Court of Australia:

> The law has not as yet been able to formulate any precise or comprehensive definition of the circumstances in which a person is constituted a fiduciary in his or her relations with another (*Breen v. Williams* (1996) 186 CLR 71 at 92 *per* Dawson and Toohey JJ).

The High Court has decided that in Australia the relationship between a doctor and patient is not a fiduciary relationship, but essentially a contractual relationship whereby the doctor undertakes to treat and to advise the patient and to use reasonable skill and care in so doing (ibid. (1996) 186 CLR 71 at p. 78 *per* Brennan CJ; pp. 89–90 *per* Dawson and Toohey JJ; and p. 102 *per* Gaudron and McHugh JJ). Importantly, the High Court noted that it is of significance that a fiduciary acts in a representative character in exercising his or her responsibility (ibid. at pp. 92–3, 101 and 113). As to fiduciary duties or obligations, the High Court recognised that notwithstanding the fact that a doctor–patient relationship is not a fiduciary one, fiduciary duties may be superimposed or concurrent with contractual obligations (ibid. at pp. 83, 89, 93–4, 107 and 132–3). Fiduciary duties or obligations arise from either of two possible sources—agency or a relationship of ascendancy or influence by one party over another, or dependence or trust on the part of that other (ibid. at pp. 82, 134).

Even where there is a fiduciary relationship between a professional and a client (for example, between a solicitor and his or her client) it is important to acknowledge that fiduciary obligations do not extend to the entire relationship. As Chief Justice Brennan (as he then was) pointed out in *Breen v. Williams* (1996) 186 CLR 71 at p. 82):

> It is erroneous to regard the duty owed by a fiduciary to his beneficiary as attaching to every aspect of the fiduciary's conduct, however irrelevant that conduct may be to the agency or relationship that is the source of fiduciary duty.

Similarly, Justices Dawson and Toohey observed in the same case (at p. 92): 'Whilst duties of a fiduciary nature may be imposed upon a doctor, they are confined and do not cover the entire doctor–patient relationship.'

So although not all relationships between a professional and client are fiduciary relationships, it is clear that some are and others may have fiduciary duties superimposed on them. To the extent that fiduciary duties arise from 'a relationship of ascendancy or influence by one party over another, or dependence or trust on the part of that other' it would seem likely that there will be a community expectation that the profession and its members will act in the public interest first and foremost. That is, ahead of the interests of the members of the profession.

**Whistleblowing in the Professions**

Two key issues merit further consideration in respect of reporting contraventions of the law perpetrated by professionals. First, given the definition of a profession as set out earlier (in particular the emphasis on ethics and on putting the welfare, health and safety of the community ahead of other considerations), should a profession as a whole support and encourage whistleblowing? Second, given the importance of self-regulation as a characteristic of the professions, how do professions or their regulating associations encourage whistleblowing from within the profession and support or protect professionals who engage in whistleblowing?

In respect of the first issue, it could be suggested that governing professional associations have a major role to play in ensuring and maintaining the public's confidence of the profession they represent by adopting a formal and public policy on whistleblowing. That is, a clear statement of the particular profession's commitment to complying with applicable laws and to reporting conduct that might be in breach of the law. Since ethical behaviour and putting the community's welfare ahead of other interests is a hallmark of a profession, such a leadership approach to the issue of whistleblowing should be regarded as consistent with the core attributes of a profession. Views of this kind have been expressed in relation to the conduct of both the accounting and the legal professions. For example, with respect to accountants:

> The accounting profession, in adopting a code of ethics and undertaking a measure of self-regulation, has indicated to society that it sees its members as operating ethically and within the law. It is expected that they will do more than their supervisors require, and will be prepared to assume responsibility. While they

are not expected to become martyrs, accountants are expected to respond appropriately to behaviour that breaches the law (Jones 1996, p. 56).

This poses some problems for the profession which, having promoted its integrity, needs to prepare for whistleblowers in its ranks. Procedures will be needed for whistleblowers to use. Businesses and governments are often involved, sometimes inadvertently, in illegal or unethical practices. Accountants often know of such practices. To be effective as whistleblowers, they will need to tell people either inside or outside the organisations involved (Barnett, Cochrane and Taylor 1993, p.127; Jones 1996, p. 56).

While the accounting profession prominently encourages ethical behaviour, it has yet to set up such mechanisms or to start changing the culture of its public practices. Unless this happens, accountants face increasing risk of prosecution or criticism for failing to report or prevent illegal behaviour within its own practices and by their clients' businesses. Accountants may not always be able to prevent illegal behaviour by their clients, but by failing to report it or failing to comment on it to the client, they are silently condoning it, and thus have to accept some responsibility for it (Jones 1996, p. 57).

Similarly, Professor Stephen Corones (1998, pp. 783–4) has recently observed in relation to lawyers:

Lawyers are frequently involved in negotiations by their clients. They frequently have knowledge about their clients' affairs and the nature of their clients' businesses. If, during the course of negotiations, they are aware that their client makes a misrepresentation and they do nothing to correct the misrepresentation, they will be 'involved in' the contravention of s. 52 by their client and incur an ancillary liability under the Act.

If a client makes a false statement during negotiations in the presence of a solicitor, the solicitor should take the client to one side and counsel the client to correct the misleading information. If the client refuses to do so, an ethical and prudent solicitor will cease to act for the client and should correct the misinformation.

As to the second key issue identified above, considerable effort will be required by professional associations to balance some possibly competing tensions. To put in place an effective whistleblowing policy, a profession— either at the professional association level or individual firm level—would need to look at the following series of important issues: resources; guarantees of confidentiality; mechanisms for keeping the whistleblower informed of investigation outcomes; incentives to come forward; mechanisms for distinguishing genuine from non-genuine whistleblowers; whether the reporting or disclosure should be internal or external (if external who would the disclosure be to an appropriate enforcement agency or to the media or other person/body); and mechanisms for reviewing the policy on a periodic basis. It is acknowledged that a professional association's practice or role in speaking out publicly on behalf of the profession may, of course, create tensions with implementation of any whistleblowing policy.

## Conclusion

Given the pace and stresses of modern life, and the fact that despite the high degree of learned training, professions are made up of human beings, it is inevitable that a small percentage of professionals will engage in illegal conduct or be involved in illegal conduct committed by others. The recent cases involving the death of solicitor Max Green and the loss of large sums of money from trust funds (Cant 2000, p. 3), and the inquiries and referral to the Director of Public Prosecutions of numerous Magnetic Resource Imaging contracts for possible legal action against various radiologists (Gray 1999; Niesche and Marris 1999; Steketee 1999) are examples.

Arguably, in order to maintain the public's confidence and trust in their activities, the professions, professional associations and individual professional firms should take a leadership role, in the public interest, by adopting and publicly committing the professions and their members to support a whistleblowing policy including protection of whistleblowers. Leading by example in this way would clearly demonstrate the concern which professionals have for maintaining high ethical standards and putting the community's interest before other interests.

## Notes

1   In 1997, membership of the Australian Council of Professions Ltd comprised: Australian Medical Association Ltd; the Institution of Engineers Australia; the Royal Australian Institute of Architects; Australian Dental Association Inc; the Australian Veterinary Association Ltd; Australian Society of Certified Practising Accountants; the Institute of Chartered Accountants in Australia; the Institution of Surveyors Australia Inc; Pharmaceutical Society of Australia; the Institute of Actuaries of Australia; the Australian Institute of Quantity Surveyors; Australian Physiotherapy Association; and the New South Wales Council of Professions.

2   ACCC (1998). Reproduced in the Appendix to this chapter.

**Appendix: Cooperation and Leniency in Enforcement**

*Introduction*

Commitment to active enforcement of the law is fundamental to the achievement of the Commission's objectives of promoting competition and fair trading.

It is not possible for the Commission to pursue all potential or alleged breaches of the Trade Practices Act or other legislation under which it has responsibilities. The effective use of resources in the public's best interests require that the Commission have clear priorities in its selection of matters for enforcement and that it chooses the enforcement vehicle most appropriate to the circumstances.

This statement deals with one aspect of the Commission's approach to enforcement—its policy on the adoption of leniency in circumstances flowing from cooperation. Because the policy continues to evolve in the light of Commission experience and changing markets, it is presented in terms of flexible guidelines.

There are separate, but in many respects similar, guidelines in respect of individuals and corporations. It is emphasised that they are flexible and intended only as an indication of the factors the Commission will consider relevant when considering leniency.

The Commission's purpose in publishing this policy is twofold:

• to promote awareness of it; and
• to encourage participants possibly in breach to come forward to assist Commission investigations.

Recognition of such cooperation and assistance takes a variety of forms, for example, complete or partial immunity from action by the Commission, submissions to the Court for a reduction in penalty or even administrative settlement in lieu of litigation.

The policy on litigation necessarily relates only to civil matters. The Commission does not have power to grant immunity for actions for criminal conduct under Part V of the Trade Practices Act. In such cases the discretion lies with the Director of Public Prosecutions.

*Individual Conduct*

The following guidelines apply to directors, managers, officers or employees of a corporation who come to the Commission as individuals and not on behalf of the corporate entity with evidence of conduct contravening the Trade Practices Act (or other legislation administered by the Commission).

Leniency, including immunity, is most likely to be considered appropriate for individuals who:

- come forward with valuable and important evidence of a contravention of which the Commission is either otherwise unaware or has insufficient evidence to initiate proceedings;
- provide the Commission with full and frank disclosure of the activity and relevant documentary and other evidence available to them;
- undertake to cooperate throughout the Commission's investigation and comply with that undertaking;
- agree not to use the same legal representation as the firm by which they are employed;
- have not compelled or induced any other person/corporation to take part in the conduct and were not a ringleader or originator of the activity.

Immunity would not be granted where the person seeking leniency has compelled or induced any other person/corporation to take part in the conduct or was a ringleader or originator of the activity.

*Corporate Conduct*

The guidelines governing policy on leniency toward corporations necessarily differ in some respects, but are similar in spirit.

Leniency is most likely to be considered for a corporation which:

- comes forward with valuable and important evidence of a contravention of which the Commission is otherwise unaware or has insufficient evidence to initiate proceedings;
- upon its discovery of the breach, takes prompt and effective action to terminate its part in the activity;
- provides the Commission with full and frank disclosure of the activity and all relevant documentary and other evidence available to it, and cooperates fully with the Commission's investigation and any ensuing prosecution;

- has not compelled or induced any other corporation to take part in the anti-competitive agreement and was not a ringleader or originator of the activity;
- is prepared to make restitution where appropriate;
- is prepared to take immediate steps to rectify the situation and ensure that it does not happen again, undertakes to do so and complies with the undertaking;
- does not have a prior record of Trade Practices Act, or related, offences.

Immunity would not be granted where the corporation seeking leniency has compelled or induced any other person/corporation to take part in the conduct or was a ringleader or originator of the activity.

It is not necessary that all the above criteria be met in order for leniency to be granted. The Commission assesses each case on its merits.

*Submissions to the Court*

It is the responsibility of the Court to determine penalties for contraventions of legislation administered by the Commission.

However, the Commission is free to reach an agreement with parties as to joint submissions to be placed before the Court for adjudication. It exercises this right if it is satisfied that a corporation or individual, which has not been granted an immunity, has cooperated with it in a substantive way.

In determining whether to reach an agreement on penalties, and what the agreement should be, the Commission takes into consideration factors including:

- whether the company or individual has cooperated with the authorities;
- whether the contravention arose out of the conduct of senior management, or at a lower level;
- whether the company has a corporate culture conducive to compliance with the law;
- the nature and extent of the contravening conduct;
- whether the conduct has ceased;
- the amount of loss or damage caused;
- the circumstances in which the conduct took place;
- the size and power of the company;
- whether the contravention was deliberate and the period over which it extended.

*Procedure*

Individuals or corporations wishing to take advantage of the Commission's policy on leniency should approach the Chairman or General Manager of the Commission. The Commission determines each request on a case-by-case basis.

The Commission is open to the discussion of hypothetical scenarios in relation to involvement in conduct that contravenes legislation for which it is responsible.

Informants or their legal representatives may freely approach the Commission in an attempt to gain some indication of the likelihood of immunity or leniency in penalties. The Commission will not be able to give definitive answers in such cases, but will provide guidance as to the probable course of action it would take (ACCC Oct. 1998).

Chapter 12

# Preventing Corruption in Government: A Transparency International Perspective

Peter Willis[1]

## Introduction

The court of King James I of England was once described in the following terms:

> This is a tale of extravagance, waste, corruption and vice...Unprecedented sums of money were squandered...Titles and government offices were bought and sold. Through monopolies, tax-farming and the appropriation of public land for private purposes the entire national economy was fleeced by parasitic rulers and their cronies...(Lever 1971, p. 15; cf. Denning 1981, p. 22).

It was what might generally be described as a 'corrupt government'. Although Australia has historical links to the country in which such corruption once existed, Australia is now perceived as being one of the least corrupt countries in the world—see Transparency International's latest *Corruption Perception Index* (Transparency International 1999).

How, then, has Australia achieved this position, and what systems have been created to guard against corruption in government? This chapter examines historically how Australia has sought to build clean government, by examining six attributes of its system: the honest elections of honest politicians; the presence of honest, neutral and qualified public servants; auditing and accountability of public receipts and expenditure; independent investigation and adjudication of complaints against government; free access to information; and finally, the independent prosecution of crimes and the presence of independent, unbiased and honest judges.

These are not the only elements underpinning clean government. The rule of law (respect for the independent and impartial application of the law) and a vigorous and free press are also vital. The present chapter will refer to these in passing only.

151

*Corruption Defined*

This chapter adopts a definition of 'corruption' used by Transparency International. Transparency International is a non-governmental organisation founded in 1992 in Berlin by a group of individuals with experience in senior positions in the World Bank, the Commonwealth Secretariat, as well as business and aid backgrounds. Transparency International aims to build coalitions to fight corruption, which it defines as 'the misuse of public power for private profit'. Corruption can also be defined as representing non-compliance with the 'arm's-length' principle, under which no personal or family relationship should play any role in economic decision-making, be it by private economic agents or by government officials. The arm's-length principle is seen as fundamental to the efficient functioning of any organisation. Transparency International, adopting Tanzi (1994), argues that once the arm's-length principle has been breached and a distinction made based on relationships, corruption will often follow.

Transparency International classifies corruption into four broad groups: (1) bribes that are paid for access to a scarce benefit, or to avoid a cost; (2) bribes that are paid for receipt of a benefit (or avoidance of a cost) that is not scarce, but where state officials must exercise discretion; (3) bribes that are paid, not for a specific public benefit itself, but for services connected with obtaining a benefit (or avoiding a cost), such as speedy service or inside information; and (4) bribes that are paid to prevent others from sharing in a benefit or to impose a cost on someone else.

The first category includes any bureaucratic decision where the briber's gain is someone else's loss—for example, access to import or export permits, foreign exchange, a government contract or franchise, concessions to develop oil or other minerals, public land allocation, the purchase of a newly privatised firm, access to scarce capital funds under state control, a license to operate a business when the total number of licenses is fixed, access to public services such as public housing, subsidised inputs or heightened police protection for a business. In all these examples there may be competition between bribers which can be manipulated or even created by bureaucrats or politicians. If public servants have the discretion to design programs, they may be able to create scarcity for their own pecuniary benefit or over-allocate resources (a phenomenon known as 'supply stretching').

Examples of the second category include: reducing tax bills or extorting higher payments when no fixed revenue constraint exists; waiving of customs duties and regulations; avoidance of price controls; award of a license or permit only to those who are deemed to 'qualify'; access to open-ended public services (entitlements); receipt of a civil service job; exemption from enforcement of the law (especially for victimless and white-collar crime); zoning board approval for a building project; and lax enforcement of safety or environmental standards. Bureaucratic discretion can often lead to the extortion of bribes. Police can pay gangs to threaten businesses, while at the same time accepting bribes from these same businesses for their protection. Similarly, politicians can threaten to support laws that will impose costs or promise to provide specialised benefits in return for payoffs.

The third category is linked to the first two categories and relates to attempts at securing a better service rather than a benefit *per se*—for example, inside information on contract specifications; faster service; reduced paperwork; advance notice of police raids; reduced uncertainty; or a favourable audit report that would keep taxes low. Bureaucrats can often generate the conditions that produce such bribes. Officials can introduce delays and impose rigid application requirements.

The final category, like the first, also includes winners and losers. Examples include cases where one operator of an illegal business pays law enforcement agencies to raid his competitors. Owners of legal business might seek the imposition of excessive regulatory constraints on competitors or attempt to induce officials to refuse to license a potential competitor.

In the first and last categories, where there are direct losers, the organisation of the potential bribers may be important in determining the size and prevalence of corruption. If there are only a small number of potential beneficiaries, they may simply share the market monopolistically among themselves and present a united front to public officials, avoiding the need to resort to bribery. These cases demonstrate why the elimination of corruption should not be an end in itself. A policy encouraging the monopolisation of an industry could reduce corruption, but would have few social gains. The benefits, instead of flowing in part to public officials, would flow into the pockets of monopolistic firms. If these companies are, in addition, foreign-owned—and repatriating profits—or international criminal concerns, the benefits will mostly flow out of the country. Examples like these illustrate how the problem might not be corruption *per se*, but the monopoly rents that give rise to payoffs.

How, then, has the adoption of the six principles referred to above led to such forms of corruption being minimised?

**Honest Elections of Honest Politicians**

An elected national parliament lies at the heart of any integrity system, based on democratic accountability. Its task is simply stated: to express the sovereign will of the people through their chosen representatives, who, on their behalf, hold the Executive accountable on a day-to-day basis.

Watchdog, regulator and representative, the modern parliament is at the centre of the struggle to attain and sustain good governance and to fight corruption. To be fully effective in these roles, parliament must be comprised of individuals of integrity. If seen as a collection of rogues who have bought, bribed, cajoled and rigged themselves into positions of power, a parliament forfeits whatever respect it might otherwise have enjoyed and effectively disables itself from promoting good governance and minimising corruption— even if it wants to do so.

Clean elections and parliamentarians do not guarantee honest and clean government, nor do they eliminate all corruption. They can only reduce its extent, significance and pervasiveness.

*Before the Anti-bribery Rules*

Almost 80 years ago, Mr Justice Higgins of the Australian High Court wrote:

> Comment has been made on the peculiar fact that there are so very few cases bearing directly on the bribery of members of Parliament. Unfortunately, it can not be said that this is testimony to the virtue of members; for according to Hallam's Constitutional History [p. 733], bribery of members was often exercised, and especially by King William III, out of secret service funds (*R v. Boston* (1923) 33 CLR 386, p. 407).

This presents a mildly critical but otherwise rosy picture of English parliamentary life and you could be forgiven for thinking that the problems it mentions occurred around 1700 or a Long Time Ago. But the truth is much more shocking and sobering. Put most simply, bribery of members of parliament was not the aberration of a single reign. Corruption was the main means of securing election to parliament and of forming government and of staying in government for over 100 years. Then for 50 years longer, election to parliament remained a haphazard and gerrymandered affair, culminating in the cataclysm of English politics known as the Reform Act of 1832.

In the days before universal franchise required, and mass communication allowed, unifying ideologies or party platforms to be spread nationwide, elections were fought on local issues; to create some unity to form government to pass the annual appropriation of revenues for government purposes, 'Ministers and magnates imposed some sort of pattern by "influencing" the elections...A member toed the line because of one, or a combination of devices' (Williams 1960, pp. 138–9, 150, 152–3, 174)—the conferral on the member or a friend or relation (or, at least, the promise of) first, a 'place' (a job on the government payroll—the positions included posts in the civil service, the court and the Royal household [now outlawed by the Constitutional prohibition on holding 'an office of profit under the Crown']); secondly, a pension, privately granted or individually slipped into legislation; thirdly, a lucrative government contract (now outlawed by basic 'conflict of interest' provisions); and fourthly, a government borough, where the electoral expenses of considerable sums were met by the government out of general revenue or secret reserves. Thus Lord North, Prime Minister could write to King George III accounting for the election of 1782: 'the whole expense is £103,765/15s/9d, ...a sum larger, but not very considerably larger, than has been paid on other such occasions of similar nature...'(17 April 1782).

This was an *enormous* sum—not spent on official Electoral Commission machinery, but in paying candidates and the controllers of the seats. There were six different franchises possible—the variety and type of seat and the means of controlling them were arcane: there might be as few as 37 votes or over 2,000. In some, it was sufficient to own the titles to all the land to control the votes; in others it was necessary to wine, dine and woo the handful of voters; in others to curry favour on a broader scale (Williams 1960).

The great saving of the English Parliament throughout the century was that the managers controlled less than half the votes and, despite the corruption, there was a culture of intellectual independence, a tolerance of dissent and acceptance of the rise *and fall* of parties. The paradox, as expressed by one law reformer, was that buying a seat in parliament out of your *own* resources was 'almost the only mode by which parliament was accessible with honour to those who had no family connection' or local patron (Williams 1960, p. 173). There were thus clean bribes and tainted bribes (with strings attached)!

*How Change Came About*

Periodically over the century from 1729 to 1832, titanic battles were fought, little by little to overcome these deeply embedded features. Persistently, the reforms were piecemeal, inconsistent, full of loopholes and fiercely resisted. They came in bursts after long lulls, not in a continuous stream. Naturally resistance came from those whose interests were threatened; but it also arose from those who were concerned at the by-products of the proposed reforms and from fear of the unknown and from reaction to the flaws and tactics of the reformers. Further, the pattern often required some overwhelming scandal or crisis to galvanise opinion or provide the impetus for the final battle, bringing the doubters and the 'middle' across to the side of the reformers.

The pace and 'system' of reforms can be judged by considering the dates and nature of the keynote reforming Acts (extracted in Williams 1960, pp. 190–4, 198–9, 206–8).

The Anti-Bribery Act (*Last Determination Act 1729*, 2 Geo II c 24), called 'an Act for the more effectual preventing bribery and corruption in the election of members to serve in Parliament', made provision for a candidate to require every voter to take an oath that they had not been bribed. If no candidate or group of voters called for the oath, it was not required.

The *Place Act 1742* (15 Geo II c 22) was an attempt to address the conferral of paid government positions on parliamentarians: minor civil servants were not allowed to be MPs. It built on two Acts of 1700, which precluded excise and customs officers from sitting in the House of Commons. Later (1782) it became necessary to preclude these officers from voting at elections—clearly the appointment to these lucrative posts carried a trade-off in voting rights.

Burke's *Place Act 1782* (22 Geo III c 45) was a more vigorous attempt to address another way in which government conferred financial benefits on their supporters, by providing that persons concerned in any contract, commission or agreement made for the public service could not be MPs.

Similar ideas are reflected in Australian constitutions (for example, Constitution of Australia, section 44 (v); *Constitution Act 1975* (Vic.), section 54), although its ambit is still debated and uncertain, due to a case involving a Senator's family company's dealings with Government in 1974. In an extraordinary decision, Chief Justice Barwick of the High Court of Australia described the section as 'vestigial', noting that it 'finally disappeared from British Parliamentary life' in 1957. The judge drew a distinction between 'protection of the independence of parliament' (its original purpose) and a provision 'to protect the public against fraudulent conduct of members of the House, carried out perhaps behind the shield of a corporation of small membership' and he confined the interpretation of the provision accordingly.

As a result he held that an MP with a shareholding in a private family company which supplied timber to the Government Works Department did not have 'a direct or indirect pecuniary interest in any agreement' with Government (*Re Webster* (1975) 132 CLR 270, pp. 278–9).

The *Civil Establishment List Act 1782* (22 Geo III c 82) systematised government payment and disbursement procedures; banning secret pensions from government funds (see Australian Constitution section 44 (iv)).

The Anti-Bribery Act (Curwen's Act 1809, 49 Geo III c 118) recited and then closed all the most obvious and widely-used loopholes which the 1729 Act left untouched and was far more effective in restricting bribery and influence peddling.

The legislation of 1782 to 1785 noted here and below, was catalysed by a famous denunciation of patronage, Royal power and corruption in the public service and government led by Edmund Burke and Charles James Fox in 1780. Burke's speech was privately published in pamphlet form and was immediately and widely distributed (there was no Parliamentary *Hansard* in those days), building widespread support among voters and the non-voting general public alike.

This provided an impetus to break down the century-long procedures and habits. Yet the battle for 'economical reform' took several generations to work its way through the English political system. Accompanying the campaign was a high profile prosecution for corruption of a public official by the House of Commons. This was the excruciatingly drawn-out impeachment of Warren Hastings, Governor-General of Bengal, in the House of Lords between 1788 and 1795. Although ending in exhausted acquittal, it too played its part in warning the corrupt of the change in sentiment and standards which the campaign brought about (Marshall 1965).

Again, irony abounds and reminds us that there is no inexorable law of progress, however much it all appears a neat process in hindsight: the initial period of reform was interspersed by an election at which William Pitt was assured by the King's parliamentary agent that a favourable majority would be obtained through bribery of the voters (Stephenson and Marchman 1937, p. 669).

*Life after the Changes—The Australian Inheritance*

Australia inherited these developments when the colonies achieved 'representative government' (elected law-making parliaments and elected ministries) from 1851 onwards.

Notwithstanding these great changes and the observation of the High Court, late colonial and the early post-Federation state politics seemed filled with corruption and dubious transactions. Equally from contemporary times, there are enough examples of corruption of members of parliament and ministers, to remind us of the temptations and occasions of power and the need for vigilance.

An early case after the grant of responsible government, involved an attempt to bribe a New South Wales member to vote in favour of a compensation claim for land damaged by goldminers and cattle. The bribe was a modest £20 (*R v. White* (1875) 13 SCR (NSW) (L) 322).

In Victoria, none was more controversial or brazen than the market gardener's son turned land speculator and railway promoter, MP (Speaker and eventually Premier) Sir Thomas Bent. Although looked upon askance by the respectable news media of the day, he remained generally untouchable and led a charmed life, blustering and bullying his way out of tight spots for over 40 years (Glass 1993).

In New South Wales, rural rather than metropolitan land and commodities dealings by and through MPs and influence peddling and bribing ministers led to a series of Royal Commissions throughout the first 20 years of the twentieth century (Evatt 1945, pp. 173, 181, 204). The Minister for Lands at the turn of the century was found to have systematically extorted half of amounts paid to land agents by clients for the grant of leases which he admitted breached the relevant Land Acts. The Minister had received £27,600 in cash during his three years in office; another MP, a practising land agent, £20,300; another land agent admitted receiving £15,000, which he said he split equally with the Minister. It all first came to light when a disgruntled client sued for the return of his payment. The Minister, the land agent/MP and the other agent were all charged with bribery. The jury could not agree and was discharged. Thereupon, the Government dropped the charges and kindly allowed the Minister to 'retire' from Parliament voluntarily—at least on this occasion, his professional peers judged his actions intolerable. He was disbarred from legal practice and died in disgrace.

Notwithstanding this example, soon after another New South Wales backbench MP was charged, with two others (and their clients, unknown), with agreeing to accept and offer 'large sums of money' to the MP for him to influence the Minister for Lands to inspect and purchase land.

The MP took a nice point of law to the High Court. He argued that his actions were not corrupt within the defined common law offences as they involved no act by him in Parliament—he was merely going to lobby the Minister outside Parliament—and, moreover, that the land was for sale at a fair value. By a majority of four to two, the High Court held that this too constituted the offence of bribery of a public officer (*R v. Boston* (1923) 33 CLR 386).

In the light of the recent United Kingdom 'cash for questions' controversy, which contributed to the downfall of the Major Conservative Government in 1997 (Robertson 1998), it is fascinating to realise that the High Court of Australia had posed in 1923 the question:

> how far may a member of the Legislative Assembly of NSW (and the same may be said as to any member of Parliament in Australia) without incurring any real personal responsibility—that is, other than political rejection—make his public position the subject of profitable traffic by engaging in departmental intervention on behalf of individuals in return for private pecuniary consideration to himself? (*R v. Boston* p. 395 *per* Isaacs and Rich JJ).

The answer is that, at least in Australia, a member may not: being elected as a Parliamentarian is to be elected to serve the state; this brings with it a duty owed to the public and a public trust. It is contrary to the duty and trust to accept money to exercise influence as an MP whether in parliamentary debate and votes or merely by letters and lobbying outside the chamber. The High Court clarified (and, in the view of some commentators at least, further extended the ambit of) this offence in 1992, deciding that it was also an offence to bribe a Minister for him to attempt to influence a decision by an authority for which he had policy responsibility but over which he had no direct legal control (*R v. Herscu* (1991) 173 CLR 276; Starke 1992).

Further scandals erupted in New South Wales in 1919 when a Royal Commission into construction contracts and other operations of the state Wheat Board left a cloud over the Minister for Agriculture, a personal friend of some of the tenderers under investigation (Evatt 1945, pp. 454ff, 480–1).

With elections pending in 1920 (which in fact produced a hung parliament and a minority Labor government), there was an election-eve attempt (as revealed by yet another Royal Commission) to bribe a member of the Labor party, with an offer of £500 for him to vote to close the Wheat Board enquiry down.

The recent experience of Tasmanian businessman, Edmund Rouse, convicted for attempting to bribe an opposition MP so as to allow the retiring government to remain in power after the 1989 state election produced a parliament potentially controlled by minorities, is a recent and more overtly 'political', but nonetheless classic, example of the perversion of democracy which bribery of MPs threatens.

Other convictions of recent times include the NSW Minister for Corrections who took bribes for the early release of prisoners (*Hilton v. Wells* (1985) 157 CLR 57, involving Rex Jackson), and the property developer and the Queensland Minister for Local Government who paid and received two bribes of $50,000 each for influencing a local council to facilitate a large building development (*R v. Herscu* (1991) 173 CLR 276, involving Russ Hinze).

The Queensland case arose in the context of a far-reaching and systematic pattern of corruption over many years which long seemed untouchable. It was brought to book by a combination of lone voices, investigatory journalism and straight politicians who appointed a Royal Commission, which documented the failings in great depth in the Fitzgerald Report (1989). Several ministers and the Commissioner of Police were convicted and jailed; the Premier of the state was similarly charged.

Not much later, in Western Australia, a related saga unfolded, in the 'WA Inc' Royal Commission (1992).

*Summary*

These few examples show how corruption survived the range of defences erected over the centuries and inherited by Australia when it broke out of its containment. Although Australia has come a long way, it took a considerable time for its system of government and parliament to become relatively free and clean. While Australia now claims to have removed endemic corruption— corruption which is built in to the very system or culture of public life—it has not gone away and the presence of corruption in our own polity is an ever-present threat. Both vigilance and persistence are required to combat corruption and it can take a long time for suspected or rumoured instances to be officially investigated. In addition, it remains even harder to 'prove' corruption to the standard of the criminal law. In a recent paper, Justice Denis Mahoney, then President of the New South Wales Court of Appeal, argued that the elements of the general criminal law protections against misuse of official power are too difficult to prove (Mahoney 1996). Enormous damage can be done in the meantime and cultures can be corrupted, so that the ritualistic cleansing, by a high-profile prosecution to remove a single 'bad apple', is not enough.

## Honest, Neutral and Qualified Public Servants

The official image of the public service is that it is composed of hard-working, competent, dispassionate men and women, providing advice to honest, upright and disinterested ministers and carrying out the decisions of government taken in the national interest.

Notwithstanding popular culture to the contrary (epitomised not only in clichés and caricatures of jokes, but in film and television), this remains the foundation myth (used in its sociological or ethnographic sense) and goal.

Yet dig behind the façade and we find that the edifice is of very recent construction. This can be seen in examination of the laws about misconduct generally, bribery in particular and in the history of the entry qualifications required for recruitment to the public service.

### *Public Service/Private Patronage*

Before turning to the laws, the questions of the selection and promotion of public servants needs to be addressed. As we have already seen, eighteenth century government was based on an elaborate web of what the polite called 'patronage'(as the great reforming nineteenth century British Prime Minister W.G. Gladstone described it: Matthew 1986, p. 85), but which we can call corruption.

The laws in large part were designed to prevent and punish individual misbehaviour—embezzlement in the personal interest of the embezzler, dereliction of duty of a kind out of the ordinary for the standards of the day (recognising that those standards were not those of today at all). But these laws are only of benefit to us if we have nothing worse to worry about. It is similar to the 'anti-corruption campaigns of contemporary Vietnam or China— an official who takes bribes for themselves is a criminal, but an official who takes the same amount for the Party is a Stakhanovite, Socialist Hero First Class.

In eighteenth-century England, the secretaries and under-secretaries of state, the senior government servants of the day (equivalent to our ministers and senior executive service):

> like so many other characters in constitutional history, were at some stage of the metamorphosis from personal servant to state official. Some regarded themselves as working for the king [we translate that as working for the impersonal State; but at that time, the King was still an active though constrained ruler]…they were thus semi-permanent, and independent of party…On the other hand, ministers needed servants they could trust, appointed by themselves…and so some civil servants did come and go with governments. These latter were certainly not politically neutral, but neither [in fact] were the former, so long as the king was in politics (Williams 1960, p. 174).

The gradual removal of the Crown from daily political battle led in equal measure to the removal of the body of the public service from partisan politics. Thus a step towards the 'neutrality' of the public service which we take as a bulwark of our version of democracy.

Two barriers to the creation of our modern public service remained. First, in the eighteenth century, 'it was well accepted that an office constituted a form of property, particularly the longer and more secure the tenure and the more pronounced the rights and pecuniary benefits attached to it' (Chester 1981, p. 18).

Moreover, the recruitment of the public service remained locked in the patronage system. The history of the campaign for the reform of the Civil Service in the United Kingdom is summarised in Peter Hennessy's *Whitehall* (Hennessy 1990, pp. 26–50). In summary, said Sir Charles Trevalyn, the prime designer of the modern meritocratic public service in the United Kingdom in 1851, the public service was staffed with 'sickly youths whose parents and friends…endeavour to obtain for them employment in the service of the Government…where they may obtain an honourable livelihood [that is, a good salary] with little labour and no risk …' (Northcote–Trevalyn Report 1851).

*How Reform Came*

With the support of a committed and powerful political sponsor (Gladstone, as Chancellor of the Exchequer and as Prime Minister) and a propitious crisis and scandal over supplies to the Crimean War, a 15-year campaign by a group of zealots at the heart of Whitehall and academia produced the Northcote–

Trevalyn Report. This established the prime features of the 'Westminster' model of the public service/civil service: entrance based on merit (competitive examinations) rather than patronage and connection and a series of rules and expectations, to create and govern a body of advisers with 'sufficient independence, character, ability and experience to be able to advise, assist and, to some extent, influence those who are from time to time set over them'. As the foremost modern Whitehall-watcher, Peter Hennessy, puts it:

> Once achieved, the principle of the great reform—that recruitment to the Civil Service should be determined by merit and not by connection—acquired the status of a self-evident truth. It did not appear that way to substantial sections of Victorian society, from the Queen down, and it was long in the making, careful in the planning and hard-fought in the implementation (Hennessy 1990, pp. 31–2).

If there were any lesson for us to bear in mind as the International Monetary Fund and other multilateral agencies prescribe anti-corruption reforms and institutions as they dispense economic wisdom and reconstruction advice for Indonesia and all the rest, this passage, and the 15 years of work it summarises, contains the most important.

It reminds us that what is commonplace and unquestioned for us today has been controversial and a close-run thing in times past.

Some reform campaigns fail ever to get off the ground, while others attract leaders and writers of genius, who capture the moment, galvanise supporters and organise effectively to carry the change to fruition; others fail at later stages, for lack of follow-through.

## Legal Controls Over Serious Misconduct

Australia has inherited from English law the offence of 'misconduct in a public office' or 'abuse of public office' (Halsbury's Laws of Australia, para. 130-12335). Legal historians can trace the origins of the offence of misconduct back 800 years (*R v. Dytham* [1979] QB 722). However, this makes it sound stronger and more developed than it was. The systematic application of the offence and its development were cemented in a period stretching from the early years of the 1700s and through to the middle of last century (that is the period in which clean politics and a clean public service were emerging step by step). Thus:

> By at least the middle of the eighteenth century the [judge-made] common law had evolved a general, though ill-defined, offence variously described as 'official

misconduct', 'breach of official trust' or 'misbehaviour in a public office'. To this day the precise metes and bounds of this offence remain uncertain. Indeed, there has been—and still is—a tendency to regard 'official misconduct' as but a descriptive formula for a series of specific but interrelated offences such as oppression, neglect of duty, abuse of official power, fraud in office etc [to say nothing of the precise but narrow offences of bribery and extortion of and by public officials] (Finn 1978, pp. 307–8).

The English judges typically fashioned and extended and defined offences of this kind in individual court cases, with an eye to what had been said and done in the past (through the doctrine of precedent) but, mostly, on a far from systematic basis. The law evolved in a complex relationship with history and with contemporary stimulus or the day-to-day practices (or outrages) which brought cases before the courts. Then from time to time, senior figures summarised and synthesised these stray examples. So a great clarifying judge of the late eighteenth century, Lord Mansfield proclaimed in the leading case on this offence:

> The law does not consist of particular cases but of general principles, which are illustrated and explained by these cases. Here are two principles applicable: first, that a man accepting an office of trust concerning the public, especially if attended with profit, is answerable criminally…for misbehaviour in…office…Secondly, where there is a breach of trust, fraud or imposition in matter concerning the public…it is indictable [as a criminal offence] (*R v. Bembridge* (1783) 3 Dougl 327 at 332; 99 ER 679, p. 681).

(There is an interesting irony when one considers that a previous Lord Chancellor, Lord Macclesfield, well known for accepting 'presents' from litigants, was eventually dismissed from office for demanding bribes from candidates for the appointment to judicial office. When offered £5000, he replied 'Guineas are handsomer' (Denning 1981, p. 722).)

The offence of misconduct in public office covers a number of actors and actions. A 'public officer' is any person in public authority, covering members of parliament and municipal councillors, public servants, judges, magistrates and police.

While most prosecutions have arisen out of official corruption, dishonesty is not an essential element of the offence—it can be constituted by deliberately failing to act or acting seriously negligently (*R v. Bembridge* (1783) 3 Dougl 327 at 332; 99 ER 679, p. 681). A public officer commits an offence if they wilfully refuse to perform a duty which they are bound to perform or if they make a decision in a matter in which they have a direct financial interest.

The cases in which prosecutions have been brought are obvious enough examples and in the current age, no doubt isolated. The Law Reports tend to reflect 'successes'—cases where bribery or other misconduct has been discovered, reported and prosecuted. As we know well from Royal Commissions and other special investigations, there are other instances where this does not occur.

The sample of cases includes: attempted bribery of a police officer to protect illegal gambling establishments in Western Australia (*R v. Small* (1903) 5 WAR 85); a Welsh Court official responsible for the investment of trust funds of litigants (injured children) who paid them over to the party's trustees who lent them back to the Court official (*R v. Llewellyn-Jones* [1968] 1 QB 429); an Australian resident who sent $100 to an official interpreter in an Australian Embassy overseas to influence a visa application (*McDonald v. Bojkovic* [1987] VR 387); police passing confidential official information to a private investigator (*Question of Law (No 2 of 1996)* (1996) 67 SASR 63 and *Wright v. Queen* (1964) 43 DLR (2d) 597); and a Commonwealth public servant conducting a tender who passed information about other bidders to a prospective tenderer and was offered a bribe to rig the tender process (*Dau v. Emanuele* (1995) 60 FCR 270—described by Justice Higgins of the Federal Court as 'the longest trial ever recorded with the exception of the trial of St Paul in Rome and the impeachment of Warren Hastings as Viceroy of India'— the case took eight years and two months to complete). In this last case, the public servant then reported the offer to his superiors and they laid a trap for the bidder. The conviction of the bribe-payer was overturned on appeal on the basis that the public servant induced the subsequent offer of bribes with lies and heavy hints when one word could have dissuaded the offer.

A civil servant at Britain's Ministry of Defence, was imprisoned for four years for taking at least the equivalent of US$2.25 million in bribes. But in an analysis carried out for Transparency International in the United Kingdom, he is said to have caused up to US$200 million in financial damage. This included the cost of job losses at the factory in Britain which failed to gain the orders (they went abroad), loss of profits leading to lower values for privatisation exercises, the loss of highly developed skills, the higher price paid than was necessary, and the purchase in at least one instance of a fuse which was useless as it was 'ineffective in practice and battle conditions'(Pope 1996).

More generically and systematically, Transparency International has found that corruption is most commonly found in the following areas of the civil service: public procurement, customs, taxation, police (especially traffic police), immigration, licences and permits (including drivers' licences), provision of services where there is a state-owned monopoly (for example, telephone connections), construction permits and land zoning, and government appointments.

## Public Procurement

Mention the subject of corruption in government and most people will immediately think of bribes paid or received for the award of contracts for goods or services, or—to use the technical term—procurement. Whether this is really the most common form of public corruption may be questionable but without doubt it is alarmingly widespread and almost certainly the most publicised. Hardly a day goes by without the revelation of another major scandal in public procurement somewhere in the world.

It has been the cause for countless dismissals of senior officials and even for the collapse of entire governments. It is the source of considerable waste in public expenditures, estimated in some cases to run as high as thirty per cent or more of total procurement costs. Regrettably, it is more talked about than acted upon. Few activities create greater temptations or offer more opportunities for corruption than public sector procurement. Every level of government and every kind of government organisation purchases goods and services, often in quantities and monetary amounts that defy comprehension.

The people doing the buying—either those carrying out the procurement process or those who approve the decisions—are spending 'other people's' money. To the non-specialist, the procurement procedures appear complicated, even mystifying—often they are—and so they may be manipulated in a variety of ways without great risk of casual detection. And the would-be corrupters, on either side of the transactions, too often find ready and willing collaborators.

What can be done to combat corruption in procurement? The first prerequisite is to recognise that it is a problem and an unnecessary, unacceptable way of doing business. The second is to do something about reducing or eliminating it. This involves process design, education and regular external review and audit.

## Preventing Corruption

Having evolved as we have, how do we prevent corruption? In the view of Transparency International, the responsibility for maintaining standards and minimising corruption within the public service falls fairly and squarely on the public administrator. The criminal law is a reserve weapon. As the President of the New South Wales Court of Appeal has argued, it is attended with difficulties of proof and the political difficulty of forcing an institution (be it government or police force or whatever) to act against itself if something more than isolated malefaction is involved (Mahoney 1996, p. 25).

Moreover, Transparency International suggests that the criminal law is too blunt an instrument to deal with corruption in the public service for three further reasons. These are, first, because it is concerned only with minimum standards; second, it emphasises enforcement rather than prevention; and third, because the burden of proof is on the government (in corruption cases usually only the officials involved know the facts).

If properly conceived, regulations governing corruption in the public service must focus on conflicts of interest and be directed towards erecting a system designed to protect the public decision-making process. Rather than detecting and punishing the wrongdoer after the fact, such a system reduces the risk of corruption occurring in the first place. For the system to be effective, responsibility for avoiding corruption should not be a centralised task within the public administration, but one which is an overall managerial function involving all levels of managers within the public service.

## Auditing and Accountability of Public Receipts and Expenditure

Elected parliaments are the essence of democracy, yet democratisation in itself presents an opportunity to control systemic corruption by opening up the activities of public officials to public scrutiny and accountability. It has been suggested that democracies, more so than any other political system, are better able to deter corruption through institutionalised checks and balances and other meaningful accountability mechanisms. They reduce secrecy, monopoly and discretion.

Public officials must be held accountable to the public and to the legislature for their performance and stewardship of public funds and assets. The currency of financial accountability is information, but ministers and officials are unlikely to always agree with members of the legislature as to the quantity and quality of information that should be provided. As such, the Office of the Auditor-General stands at the pinnacle of the financial accountability pyramid.

*The Office of the Auditor-General*

For Transparency International, the Auditor-General is, in many ways, the linchpin of a country's integrity system. As the officer responsible for auditing government income and expenditure, the effective Auditor-General acts as a watchdog over financial integrity and the credibility of reported information.
The classic description of the role of the Office is that:

> the [Auditor-General] audits the Appropriation Accounts on behalf of the [Parliament]. He is the external auditor of Government, acting on behalf of the taxpayer, through Parliament, and it is on his investigations that Parliament has to rely for assurances about the accuracy and regularity of Government account (United Kingdom, House of Commons Public Accounts Committee 1981).

The typical responsibilities of the Office of the Auditor-General also include ensuring that the Executive complies with the will of the Legislature, as expressed through parliamentary approval of government expenditure (appropriations); promotes efficiency and cost effectiveness; and prevents corruption through the development of financial and auditing procedures designed to effectively reduce the incidence of corruption and increase the likelihood of its detection.

*Independent Auditing in the Public Interest*

The importance of proper and independent scrutiny of expenditure as a means of controlling corruption was not lost on Edmund Burke, James Charles Fox and the other British Parliamentarians who led the movement for 'Economical Reform' in the 1780s. That led in due course to changes in electoral procedure, as we have already noticed. Equally importantly, it led to the passage of two important Audit Acts: the *Audit Commission of Enquiry Act 1785* (special commission appointed to audit receipts of all government and state officers) and the *Audit Act 1785* (abolishing private right of audit and creating an Audit Commission for all public accounts).

These Acts laid the foundation for the institutionalisation and independence of the audit function. Most particularly, they made auditing a matter of public interest and parliamentary responsibility, rather than purely internal or ministerial concern. After all, the oldest formal government department in the United Kingdom was the Treasury or Exchequer, responsible for tallying and counting royal income and supervising its disbursement (Hennessy 1990). And it is remarkable that, as noted above, in reporting to King George III on the outcome of the systematic bribing of candidates and voters in the 1782 elections, the Prime Minister reported down to the last penny. Burke's audit reforms were adopted because of express concern that government funds were otherwise wasted and misused, both for party and personal gain.

A further step was taken in the United Kingdom in 1866, when the Auditor-General became responsible for more broadly based 'efficiency audits' as well as classical financial tallies, reporting 'on wasteful government expenditure with the aid of several hundred inspectors working permanently in the departments and 'engaged in an internal and continuous, and to large extent preventative, check on maladministration' (Wade and Forsyth 1994, pp. 82–3).

In Australia, Transparency International viewed with alarm the changes to the function and operations of the Victorian Auditor-General passed by the Liberal government and now reversed, precisely because it seemed to have been promulgated as a response to the Auditor-General fulfilling his functions in this field too effectively. Transparency International does not object to contracting out as such—it depends on the context: the existing resources, capacity, integrity and technical expertise of the Auditor-General's office and of the private sector. None of these factors made the 1996 changes in Victoria necessary or compelling. These have now been reversed by legislation in 1999.

## Independent Investigation and Adjudication of Complaints against Government

What can the ordinary citizen do when things go wrong, grievances arise and complaints about government bureaucracy fall on deaf ears? One option is to turn to the legal system, but courts are slow, expensive, public and far from user-friendly.

### Claims against the Government

For centuries, the English tradition said it was not possible to sue the government directly. Instead, an aggrieved party attempted to sue the individual decision-maker or, in conformity with the standards of politeness and deference to regal authority, it was necessary to petition the Crown to right the wrong suffered by the citizen. This was not only quaint, but cumbersome, expensive and, originally, discretionary as to the outcome (Somervell 1959; Wade and Forsyth 1994, pp. 821–2).

By contrast, the Australian colonies in the nineteenth century swept away these procedural contortions and legislated that citizens could directly sue the government (embodied in the Crown) for breach of contract and for tort (breach of duty of care): Claims against the Government Act or Crown Proceedings Acts of South Australia (1853), New South Wales (1861), Queensland (1866), Commonwealth (1901), Victoria (1955) (Finn and Smith 1992, Sawer 1968, pp. 18, 24).

These acts provided remedies where government officers or decisions breached the established law. They did not offer review for simple mistakes or reconsideration for mistaken policies. With the complexity and extent of government intervention in all areas of society in the twentieth century, concomitant with the development of the Welfare State, additional grounds for dealing with complaints of a non-legal nature were needed. Through a decade of campaigning across the common law world commencing in the late 1950s and early 1960s, Australia, New Zealand and the United Kingdom borrowed the office of the Ombudsman.

## The Ombudsman

Although the word 'ombudsman' is Scandinavian in origin, the first ombudsman flourished in China over 2,000 years ago, during the Han dynasty. However, antiquity did not guarantee continuity, and it was left to the Scandinavian countries to reinvent the office in the nineteenth century and to mould it into its modern form (Sawer 1968, pp. 6–9; Wade and Forsyth 1994, pp. 81–2). Sawer also invoked the Roman *censors*: a pair of officials with sweeping powers to call to account all other officials in office in the previous five years, in the Roman Republic 200 BC to 80 BC (contemporary with the Han dynasty).

The institution was thought to be unique to the needs of the Scandinavians until the early 1960s when New Zealand introduced its first Ombudsman (Sawer 1968, pp. 25–34). Throughout the 1960s, Sawer and others were ardent campaigners in Australia for the role and had to fight fiercely against governments comfortable with the status quo. There was an international aspect to the campaign, as he worked closely with Liberty in the United Kingdom (Wade and Forsyth 1994) and the Danish and New Zealand Ombudsmen were effective ambassadors for the office.

The implementation of the office in New Zealand was followed by the United Kingdom (1967) and in Australia: Western Australia (1971), South Australia (1972), Victoria (1973), Queensland and New South Wales (1974), the Commonwealth (1976) and Tasmania (1978) (Sykes, Lanham, Tracey and Esser 1997, para 2803ff). The early introducers were often newly-elected governments, of the left or of the centre, as with the later pattern of the introduction of freedom of information legislation.

Once the introduction was achieved and the office operated effectively and without causing destruction or riotous revolution, the long period of stout resistance was forgotten. As Sir Guy Powles, the common law world's first Ombudsman, later observed, citizens found the office to be useful in dealing with the powerful engines of authority and the concept quickly spread to the rest of the world. Today, the office of the Ombudsman is found in operation in over 100 countries and localities and in numerous private industry schemes (for example, banking, insurance and legal services) (Wade and Forsyth 1994, pp. 81, 105).

In essence, the Ombudsman constitutes an office which independently receives and investigates allegations of maladministration. The primary function of the ombudsman is to examine:

(i) a decision, process, recommendation, act of omission or commission which is contrary to law, rules or regulations, or is a departure from established practice or procedure, unless it is bona fide and has valid reason; is perverse, arbitrary or unreasonable, unjust, biased, oppressive or discriminatory; based on irrelevant grounds; or, involves the exercise of powers or the failure or refusal to do so for reasons of corrupt or improper motives such as bribery, jobbery, favouritism, nepotism and administrative excesses; and

(ii) neglect, inattention, delay, incompetence, inefficiency and ineptitude in the administration or discharge of duties and responsibilities.

As a high-profile constitutional institution, the office is potentially better able to resist improper pressure from the executive than are other bodies. The Ombudsman is constituted 'an officer of the Parliament' echoing the role and independence of the Auditor-General, as well as following the Scandinavian precedent (Wade and Forsyth 1994, pp. 82–4; Sawer 1968, p. 26).

The Ombudsman can perform an auditing function to stimulate information flows which will reveal and contain the limits of corruption in government. The confidentiality of these procedures gives the office an added advantage in providing a shield against the possible intimidation of informants and complainants. The office of the Ombudsman also acts to prevent corruption and maladministration. It can recommend improvements to procedures and practices and act as an incentive for public officials to keep their files in order at all times (Wade and Forsyth 1994, pp. 81, 93).

The spread of the office of Ombudsman following its adoption in New Zealand is the ultimate testament to the practical success and benefit of the office. It is a worthy and necessary part of the modern armoury against bad government. As such it plays some part in the prevention of corruption.


## Access to Information

The fight for information takes place between the public who want it and those in power who do not want them to have it. In the words of James Madison (1780):

> A popular government without popular information or the means of acquiring it is but a prologue to a farce or a tragedy, or perhaps both. Knowledge will forever govern ignorance; and a people who mean to be their own governors must arm themselves with the power that knowledge brings.

Madison's philosophy suggests that there can be no democracy without freedom of information, that secrecy impedes the political education of a community so that electoral choices are not fully informed, opportunities for individuals to respond meaningfully to political initiatives are blunted, and a political climate is generated in which the citizen views government not with responsibility and trust, but with malevolence and distrust.

The right to know is linked inextricably to accountability, the central goal of any democratic system of government. Informed judgment and appraisal by public, press and parliament alike is a difficult, even fruitless task if government activities and the decision-making process are obscured from public scrutiny. Where secrecy prevails, major resource commitments can be incurred, effectively closing the door to any future review and rethinking in the light of an informed public debate. There are, of course, other mechanisms within government such as parliament, the courts or an ombudsman, that act as a check on the abuse of power by an Executive. However, for these to be effective, their own access to information is an imperative. Given that such a right is worthy of recognition, how best can it be guaranteed?

*A Freedom of Information Act*

If governments simply behaved in an open fashion, making information widely available to the public and affected individuals, there would be no problem. This approach has been tried (for example in the early 1990s in the United Kingdom through the introduction of a much publicised 'Citizen's Charter' (see Wade and Forsyth 1994, pp. 106–7), but has generally failed to make much headway. Providing information that reflects well on an administration presents little difficulty; however, when the information reflects the opposite, the voluntary approach is most vulnerable. Where the release of information is a matter of discretion, be it of politicians or of administrators, the temptation to give themselves the benefit of the doubt when the information is embarrassing is too often irresistible.

That should not stop a government from making a concerted effort to encourage attitudinal changes which would relax restrictions on disclosures and increase the accessibility of decision-makers to press and public alike. But the problem with administrative guidelines will always be that, at the end of the day, discretion remains. And discretion, it is argued, runs counter to the fundamental principle of natural justice—for the administration is the judge in its own cause. The same argument stipulates that the dispute over access to information should be determined by a third, and neutral, party.

Legislation is therefore the only alternative. Hence the demand for freedom of information (FOI) legislation. Not only can FOI legislation establish a right of review (for example, by the Ombudsman), it can also establish practices which must be observed, even by those least willing to do so. It can reverse the usual presumption in favour of secrecy. Citizens are given the legal right of access to government documents without having to first prove special interest, and the burden of justifying non-disclosure falls on the government administration. Time limits within which requests must be handled can be imposed and an unimpeachable right of access to certain categories of information can be conferred.

The earliest legislation governing open records dates back to 1776 in Sweden. That country's present law is unique in that it is one of the four laws which together comprise the constitution of the country. The law outlines the main principles of the open records scheme, but the detailed provisions are contained in an ordinary Act, the Secrecy Law (Pope 1996). Similar, but nowhere near as rigorous, systems were introduced throughout Scandinavia in the 1970s and, most influentially for Australia, in the United States in

1966–67, as the result of an eight-year campaign by a senior congressman. Since then, the concept of open records legislation has started to emulate the spread of the office of Ombudsman across the world.

In Australia, freedom of information legislation grew out of a wave of administrative law reform studied and pioneered by the Coombs Royal Commission on Government, established by the Whitlam Government and adopted by Robert Ellicott, as federal Attorney-General in 1976. The same impetus gave rise to the Federal Ombudsman Act. The first federal FOI legislation was eventually passed in 1982, four years after its introduction (Curtis 1980; Sykes, Lanham, Tracey and Esser 1997, para. 1912). Chronologically, although not spiritually, it represents an exception to a telling rule explained to me by one minister, that 'FOI is legislation that only new governments introduce, in their first year in office'. In testament to that rule, FOI has eventually been adopted in all states, following changes of government: Victoria (1982), New South Wales and the Australian Capital Territory (1989), South Australia (1991), Tasmania, Queensland and Western Australia (1992).

FOI was not introduced as an expressly anti-corruption device, but there is no doubt it contributes to the battle against corruption in several ways. First, it creates an assumption of openness, reversing the common law and the natural tendency and inclination of the public service of old (Murphy 1997). In this respect, FOI is a key part of what the Western Australia Inc. Royal Commission compellingly describes as 'architectural principles' for Australian government (Western Australia 1992, Part II, para. 1.2.5–8). The two principles are popular participation in and election of government and the trust principle—the institutions, officials and agencies of government exist for the public to serve the interests of the public. All government must be constructed with three goals in mind: first, government must be conducted openly; second, public officials and agencies must be accountable for their actions; and third, there must be integrity both in the processes of government and in the conduct expected of officials.

In addition, remembering that corruption relies on secrecy, FOI provides a window into the darkest recesses. The power of FOI in the scrutiny of administration is exemplified in recent Victorian politics and is the subject of a Royal Commission.

Overall, it is not so much the usefulness of FOI on its own, but the combination of the tool with all the other mechanisms available which assist in reinforcing accountability and transparency, and perforce in restricting the opportunities for corruption to extend its grip.

## Honest and Independent Prosecutors and Judges

An independent, impartial and informed judiciary holds a central place in the realisation of just, honest, open and accountable government. Indeed, a judiciary must be independent if it is to perform its constitutional role of standing between the government and the people, and reviewing actions taken by the government and public officials to determine whether or not they comply with the standards laid down in the Constitution and with the laws enacted by the legislature.

On occasion, public confidence in the fairness and openness of systems of accountability will depend solely on the trust they have in the individuals charged with investigating particularly controversial issues. Moreover, if these issues actually touch on the inner workings of government, or even on the judicial or investigative process itself, the public naturally is suspicious of whether prosecution and thorough investigation will occur (Mahoney 1991, p. 25; Evatt 1945, pp. 181 and 454). Moreover, those ordinarily charged with the duty of investigation may find themselves in a situation in which they cannot perform their tasks without the trust and support of the public. For these reasons, the placing of the decision to prosecute in an independent non-political office is important. For these reasons, the Director of Public Prosecution was adopted in Australia in the 1980s, commencing with Victoria in 1982 and the Commonwealth in 1983. Events almost immediately highlighted the importance of the function (Temby 1985). Arguably, the independence of the office and the vesting of a discretion to prosecute in hands outside the Government's is a critical element in the modern fight against corruption in government.

## Conclusions

A survey of the National Chapters of Transparency International conducted in 1995, found that corruption in the public sector takes much the same form and affects the same areas whether one is dealing with a developed country or a developing one (Pope 1996, p. 10). The areas of government activity most vulnerable to corruption were: public procurement; rezoning of land; revenue collection; government appointments; and local government. The methodologies, too, were remarkably similar, including cronyism, connections, family members and relatives, political corruption through donations to political campaigns, kickbacks on government contracts (and subcontracting consultancies) and fraud of all kinds.

Corruption and its forms and mannerisms is, therefore, not unique to any one country. Corruption in China, where many bureaucrats have 'commercialised their administrative power', is really no different than in Europe, where political parties have taken huge kickbacks for public works projects. In Italy, the cost of road construction has reportedly dropped by upwards of 20 per cent since the 'Clean Hands' assault on corruption. Slush funds have been established in Swiss bank accounts for illicit political party financing, and suspicions are that these funds have been 'leaked' into private pockets. Kickbacks, too, have been paid to political parties for defence procurement, and companies have wined, dined, entertained and bribed officials (especially across international borders) to obtain business both illegally and unfairly, and not infrequently with disastrous consequences.

*Removing Corrupt Incentives*

The would-be reformer of corruption can be at a loss as to where to begin. History is littered with postures at reform—with grandiose promises and the conspicuous inability to deliver. In some cases, the intentions are genuine: newly-elected leaders arrive determined to clean out the stables, but are quickly overwhelmed by the size of the problem facing them. Others simply posture, making speeches, signing laws—all in the absence of any expectation that meaningful change will follow. Time and again, optimistic electorates have returned governments pledged to confront corruption firmly and effectively. Governments have fallen over their inability to counter the phenomenon; others have been elected in the hope that they can do better. Yet, very few can point to enduring progress. A telling example is the former President of South Korea, Roh Tae Woo, who at his inauguration vowed that he intended to be the cleanest President in his country's history. He was convicted of major corruption charges.

An analysis of the failure of past efforts has identified a number of causes. The first concerns the limits of power at the top. An incoming president may wish to tackle the challenge effectively but has, by definition, inherited a corrupt governmental machine which impedes efforts for change. Similarly, there may be an absence of commitment at the top. Lower-ranking political and administrative figures may wish to effect change but be severely restricted by an absence of commitment at the leadership level. Overly ambitious promises may also lead to unrealistic and unachievable expectations. Those who promise what they cannot deliver quickly lose the confidence of those around them and those looking to them for effectiveness.

Reforms may take place piecemeal and in an uncoordinated manner so that, in the end, no-one can be said to 'own' the reforms in the sense of being personally committed to them and being driven to see them implemented effectively and kept up to date. Reforms may also rely too much on the law, which is an uncertain instrument in trying to change the way people behave, or too much on enforcement, which leads to repression, apparent abuses of power and the emergence of another corrupt regime. Sometimes reforms tend to overlook those at the top and focus only on the smaller fry, the assumption being that those at the top either do not need reform or that they would be openly hostile towards anyone who attempted it. As a result, the law is seen as being applied unevenly and unfairly, and soon ceases to be applied at all. Reforms might also not have a specific and achievable focus and fail to deliver any real change to the public (without which the public belief essential to successful reform quickly ebbs away).

Finally, institutional mechanisms may not be constructed, even where reform is real, to carry reforms forward after their initial proponents have passed from the scene. One example is that of Justice Plana in the Philippines. He reformed the tax administration, raising its ability to implement tax collection fairly and effectively. As soon as he was promoted, the reforms began to unravel. Soon the situation was as parlous as it was before he began (Klitgaard 1988).

As we have seen, reform must always face a host of vested interests: those who benefit by the status quo are potentially at risk in this process. Many are in positions in which they can derail reforms; some are so powerful—or so determined—that they may resort to violence. The potential dangers to reformers in such countries are real. The changes inherent in a comprehensive and effective overhaul of a country's integrity system may be considerable, and call for special political and managerial skills.

Yet not everyone who is part of the status quo is wedded to it. The lessons of the battles to reform corruption in parliament in the United Kingdom is that there will be those who, realising that the rules have changed, will go along with reforms that prevent future corruption. The task is always to keep the momentum for change towards corruption-free structures.

*Creating the Foundation for Corruption-free Government: An Environment of Integrity in Public Life*

A lesson of the modern world is that the public—civil society—plays a powerful role in curbing corruption, if it can be mobilised and organised.

The public is entitled to expect from their leaders standards of behaviour which contribute to the public good and are themselves bulwarks against corruption.

The Nolan Commission in the United Kingdom (1995) suggested the application of seven principles to all aspects of public life.

*Selflessness:* Holders of public office should take decisions solely in terms of the public interest. They should not do so in order to gain financial or other material benefits for themselves, their family or their friends.

*Integrity:* Holders of public office should not place themselves under any financial or other obligation to outside individuals or organisations that might influence them in the performance of their official duties.

*Objectivity:* In carrying out public business, including making public appointments, awarding contracts or recommending individuals for rewards and benefits, holders of public office should make choices on merit.

*Accountability:* Holders of public office are accountable for their decisions and actions to the public and must submit themselves to whatever scrutiny is appropriate to their office.

*Openness:* Holders of public office should be as open as possible about all the decisions and actions that they take. They should give reasons for their decisions and restrict information only when the wider public interest clearly demands.

*Honesty:* Holders of public office have a duty to declare any private interests relating to their public duties and to take steps to resolve any conflicts arising in a way that protects the public interest.

*Leadership:* Holders of public office should promote and support these principles by leadership and example.

The establishment and maintenance of integrity in public life and public service requires a number of elements, including legislation—regulations and codes of conduct; a society whose religious, political and social values expect honesty from politicians and officials; professionalism among officials; a sense of elitism among senior civil servants; and a political leadership which takes both public and private morality seriously.

Together, these elements establish and foster a tradition of ethical public life and an ethical environment in which politicians and officials are generally assumed to be honest. Within such an environment it is also assumed that the laws and means of detection and investigation are sufficient to make it risky and costly to break the rules, accept bribes and become involved in fraud (Doig 1994, p. 4).

## Guarding the Guardians—Perpetual Vigilance

The example set by leaders and high-ranking public officials is crucial to the achievement and maintenance of an effective national integrity system. But who will guard the guardians? The objective in any integrity system is to build a system of checks and balances within the framework of agreed fundamental principles (usually enshrined in a written constitution or basic law). In effect, a self-sustaining 'virtuous circle' is achieved, in which the principals at risk are all monitored, by themselves and by others.

The challenge is to construct a transparent and accountable system, which has two primary objectives: the first is to prevent fraud from taking place, and the second to make the principal players believe that there is a realistic chance of fraud being detected.

As argued above, monitoring corruption cannot be left only to public prosecutors and to the forces of law and order. Action cannot depend solely on detection and criminal prosecution. Rather, action must include a combination of interlocking arrangements. In part, this approach includes improving the transparency of relationships, and to the extent possible, preventing the development of relationships which can lead to corruption. It includes transparency in the financial affairs of key players and the prospect of reviews being conducted by independent institutions which are likely to be outside any particular corruption network.

## Organisational Change

Organisational change within the civil service can help minimise the opportunities for corrupt practices. Singapore, for example, began its successful anti-corruption program in the early 1970s by instructing permanent secretaries (heads of government ministries) to make their officers aware of the government's serious efforts to eradicate corruption and to advise them to report any cases of corruption (Quah 1989). The permanent secretaries were also requested to take appropriate measures in those departments particularly exposed to corruption. Such measures included: improving work methods and procedures to reduce delay; increasing the effectiveness of supervision to enable superior officers to check and control the work of their staff; rotating officers to ensure that no officer or group of officers remain too long at a single operational unit; carrying out surprise checks on the work of their officers; making the necessary security arrangements to prevent unauthorised persons from having access to a department's premises; and reviewing the anti-corruption measures taken once in three to five years with the aim of introducing further improvements.

Of course, this has not eliminated all corruption. A recent case, involving money paid by the briber to an Australian bank account led to the conviction of a senior Singaporean public procurement official. However, the systemic propensity for corruption has been greatly diminished.

*Program and Policy Reform*

Public programs that are riddled with corruption can sometimes be reformed by their redesign or elimination (Rose-Ackerman 1978; Klitgaard 1988).

*Involving Civil Society*

Although corruption can never be completely monitored, it can be controlled through a combination of ethical codes, decisive legal prosecutions against offenders, organisational change and institutional reform. Surrounding it all, and monitoring the monitors, should be a vigilant civil society and free and critical media.

Where genuine attempts to combat corruption have been unsuccessful, there has generally been one missing ingredient—the involvement of civil society. The *Times of India* has observed that: 'people's acceptance of corruption as a fact of life and their general despondency need to be tackled first' (Editorial 1964, cited by Bayley p. 723). Many people in civil society have a fundamental interest in an effective integrity system, including the private sector, religious leaders, the press, the professions and, above all, the ordinary citizen who bears the brunt of corruption on a daily basis.

That civil society is crucial in any successful anti-corruption strategy is clear. Some of the solutions lie within civil society itself—for example, the need to reverse public apathy or tolerance of corruption. But civil society is also part of the problem. The notion that state activities can take place in a vacuum simply does not stand up. It is often the general public that is paying the bribes. The point of interface between the private and the public sectors is also often the point at which grand corruption flourishes and the largest bribes are paid.

Thus, any attempt to develop an anti-corruption strategy that fails to involve civil society is neglecting one of the most potentially useful and powerful tools available. Of course, in many countries where corruption is rife, civil society is weak, apathetic or only in the early stages of mobilisation and organisation. These are not reasons to neglect its role, however, as the very involvement of an emerging civil society can, of itself, provide strength and stimulus for further development of an anti-corruption strategy.

This, too, is a lesson of our history and one we do well to bear in mind at all times.

## Note

1    The views expressed in this chapter are those of the author alone, other than statements which are expressed as the views of Transparency International: these are based on Pope (1996).

# PART IV
# NEW PROFESSIONS AND NEW
# REGULATORY APPROACHES

Chapter 13

# Occupational Regulation of Complementary Medicine Practitioners

Anne-Louise Carlton[1]

## Introduction

Although there has been a significant growth in recent years in the use of various forms of complementary medicine both in Australia and overseas (Carlton 1998, p. 81), there are difficulties associated with quantifying the nature and extent of risks to public health with the practice of complementary medicine and also in assessing whether existing regulatory safeguards and complaints mechanisms are satisfactory.

Professional registration via statute is an important form of regulation in the health care sector. The purpose and functions of the registration system are not determined by the health practitioner group alone, but are set out in legislation and subject to public scrutiny. Such a system provides an effective mechanism for establishing and enforcing standards for practitioner training and practice, and for consumers to have complaints against practitioners addressed.

Under the Australian Constitution, the power to establish statutory registration systems resides with state and territory governments. In recent years, no state or territory has introduced statutory regulation of any complementary medicine profession and some mainstream professions have been deregistered following assessment under National Competition Policy. In Victoria, for example, the last professions to be regulated were chiropractic and osteopathy, which occurred in 1978.

In 1995, the Victorian Department of Human Services commenced a review of the practice of one form of complementary medicine—Traditional Chinese Medicine (TCM). Pressure to examine the regulatory requirements for TCM arose from the significant increase in its use, representations from the profession, and an increase in consumer complaints to the Victorian

Department of Human Services Drugs and Poisons Unit concerning the effects of some herbal preparations adulterated with potent Western pharmaceuticals. The purpose of the review was to establish a profile of the workforce, assess the risks and benefits of the practice, and determine the need, if any, for occupational regulation and regulation of prescribing and dispensing of Chinese herbal medicines.

Additional impetus to examine the need for occupational regulation of complementary medicine professions was provided by the recent introduction of the Commonwealth Government's Goods and Services Tax (GST). The Commonwealth's legislation, *A New Tax System (Goods and Services Transition) Act 1999* (Cth), makes provision for practitioners of naturopathy, acupuncture and herbal medicine to be eligible to provide GST-free services for a period of three years from proclamation.

From 1 July 2003, only practitioners recognised under state law or a national registration scheme will be entitled to provide services GST-free. This is designed to bring the treatment of appropriately qualified naturopaths, acupuncturists and herbalists in line with that of other health service providers (Office of Prime Minister, 31 May 1999, p. 1). The Commonwealth has set aside $500,000 to assist with the establishment of registration systems for these professions.

Bearing these matters in mind, the present chapter examines some definitional issues arising out of the regulation of the complementary medicine professions, looks at the national criteria and process for determining whether occupational regulation via statute is required for currently unregulated health professions, and considers some examples and difficulties arising out of self-regulation of unregulated professions.

It also examines the Victorian model of health practitioner registration and the Victorian review of TCM and provides an overview of the recently passed *Chinese Medicine Registration Act 2000* (Vic.). Two particular issues will also be addressed, namely, how the new legislation will regulate the profession of TCM, including the practice of acupuncture and the prescribing and dispensing of Chinese herbs, and how the legislation will complement other forms of regulation of complementary medicine.

**Definitional Issues**

There are two main groups of unregistered health practitioners within the Australian health care system: those who work within what might be classified as 'mainstream' or 'orthodox' health care services such as social workers, occupational therapists, speech therapists, dietitians and counsellors; and those who work within an 'alternative or complementary medicine' framework.

The first group is relatively easy to define although the above list may be incomplete, and there are increasing numbers of practitioners within these professions who are adopting therapeutic approaches or techniques which better fall under the umbrella of 'complementary medicine'. There are, however, difficulties in defining and identifying practitioners who work within a 'complementary or alternative medicine' framework. This appears due to a number of factors.

First, 'complementary medicine' is an umbrella term used to describe a range of techniques, modalities and diagnostic tools as well as disciplines, professions or occupations. Little work has been done on defining its scope. Secondly, there is an evolutionary process in the development of any profession with some complementary medicine practices beginning as isolated techniques but gradually evolving into discrete professions. Thirdly, there is often prejudice and a lack of understanding of the nature of complementary medicines and therapies on the part of 'mainstream' health care providers and, finally, there is an absence of clear definitions and precise lines of demarcation in the practice of some forms of complementary medicine as the Social Development Committee of the Parliament of Victoria (1986, pp. 61–2) has described:

> The term 'alternative medicine' is used interchangeably with terms such as 'complementary medicine', 'holistic medicine', 'traditional medicine', 'unorthodox medicine', 'fringe medicine', 'natural therapy' and 'drug-free therapy'. Similarly 'naturopathy' is a general term used interchangeably with 'natural therapy' and covers the use of a wide range of natural therapies. Thus the practice of naturopathy can include the use of therapies such as herbalism and homoeopathy which are also specialist modalities in their own right.

There appear to be three common features of most alternative or complementary medicine practices. These are a belief in an inherent 'vital force', 'energy' or 'qi' which is basic to human life; an underlying philosophical approach which views the body holistically and recognises that living organisms have inherent self-regulating and self-healing (homeostatic) capacities and a natural ability to resist disease; and a defined role for practitioners to assist patients to restore homeostasis in order to maintain or achieve optimal health or minimise the impact of disease.

A distinction must be made, however, between complementary medicine disciplines or occupations (such as TCM, naturopathy/western herbal medicine, homoeopathy and massage therapy) with established bodies of knowledge which incorporate a range of diagnostic and treatment techniques or modalities, and the techniques or modalities themselves, such as iridology, acupuncture and herbal medicine.

There will be different policy and regulatory responses required from government—for example, statutory registration, co-regulation or self-regulation—depending on the nature of the practices and associated risks, and also on the stage of development or evolution of the different disciplines. For the purposes of the present analysis, those professions which have established tertiary training and statutory registration systems but are sometimes considered 'complementary' or 'alternative' can be excluded from discussion. In Australia, these are the professions of chiropractic and osteopathy.

## Occupational Regulation of Complementary Medicine Practitioners

In 1995, the Australian Health Ministers Advisory Council (AHMAC), a meeting of all heads of state, territory and Commonwealth health departments, agreed that before any jurisdiction proceeds with a proposal to register a previously unregistered health occupation, a majority of states should agree that such registration is required. AHMAC adopted the following six criteria for assessing the regulatory requirements of unregulated health occupations which included a series of questions to address to determine whether the criteria have been met (Australian Health Ministers Advisory Council 1995):

> *Criterion 1:* Is it appropriate for health ministers to exercise responsibility for regulating the occupation in question, or does the occupation more appropriately fall within the domain of another ministry?
>
> *Criterion 2:* Do the activities of the occupation pose a significant risk of harm to the health and safety of the public?
>
> *Criterion 3:* Do existing regulatory or other mechanisms fail to address health and safety issues?
>
> *Criterion 4:* Is regulation possible to implement for the occupation in question?
>
> *Criterion 5:* Is regulation practical to implement for the occupation in question?
>
> *Criterion 6:* Do the benefits to the public of regulation clearly outweigh the potential negative impact of such regulation?

These criteria establish assessment requirements similar to those subsequently adopted under National Competition Policy and established via the *Competition Policy Reform (Victoria) Act 1995*, namely that legislation should not restrict competition unless it can be demonstrated that the benefits of the restriction to the community as a whole outweigh the costs, and the objectives of the legislation can only be achieved by restricting competition (Competition Policy Taskforce 1996, p. 2).

A national process was also agreed to, in which unregistered professions were able to make submissions to any state or territory government requesting consideration of their case for statutory registration. AHMAC would then establish a working group to examine and make recommendations to all jurisdictions as to whether statutory registration was required.

In 1995, an application for statutory registration from a combined group of TCM professional associations was made and in 1996, the AHMAC Working Group on Criteria and Processes for Assessment of Regulatory Requirements of Unregulated Health Professions Working assessed a joint submission from the TCM profession, along with the findings of the research conducted as part of the Victorian Review of Traditional Chinese Medicine. Acupuncture and Chinese herbal medicine were considered modalities within the occupation of TCM (rather than separate professions) for the purposes of assessment against the criteria.

At its February 1997 meeting, AHMAC received the final report of the Working Group and accepted the following recommendation:

> That states/territories/the Commonwealth should determine the efficacy of their legislation and regulation to respond to the public risks identified in 'Towards a Safer Choice: The Practice of Traditional Chinese Medicine in Australia', and take remedial action to resolve any problems which are identified. This efficacy assessment should take into account possible improvements to consumer complaints mechanisms to enable consumers of alternative and/or complementary therapies to make complaints about therapies and therapists (AHMAC 1997).

## Self-Regulation of Complementary Medicine Practitioners

*What is 'Self-regulation'?*

Despite pressure over many years from the complementary medicine professions, governments have encouraged these professions to establish systems of self-regulation as an alternative to statutory registration.

Self-regulation is recommended as a regulatory tool where the implications of non-compliance are not catastrophic (Office of Regulatory Reform 1995, p. 27). It generally involves the formation of a body or association with voluntary membership, supported by voluntary standards and codes of practice and a recognised and accredited body of knowledge (Bensoussan and Myers 1996, pp. 213–14). Self-regulatory mechanisms are established in the absence of, or to complement legislation requiring mandatory registration and rely on voluntary compliance by members of the group.

Reliance on self-regulation may go some way toward minimising risks to consumers of health services and there is greater flexibility available to providers in relation to service delivery. The Office of Regulatory Reform states that self-regulation works best where there is 'sufficient availability of sanctions within the industry to require compliance' (Office of Regulatory Reform 1995, p. 27). Since membership of such professional associations is voluntary, there may be no effect upon practitioners' businesses if they are expelled from such an association for professional misconduct (New South Wales Joint Committee on the Health Care Complaints Commission 1998, p. 43). In the words of Bensoussan and Myers (1996, p. 214):

> Certification or accreditation systems provide a way of identifying those who have obtained certain qualifications. They do not prevent uncertified practitioners from undertaking the relevant occupation, but do limit the use of identified titles to certified practitioners. The regulatory controls imposed by an association on certified practitioners may be as stringent as those imposed by any government regulation.

## Principles and Key Elements of Effective Self-Regulating Professions

There are a number of principles which appear to underpin effective self-regulatory systems. First, protection of public interest should take precedence over professional interests. Second, certification, disciplinary and complaints-handling procedures should be free from bias and should observe the principles of natural justice. Third, confidentiality of complaints and other personal information should be observed. Fourth, self-regulatory systems should have effective sanctions and accessible appeal mechanisms. Fifth, there should be external scrutiny and involvement of experts from other professions to ensure transparency and credibility of the system. Finally, there should be external government and industry recognition of and support for the self-regulatory system.

There are seven key elements of an effective self-regulatory system for the health care professions:

• A certification system which incorporates the following elements: high standards of training for membership, established via a consultative process with the profession and endorsed by the relevant educational/industry authorities; an established procedure for assessing practitioner qualifications, incorporating an examination where necessary; effective incentives for practitioners to seek and maintain certification; and annual requirements for Continuing Professional Education (CPE) as a condition of continued certification.
• A Code of Ethics should be established which members agree to comply with.
• Effective procedures should exist for receiving, investigating and resolving consumer complaints.
• An established disciplinary system should be created for enforcing conduct and CPE requirements, and applying sanctions where necessary, including a process for appeals.
• Effective incentives should exist for compliance with codes of practice while sanctions should be used for non-compliance with standards of practice and other membership requirements.
• Strong institutional support for the system from the profession, educational institutions, employer bodies and government should be present.
• An effective public education campaign should be used to assist consumers to recognise and understand the difference between certified and non-certified practitioners.

*Mechanisms for Strengthening and Supporting Self-regulation*

Professional associations and other self-regulatory bodies can seek institutional support for their self-regulatory systems and thereby establish greater incentives for participation by practitioners. For example, accreditation of training courses by educational authorities such as the Australian National Training Authority (ANTA) or state and territory educational authorities can significantly improve standard of education for entry to the profession. Associations can seek provider rebate status for their members from private health funds and bodies such as the Workcover Authority. Associations can also seek government assistance with the establishment, maintenance and monitoring of their self-regulatory system, as well as government endorsement.

Eligibility to provide goods and services tax (GST)-free services can also be an incentive for membership of self-regulatory bodies recognised by government for that purpose. Professional associations can use these types of institutional support as part of an education campaign to encourage the public to make informed choices when selecting a practitioner.

*Difficulties with Self-regulation of Complementary Medicine Professions*

Relying solely on self-regulation has, however, been problematic where the practices of a profession present potentially serious risks to public health and safety. For example, where there are no statutory powers to restrict entry to a profession, those with minimal or no qualifications can set up practice and use the titles of the profession without meeting acceptable minimum standards of training and practice. This has led to widely varying standards of practice and levels of qualifications, substantial fragmentation of these professions, and no widely recognised and accepted peak bodies.

In addition, under a self-regulatory system there have been no effective methods established for enforcing compliance by public or private training institutions with educational standards which are acceptable to the profession in question.

Traditional incentives for membership of associations with high professional standards may also, in some areas, be compromised due to deregulation and the impact of National Competition Policy. For example, there has been a recent trend towards provider recognition by private health funds (and therefore access to rebates for patients) on an individual basis rather than on the basis of membership of certain professional associations.

There also exists a potential for conflict of interest. For example, some professional associations have close links with or have been established specifically to recognise graduates of particular training institutions and provide certification only for those graduates. These links are not always transparent (Bensoussan and Myers 1996, pp. 136–7).

It has also been found that the office bearers of professional associations are generally elected by members of the association rather than appointed by an independent process. Without sufficient independent (non-profession-specific) input into the procedures of certification, complaints handling and discipline, there is scope for these mechanisms to be compromised with professional interests taking precedence over the public interest.

In some cases, existing professional association complaints-handling mechanisms do not operate with sufficient independence and integrity, and associations report threats of litigation against the organisation should a practitioner be required to attend an informal hearing of a complaint (Australian College of Acupuncturists 1994, p. 2).

Finally, problems also arise with access to prescribing rights. Practitioners of Western herbal medicine, Chinese herbal medicine and naturopathy have for many years sought the legal right to prescribe herbs which are restricted under state and territory drugs and poisons legislation. A self-regulatory system is unlikely to provide sufficient controls or government and community confidence to allow prescribing rights for these groups (Ministerial Advisory Committee on Traditional Chinese Medicine 1998, pp. 30–3).

Despite over 20 years of efforts, professions such as TCM have been unable to establish a self-regulatory system that has the broad support of the majority of interest groups and sufficient incentives for compliance. There is no indication that without government encouragement and intervention efforts at self-regulation would be successful in the future. The New South Wales Joint Committee on the Health Care Complaints Commission, in its final report *Unregistered Health Practitioners: The Adequacy and Appropriateness of Current Mechanisms for Resolving Complaints,* concluded as follows:

> The Committee is not of the view that self-regulation of unregistered health practitioners through their associations is particularly effective, particularly in the National Competition Policy environment. It believes that some type of mandatory registration and complaints and disciplinary mechanism is needed. (New South Wales Parliament Joint Committee on Health Care Complaints Commission 1998, p. 49).

*Examples of Self-regulation in Complementary Medicine Professions*

*Massage therapy* The Association of Massage Therapists Australia Inc. and other massage therapy professional associations are members of the National Council of Massage and Allied Health Practitioners. The National Council has established a system of self-regulation which has a Code of Ethics; standards of training; a Code of Conduct for practitioners which addresses matters such as practitioners' duty of care, professional conduct, confidentiality and client records, insurance, first-aid, hygiene, equipment and premises; complaints resolution; and disciplinary procedures.

The Association has had discussions over several years with the Victorian Office of Fair Trading and Business Affairs, and has made a submission seeking a form of registration of the industry to be conducted on a cooperative basis between that Office and the Association (Association of Massage

Therapists 1999). The proposal has been prompted by the need for consumers to have access to reliable information on who is a qualified massage therapist and who is not, and also by problems with the interface between the massage industry and illegal sexual services. This proposal is still being assessed.

*Homoeopathy* The Australian Council for Homoeopathy Inc. has established the Victorian Register of Certified Homoeopathic Practitioners Inc., an independent incorporated body, which is intended to regulate the practice of qualified homoeopaths, to protect the public interest in homoeopathic health care. It also serves as a point of contact for complaints and disputes. Board members are drawn from the homoeopathic profession, the medical and health professions, the law, leading university academics and consumer groups.

The Victorian Health Services Commissioner acts as a consultant to the Register, and Victorian health ministers have provided an endorsement of the self-regulatory framework as 'a mechanism by which the homoeopathic profession endeavours to promote the highest standard of homoeopathic practice, and to provide avenues for dealing with patient complaints' (The Victorian Register of Certified Homoeopathy Practitioners Inc. 1997).

However, the Register and the Australian Council for Homoeopathy have made submissions to government identifying their difficulties with creating sufficient incentives for homoeopaths, particularly those who do meet the standards of training required for certification, to upgrade their skills and seek certification with the Register (The Australian Council of Homoeopathy 1998, p. III).

*Traditional Chinese Medicine* One profession where self-regulation has been closely examined recently is TCM. The Victorian Review of Traditional Chinese Medicine collected risks data from a variety of sources including patients, practitioners, professional associations, complaints bodies, court reports and a literature search of adverse events that have occurred both in Australia and overseas. This information, along with an assessment of the effectiveness of self-regulatory systems is contained in the report *Towards a Safer Choice: The Practice of Traditional Chinese Medicine in Australia* (Bensoussan and Myers 1996). No similar analysis has been undertaken in Australia for other forms of complementary medicine.

During the second stage of the review, a Victorian Ministerial Advisory Committee on Traditional Chinese Medicine assessed the data on risks associated with the practice of TCM, and examined whether self-regulation of the profession could provide sufficient protection to consumers. The review identified serious concerns with reliance on a self-regulatory framework, and four main factors that have undermined the efforts of the TCM profession to regulate itself effectively. These were the fragmentation of the profession and lack of agreement on standards; deregulation of education provision; difficulties with creating sufficient incentives for voluntary certification; and a lack of access to restricted herbs scheduled under the *Drugs Poisons and Controlled Substances Act 1981* (Vic.) (Victorian Ministerial Advisory Committee on Traditional Chinese Medicine 1998, pp. 15–16).

The Review Committee considered that, given the risks, the proposals for self-regulation of the TCM profession were unsuitable in the absence of statutory powers of enforcement of standards of training and practice and accordingly recommended statutory registration of TCM practitioners (ibid., pp. 20–1).

## Occupational Regulation of Health Practitioners—A Victorian Model

There is an established model of health practitioner registration in Victoria as there is in the other states and territories. The Victorian model was first introduced with the passage of the *Nurses Act 1993* and the *Medical Practice Act 1994*. Between 1994 and 2000, eight revised health practitioner registration Acts have been passed in Victoria, each incorporating the model provisions with some updated provisions. The remainder are currently being reviewed.

In Victoria, each regulated health profession has a registration board established under its own Act of Parliament. These boards are independent of government, and are incorporated so as to avoid personal liability for board members. Membership consists of a majority from the profession being regulated. Victorian registration boards are required to consult the Victorian Minister for Health and take notice of his or her views, but the Minister cannot direct a board. Boards are self-funding, and are responsible for setting their own registration fees and meeting all their own expenses, such as renting premises, hiring staff and paying legal counsel.

Under the Victorian model, the main powers of health practitioner registration boards are as follows (Department of Human Services 1998, pp. 10–11):

* to regulate the standards of practice of the profession in the public interest;
* to register suitably qualified persons and/or persons meeting approved competency standards so that they may practice in Victoria;

- to accredit courses which provide qualifications for registration purposes;
- to establish standards for the conduct of examinations for the purposes of registration and continuing education;
- to issue guidelines about appropriate standards of practice;
- to investigate complaints about, and inquire into, the conduct of persons registered under the Act; and
- to carry out such other functions as are vested in the Board by or under its Act.

Subject to mutual recognition principles, health practitioner registration boards in general have powers to register practitioners who have successfully completed a course of study accredited by the Board; who have a qualification that is substantially equivalent or is based on similar competencies to an accredited course; or who have passed a prescribed examination.

The purpose of regulation is to protect the public rather than professional interests. The main privilege of registration is the right to use the relevant title or to hold oneself out as being registered. With the exception of dentistry and optometry, it is *not* an offence for non-registered persons to practice the techniques of the relevant health profession, provided that they do not use certain protected titles or any title calculated to induce a belief that they are registered under the Act, claim to be registered under the Act or hold themselves out as being registered under the Act, carry out any act which is required to be carried out by or under an Act by a person registered as a practitioner under the Act, or claim to be qualified to practice as a member of the relevant health profession.

Members of boards are appointed by the Victorian Governor in Council on the recommendation of the Minister for Health, rather than being elected by the members of the relevant profession. All boards must include legal and community representation. Boards also have the power to temporarily, provisionally or conditionally register a practitioner or to grant a restricted registration.

With respect to disciplinary matters, boards have a broad range of procedures available, including informal hearings in appropriate cases and the power to immediately suspend the registration of a practitioner if that is necessary to protect the public. All registration Acts include a standard definition of 'unprofessional conduct' and all boards have powers to deal with false and misleading advertising by referring matters to the police for prosecution. Boards also have the power to enter and inspect premises with a warrant to enable thorough investigations of complaints. There is also a formal system of referral of complaints from boards to the Health Services Commissioner in appropriate cases. Disciplinary hearings are open rather than closed (with provision for closed hearings and suppression of the names of witnesses where necessary) and those who make complaints against a health practitioner have the right to be present at a hearing. Appeals from decisions of boards are made to the Victorian Civil and Administrative Tribunal.

Appendix 1 of the Victorian Government Department of Human Services Ministerial Advisory Committee on Traditional Chinese Medicine's (1998) *Report on Options for Regulation of Traditional Chinese Medicine Practitioners* provides further detail on the standard model of health practitioner registration, including the definition of 'unprofessional conduct' and the complaints and disciplinary procedures.

## The Victorian Review of Traditional Chinese Medicine

*Background*

A range of risks have been identified as being associated with the practice of TCM. Serious risks arise where TCM treatment is performed incorrectly, and/or without due regard to the clinical condition of the patient. Deaths and serious injuries have occurred in Australia and overseas arising from the practice of both acupuncture and Chinese herbal medicine. Detailed documentation of injuries and deaths arising from the practice of TCM is provided in the report *Towards a Safer Choice* (Bensoussan and Myers 1996, pp. 49–95).

The regulatory framework for TCM has been characterised by inadequate protection for the public from untrained unqualified practitioners who are in many instances using intrusive and risky techniques and modalities and widespread illegal prescribing and dispensing of Chinese herbs that have been restricted via inclusion in the Poisons List of the *Drugs Poisons and Controlled Substances Act 1981* (Vic.).

In addition, there is a lack of consistency in regulation with other registered health occupations which present similar risks to the public and legislative restrictions on competition which arguably may be difficult to justify. Qualified TCM practitioners, for example, are prevented from legally prescribing and dispensing to their patients many of the herbal medicines they have been trained to supply safely.

It is essential that the practice of TCM be safe for the public. This requires that TCM training be of a high standard, that the public and other health care professionals are able to identify practitioners who are well qualified, and that consumers have access to effective mechanisms to deal with any complaints as they arise. At present, the standard of TCM training varies widely, members of the public have difficulty in telling who is qualified and who is not, and the profession has no power to enforce qualifications and practice standards.

## The Chinese Medicine Registration Act 2000 (Vic.)

In July 1998, following receipt of the report by the Victorian Government Department of Human Services Ministerial Advisory Committee on Traditional Chinese Medicine (1998), the Australian Health Ministers Council agreed for Victoria to take the lead in developing legislation to regulate the TCM profession.

The *Chinese Medicine Registration Act 2000* (Vic.) (CMR Act) was passed by the Victorian Parliament in May 2000. Implementation commenced in December 2000 with the establishment of the Chinese Medicine Registration Board, and registration of practitioners commenced on 1 January 2002. The legislation establishes a system of registration similar to that which applies to other health practitioners in Victoria, such as medical practitioners, nurses and pharmacists, and creates a mechanism for suitably qualified practitioners to prescribe herbs that have been scheduled and therefore restricted under Victoria's drugs and poisons legislation. It is expected that the Act will provide a model for other state and territory governments to follow.

## Key Features of the Chinese Medicine Registration Act 2000

The Act provides for the establishment of a Chinese Medicine Registration Board comprising nine members appointed by Governor-in-Council on the recommendation of the Victorian Minister for Health. Membership includes six Chinese medicine practitioners, two lay persons and a lawyer. The Board has the same standard powers and functions as in the Victorian model described above.

The Board has the power to keep a register of qualified practitioners to be listed in three divisions: Chinese herbal medicine, Acupuncture and Chinese herbal dispensing. Practitioners must have the relevant qualifications required by the Board in each division to be eligible for registration.

The Board also has power to:

- approve courses which provide qualifications for registration purposes;
- endorse the Register in order to recognise postgraduate qualifications and/ or training in specialty areas such as Chinese orthopaedics and traumatology;
- endorse registration certificates of Chinese medicine practitioners and Chinese herbal dispensers in order to authorise them under the *Drugs Poisons and Controlled Substances Act 1981* (Vic.) to legally prescribe and dispense scheduled herbs;
- investigate complaints about, and inquire into the professional conduct or fitness to practice of persons registered under the Act, and to impose sanctions or conditions and limitations on their practice where necessary;
- immediately suspend the registration of a practitioner considered to be impaired or acting unprofessionally and who therefore presents a risk to public health and safety;
- secure a warrant to enter and search premises when conducting an investigation of a complaint of unprofessional conduct against a practitioner;
- develop and publish Codes of Practice which set out standards of clinical practice, for example in preparation, prescription, labeling, storage, dispensing and record-keeping of Chinese herbs;
- require evidence of satisfactory arrangements for professional indemnity insurance as a condition of registration; and
- require that registrants provide to the Board information, for example, on any criminal convictions and judgments against them in medical negligence cases.

It is an offence under the Act for an unregistered person to use titles protected under the legislation *or any other title calculated to induce a belief that the person is registered.* The protected titles are 'Registered Chinese Medicine Practitioner', 'Registered Chinese Herbal Medicine Practitioner', 'Registered Chinese Herbalist', 'Registered Acupuncturist' and 'Registered Oriental Medicine Practitioner'.

It is also an offence under the Act for a registered person to advertise Chinese medicine services in a way which is false, misleading or deceptive, including to offer gifts or discounts without setting out the conditions, to use or refer to testimonials or purported testimonials, or to create an unreasonable expectation of beneficial treatment. The Board has the power to issue advertising guidelines and the courts can require corrective advertising.

*How the Chinese Medicine Registration Act 2000 will Protect the Public*

There are a number of mechanisms by which the Act protects the public. First, the Act makes clear that its primary purpose is to protect the public rather than to promote the professional interests of TCM practitioners. Registration of TCM practitioners and dispensers ensures that members of the public who seek TCM treatment can be confident that the practitioner or dispenser has a recognised qualification and has achieved a certain acceptable standard of practice. This includes training in safe practice of the various TCM modalities, such as acupuncture and the prescribing and dispensing of Chinese herbal medicines, and a thorough knowledge of how to minimise risks associated with these intrusive practices. Practitioners are expected to have sufficient training in, and to apply, appropriate infection control procedures and to carefully screen and refer to Western medical practitioners where necessary. In addition, training is required in safe prescribing of Chinese herbal medicines, including those scheduled under the nationally agreed Standard for Uniform Scheduling of Drugs and Poisons and regulated by the *Drugs Poisons and Controlled Substances Act 1981* (Vic.).

The CMR Act also provides a mechanism by which members of the public will be able to distinguish between different types of practitioners, that is, those who are qualified to provide acupuncture services and those qualified to provide Chinese herbal medicine or other TCM services, as well as those with specialist TCM qualifications.

The Act gives the Board powers to establish and to enforce standards of training and practice and to address patient complaints against registered practitioners and Chinese herbal dispensers, including the power to conduct investigations and hearings, and to impose sanctions where necessary. The Board will also be able to impose conditions, limitations or restrictions on the practice of registrants or de-register practitioners if necessary and initiate action against individuals who hold themselves out to the public as being registered and/or endorsed to prescribe scheduled herbs when they are not.

These safeguards should operate to minimise the risks of harm to patients, and to support freedom of choice in health care.

**Regulation of Prescribing and Dispensing of Chinese Herbal Medicines**

*Amendments to the Drugs Poisons and Controlled Substances Act 1981 (Vic.)*

The CMR Act amends the Poisons List created under section 12 of the *Drugs Poisons and Controlled Substances Act 1981* (Vic.) (DPCS Act) by including a new Schedule 1. This Schedule is to include:

- Chinese herbs that have been already been scheduled under the DPCS Act either directly (for example, the commonly used Chinese herb Fu Zi is Aconitum spp., a Schedule 4 poison) or included because they contain a substance that has been scheduled under the DPCS Act (for example, the commonly used Chinese herb Ma Huang is Ephedra Spp. and contains ephedrine which is a Schedule 4 poison); and
- any additional Chinese herbs that have the potential to be toxic and dangerous if used incorrectly and it is therefore considered in the public interest to regulate their prescription and dispensing by suitably trained and registered Chinese medicine practitioners and dispensers.

The Commonwealth Department of Health and Aged Care has indicated its support for this approach, on the basis that a separate schedule would facilitate its adoption into the Standard for Uniform Scheduling of Drugs and Poisons, and therefore the adoption of uniform national standards in all state and territory drugs and poisons legislation (Commonwealth Department of Health and Aged Care 1999, p. 2).

Practitioners who obtain an endorsement from the Board will be authorised to obtain, possess, prescribe and supply the scheduled herbs in accordance with the Victorian legislation. The Board will have power to specify in the endorsement the list of Chinese herbs that each practitioner/dispenser is endorsed to prescribe and/or dispense and in what form (raw, processed, manufactured). This will allow the Board, if it chooses, to issue a number of different types of endorsement according to the level of training of the practitioner or dispenser and the form of the substances they wish to prescribe and/or dispense (for example, pills, powders and raw herbs).

The *Drugs Poisons and Controlled Substances Act 1981* (Vic.) regulates the manufacture, importing, wholesaling and labeling of drugs, in addition to the prescribing and dispensing of those drugs. By contrast, the CMR Act and associated amendments to the DPCS Act will only provide for the regulation of prescribing and dispensing Scheduled Chinese herbs to individual patients. The regulatory scheme will not provide direct controls over the manufacture, importation and wholesaling of Chinese herbs scheduled or unscheduled.

At present, the Australian Quarantine Inspection Service and the Commonwealth Therapeutic Goods Administration do not regulate the importation and wholesaling of raw Chinese herbs, unless they are a prohibited import under the *Customs (Prohibited Imports) Regulations* (Cth). It is anticipated that those prescribing and dispensing raw herbs will have the expertise to check the identity and quality of the herbs they are using or that they will seek appropriate written assurances from their suppliers. If this proves not to be the case, and the risks to the public are unacceptable, it may be necessary to strengthen the system of regulation of raw Chinese herbs analogous to the control of manufacture, importation and wholesaling of drugs under the *Drugs Poisons and Controlled Substances Act 1981* (Vic.) including, for example, requirements for importers and wholesalers to verify the identity and quality of the Chinese herbal substances they supply.

Offences committed in relation to prescribing or dispensing/supply by unregistered persons of scheduled Chinese herbs will continue to be regulated under the provisions of the *Drugs Poisons and Controlled Substances Act 1981* (Vic.). Offences committed by registered practitioners who are not authorised or who have breached their conditions of authorisation (established under their endorsement) may be regulated under the unprofessional conduct provisions of the CMR Act or under the offence provisions of the DPCS Act in relation to breaches of regulations governing possession, sale, supply, prescribing, labelling and so on. In such cases, liaison will be required between the Drugs and Poisons Unit of the Victorian Department of Human Services which is responsible for administering the DPCS Act, and the Chinese Medicine Registration Board.

*Other Controls Over Schedule 1 Herbs*

The Chinese Medicine Registration Board will have power to develop and to publish Codes of Practice for the establishment of standards of practice, including standards for prescribing, labeling, storage, dispensing and supply of extemporaneously dispensed Chinese herbal medicines (both scheduled and non-scheduled).

Breach by a registered practitioner or dispenser of a Code of Practice issued by the Board may be used as evidence of unprofessional conduct in a formal or informal hearing conducted by the Board under the CMR Act. The

Codes are expected to require practitioners to report any adverse reactions to the medicines they prescribe or dispense to the Commonwealth Adverse Drug Reactions Advisory Committee and to make clear that prescribing and dispensing of herbal medicines which contain material from endangered species will be considered by the Board to constitute *prima facie* evidence of unprofessional conduct. The definition of unprofessional conduct includes breach of any condition contained in a practitioner or dispenser's endorsed registration.

## How the *Chinese Medicine Registration Act 2000* Complements Other Forms of Regulation

*Regulation of Other Registered Health Professionals who offer TCM Services*

The Victorian Government Department of Human Services Ministerial Advisory Committee on Traditional Chinese Medicine (1998, pp. 46–8) found that large numbers of health professionals, such as medical practitioners, nurses, physiotherapists, chiropractors and osteopaths, are adopting TCM modalities, particularly acupuncture, as part of their practice.

If practitioners are already registered by another Victorian statutory registration board, then they will not be required to obtain an additional registration from the Chinese Medicine Registration Board in order to continue their practice, use protected titles and advertise their services to the public. All registration boards currently have adequate powers to receive complaints and conduct disciplinary hearings into their registrants' practice, regardless of the type of service offered or the modalities employed. This includes responsibility for addressing any breaches by the registrants of the *Health (Infectious Diseases) Regulations* 1990 (Vic.) in relation, for example, to skin penetration.

Requiring dual registration would be unnecessarily restrictive and costly. However, it is essential to ensure that registered practitioners who adopt modalities such as acupuncture are adequately trained. The CMR Act includes a schedule of consequential amendments to registration Acts governing chiropractors, dentists, dental hygienists, dental therapists, medical practitioners, nurses, optometrists, osteopaths, pharmacists and physiotherapists. These amendments create the power for these registration boards to exempt their registrants from the offence provisions of the CMR Act in order for them to use titles protected under that Act. The Victorian Ministerial Advisory Committee on Traditional Chinese Medicine recommended that exercise of these powers should be conditional on the following: first, that registrants act in accordance with an express authority in writing from their board; second, that their registration board consult with the Chinese Medicine Registration Board about the standards of training and clinical practice required before registrants are granted this exemption; and third, that all boards take reasonable steps to ensure that a person with appropriate qualifications or training in Chinese medicine practice is appointed to any hearing panel which investigates a complaint that involves the practice of Chinese medicine.

Acupuncturists, for example, who are registered under another health practitioner registration Act will have three years from the date of proclamation of the offence provisions in the CMR Act to obtain this written authority from the relevant registration board.

The reforms are designed to ensure that where these registered practitioners offer Chinese medicine services to the community, that they are adequately trained in the relevant modality, and their registration board has adequate expertise to deal with any complaints that might arise.

*Registration of Acupuncture Premises by Local Councils*

Health practitioners in Victoria (apart from exempted professions, such as medical practice and dentistry) who provide acupuncture services are required to obtain registration of their acupuncture business under section 366C(1) of the *Health Act 1958* (Vic.). These provisions are administered by local councils through their Environmental Health Officers (EHOs) who ensure compliance with the *Health (Infectious Diseases) Regulations 1990* (Vic.) which regulate the practice of skin penetration.

It is considered unnecessary for those acupuncturists who are granted registration or authorisation under the CMR Act also to be required to register under the *Health Act 1958* (Vic.) and have their premises inspected regularly by EHOs for compliance with infection control regulations. The responsibility for ensuring compliance of registered practitioners rests with the Chinese Medicine Registration Board and other boards empowered to grant authorisation to their registrants to offer acupuncture services to the public.

*Regulation of Spinal Manipulation*

The practice of TCM has traditionally included specialities such as tuina (Chinese therapeutic massage), and Chinese orthopaedics and traumatology.

These practices include use of techniques such as spinal manipulation, and are widely practised in China and to a limited extent in Australia. In some Australian jurisdictions, the practice of spinal manipulation is illegal unless carried out by certain registered health practitioners, such as medical practitioners, chiropractors, osteopaths and physiotherapists. This is not the case in Victoria where there are no legislative restrictions on the practice.

Whether or not to restrict the practice of spinal manipulation was vigorously debated in Victoria in 1995–96 with the review of the *Chiropractors and Osteopaths Registration Act 1978* (Vic.) and the passage of two new Acts governing these professions, the *Chiropractors Registration Act 1996* (Vic.) and the *Osteopaths Registration Act 1996* (Vic.).

In Victoria, it is considered that restricted use of titles such as 'chiropractor', 'osteopath' and 'physiotherapist' provides sufficient protection to the public from the risks associated with untrained practice of spinal manipulation. The CMR Act adopts a consistent approach and will not impose any practice restrictions on those who offer such services to the public within a TCM framework. The Board will, however, have the power to enter on the Chinese Medicine Register postgraduate qualifications and this may provide a method for the public to identify practitioners with these additional specialist qualifications.

If a registered Chinese medicine practitioner advertises to the public that he or she is qualified to practise in a particular TCM specialty area such as Chinese orthopaedics and traumatology and does not have the relevant specialist postgraduate qualifications, then the Board has the power to initiate an investigation under the provisions governing unprofessional conduct or those relating to false and misleading advertising, and apply sanctions if necessary.

*Regulation of Use of Medicines Containing Endangered Species*

The *Wildlife Protection (Regulation of Exports and Imports) Act 1982* (Cth.) (WP Act) controls the exportation of Australian native animals and plants, and fulfils Australian legislative requirements as a signatory to the Convention on International Trade in Endangered Species of Wild Fauna and Flora (CITES). The Act also controls the importation and exportation of certain plants and animals, and products derived from them. The species under CITES control are listed in three appendices and in schedules to the WP Act.

Serious concerns have been raised about the illegal prescribing and dispensing to the public of medicines that include material from endangered species, in breach of the WP Act (Callister and Bythewood 1995). Controls under that Act extend to importing but not to prescribing such medicines.

Arguably, an occupational regulation system such as that being implemented in Victoria could contribute to the Commonwealth Government's efforts to regulate the importation and possession of endangered species by influencing, via regulation of unprofessional conduct, the prescribing practices of registered practitioners.

The offence provisions of the WP Act which are of most relevance to practitioners and dispensers of Chinese herbal medicines are section 22, which creates an offence for a person to import scheduled specimens without the required permit or authority, and section 53 which creates an offence for a person to have in his or her possession, without reasonable excuse, any specimen which has been imported in contravention of the Act (that is, without a permit).

To date, it is understood that there have been no prosecutions for breaches of the WP Act that involve illegally imported traditional medicine products containing material from endangered species. The major impediment has been that current forensic technology is unable to prove beyond reasonable doubt that the traditional medicines contain material from endangered species as claimed on their packaging (Department of the Environment 1998).

Amendments to the WP Act in 1999 have addressed some of the evidentiary problems that have arisen with attempts to prosecute under the above provisions. The Explanatory Memorandum to the Wildlife Protection (Regulation of Exports and Imports) Amendment Bill 1998 (Cth) states as follows:

> for a prosecution to be successful under the current legislation, it must be proved beyond reasonable doubt that the product does contain an endangered species. ...the proposed amendments will enable a prosecution to be successful on the basis that a product is represented to contain material from an endangered species, and as such will overcome forensic problems...by deeming that things which are deliberately represented (for example by their packaging) to be or to contain endangered species, are covered by the Wildlife Protection Act.

There are a number of ways in which the CMR Act may reinforce and strengthen the enforcement of the Commonwealth legislation.

*Unprofessional conduct powers*   Under the standard definition of 'unprofessional conduct', it is reasonable to expect that a practitioner found guilty of an offence under the WP Act would also be found by the Board to have engaged in unprofessional conduct. Under the provisions of the CMR Act, the Chinese Medicine Registration Board will have power to investigate and to prosecute practitioners for unprofessional conduct. Complaints could be made to the Registration Board by any party, including a patient, another practitioner or the Wildlife Protection Section of Environment Australia.

On receipt of a complaint, or on its own initiative, the Board has power to make its inquiries and to gather evidence (including searching premises with a warrant and seizing relevant material); conduct a hearing (formal or informal); make a finding as to whether unprofessional conduct has occurred; and apply a suitable sanction such as a caution, reprimand, fine, conditional registration or suspension or cancellation of registration.

A finding of not guilty under the WP Act would not necessarily prevent a Chinese Medicine Registration Board from finding a practitioner guilty of unprofessional conduct, since the necessity to prove that the medicine had been illegally imported would not be necessary.

*Issuing a code of practice on use of medicines which contain material from endangered species* It is expected that the Chinese Medicine Registration Board will inform registered practitioners and dispensers that possessing, prescribing or dispensing Chinese herbal medicines which contain material from endangered species or listing them on the packaging may constitute unprofessional conduct under the CMR Act if proper permits have not been obtained under the WP Act.

A Code of Practice covering the use of endangered species in Chinese herbal medicines would be expected to set out clearly the Board's expectation that registered practitioners and dispensers have a thorough knowledge of their obligations under the WP Act and comply with its provisions. Such a Code could be taken into account by a hearing panel in determining whether a practitioner was guilty of unprofessional conduct. The Code might include requirements that practitioners and dispensers understand the following:

- the schedules attached to the WP Act and what they contain;
- the Chinese herbal medicines which contain substances scheduled under the Act;
- the alternatives to use of herbal medicines that contain material from endangered species;
- the offence provisions and the likely consequences of breaches of both the WP Act and the CMR Act;
- labeling of Chinese herbal medicines and whether medicines supplied to them contain material from endangered species; and

- that if practitioners are unable to read the labels, then they obtain from any importers or wholesalers who supply their medicines evidence of satisfactory compliance with the WP Act (that is, an assurance that the medicines supplied do not contain material from endangered species for which a permit is unavailable, or that the required permits under the WP Act have been obtained).

There are, however, likely to be limitations on the Board's powers in this area. For example, the Board's powers to regulate standards of practice and unprofessional conduct only extend to registered practitioners and dispensers. In addition, since there is no restriction on practice of Chinese herbal medicine under the CMR Act (except where herbs are used that have been scheduled under Victoria's *Drugs Poisons and Controlled Substances Act 1981*), there is nothing which would prohibit a practitioner or dispenser who has been de-registered from continuing to practice beyond the jurisdiction of the Board, as long as they do not breach the offence provisions relating to protection of title (that is, they do not claim to the public that they are qualified and registered). Further, some Chinese herbal dispensers, particularly those who supply herbal medicines via a grocery store, may choose not to register with the Chinese Medicine Registration Board unless they decide to dispense medicines that include herbs scheduled under the *Drugs Poisons and Controlled Substances Act 1981* (Vic.).

There is, however, considerable scope for a system of statutory registration of Chinese medicine practitioners and Chinese herbal dispensers, if adopted in all states and territories, to reduce the use of material from endangered species in Chinese herbal medicines in Australia and thereby to assist in wildlife conservation.

**Conclusions**

The issues that have been raised here in relation to regulation of TCM also apply to the regulation of other complementary medicine professions such as naturopathy, homoeopathy and Western herbal medicine. There is a need for further research to gather data on these professions as a basis for determining a suitable regulatory response.

There are a number of initiatives which would contribute to this process. The New South Wales Health Department is preparing a discussion paper on regulation of the profession of Chinese medicine. The Commonwealth is also examining different models of regulation in the context of taxation reforms and implementation of the GST, and the Victorian Government's policy commitments in the area of health include registration of those complementary medicine professions which involve ingestive therapies. Models other than statutory registration may be suitable except where the profession involved seeks rights to prescribe herbs that are regulated via drugs and poisons legislation. Where a profession seeks access to potentially toxic and dangerous substances, the level of protection of the public provided by statutory registration is likely to be necessary.

**Note**

1  This chapter presents the views of the author and does not necessarily reflect the views of the Government of Victoria. The author acknowledges the support of the Victorian Department of Human Services in preparation of this chapter. Some material contained in this chapter appears in an article by Carlton, A-L. and Bensoussan, A., 'Regulation of Complementary Medicine Practitioners in Australia: Chinese Medicine as a Case Example', *Journal of Complementary Therapies in Medicine* (forthcoming).

Chapter 14

# National Standards and the New National Probation Service[1] in England and Wales: Regulation of Professionals in the Community?

Graham Brooks

## Introduction

This chapter will examine the changing nature and working practice of English and Welsh probation officers, and their struggle throughout their history to retain autonomy over their 'professional'[2] work in the community. A case study is given of the new National Probation Service of England and Wales that has recently challenged the previous nature and direction of professional probation practice by suggesting that 'nothing short of deep-rooted cultural change' (Wallis 2001, p. 5) is required to improve what is seen as a well-meaning but seemingly amateurish image of the probation service if it is to be taken seriously at the present time and in the foreseeable future.

The concern of the present chapter is not so much with a change in the name of the probation service, or indeed its image, but rather with the substantial change in the 'professional' working practice(s) of its officers. Where its officers once diagnosed *the* problem(s) with individual offenders and prescribed *a* 'scientific' solution to their 'criminality' they now seem to manage aggregate groups of offenders assessed by 'risk' and sorted by dangerousness (McWilliams 1987, p. 104; Mathiesen 1983, p. 139) and resemble a law enforcement agency predominantly concerned with protecting the public (Wallis 2001).

This 'new' working practice is representative of what has been described as 'the new penology of actuarial justice' (Feeley and Simon 1994, p. 173) where all 'issues' seem to be translated into problems about the flow of offenders in and 'round' the system of criminal justice. In this way offenders seem to be becoming little more than 'bodies' that need managing as the process of dispensing 'justice' is replaced by the efficient and effective management of the system. Whilst this will at least offer beleaguered 'criminal justice practitioners' a chance to succeed, it will deny offenders the concept of *humanity* (Simon and Feeley 1995, pp. 172–4).

The present chapter suggests that such a change and denial of *humanity* is actually occurring and beginning to shape criminal justice policy in England and Wales. However, rather than look at the system as a whole we will specifically focus on the probation service and its changing working practice(s). Under pressure from the Home Office to punish and/or to manage offenders in the community, the question arises: are 'professional' probation officers actually needed to control offenders in the community?

This issue must be addressed as the 'new penology of actuarial justice' is 'dumbing-down' most of probation working practice. National Standards for the Supervision of Offenders in the Community (Home Office 1995, 2000a) are part of this new penology where an intellectually restrictive managerial culture (Gailbraith 1992; Nellis 1996) is beginning to affect 'professional' probation working practice. Prescriptive of *all* its working practice, the professional autonomy of probation officers is beginning to rapidly diminish (Clear and Karp 1999). Of particular concern are basic grade officers who are now expected to 'perform' to set standards rather than diagnose, and be 'competent' rather than 'knowledgeable'. In this way the probation service has seemingly moved from being a problem-solving agency to a performance organisation (May 1991) where it is assessed more for its 'outputs' than its 'outcomes' and what it *does* rather than what it *achieves* (Garland 1996, p. 458).

With this in mind, this chapter briefly reviews the historical development and changing working practice of the probation service from its official beginning to its present position and its changing relationship with the magistrates' court and the Home Office (McWilliams 1981, 1983, 1985, 1986, 1987; Haxby 1978). Its early beginning is charted as a voluntary religious ad hoc service (where its 'mission was moral') to one in which the 'appliance of science' through diagnostic casework was the basis of its claim to be a profession (Corner 1956) with a particular body of knowledge and specific working practice.

Focus is then specifically placed on the effect that National Standards have on probation working practice. As part of the 'new penology' it is suggested that they are a 'new control' to help regulate probation officers working in the community at a distance from the Home Office. They regulate working practice to the extent that probation officers are becoming little more than criminal justice operatives (Worrall 1997) employed to enforce set measurable (Garland 2001) 'standards' and manage offenders in the community. National Standards are then looked at in reference to and as part of the New Public Management (NPM) initiative and its continuous assessment of working practice based on economy, efficiency and effectiveness. Its pervasive influence has made the probation service more accountable to the Home Office than to its local community whilst still managing to preserve the semblance of local control (Rhodes 1994; Brownlee 1998). In this way the Home Office can avoid blame if local practice is found wanting without relinquishing control or overall direction over probation working practice.

It will be concluded that the Home Office is seemingly now as much concerned with managing officers as with offenders. The concept of the new penology of actuarial justice is beginning to be represented in probation working practice as National Standards are as much about the regulation of the probation service and its officers as they are about the identification, classification and management of offenders in the community.


**The 'Moral Mission' of Probation**


In 1876 the Police Court mission of the Church of England Temperance Society set about reclaiming the lost souls of those whose 'criminality' was thought to stem from the consumption of alcohol. Its 'mission', essentially religious, was to preach and to encourage abstinence in an attempt to save the souls of what seemed to be a growing number of individuals convicted of a drunk and disorderly offence.[3] At this time in Victorian England, and particularly in London, criminal offences relating to the consumption of alcohol had increased dramatically. Blaming the individual for the 'exceptional magnitude of the sin of intemperance' (McWilliams 1983, p. 134) encouraged the Police Court mission to become involved in the reformation of the intemperate and the restoration, physically and morally, of those convicted of a drunk and disorderly offence.

However, it has been claimed by Harrison (1971) that widespread drunkenness in Victorian England was the product of a particular socioeconomic structure and could not be dismissed as simply the lack of 'God' and/or 'morality' in an individual's life. This was not universally recognised at the time and a plea of mercy by a police court missionary to a magistrate to 'order' an offender to probation was reserved for those offenders deemed suitable and capable of moral reform only. This 'selection' by a missionary based on the possibility that an individual could respond to exhortation and religious guidance gave the justification for a plea of mercy. It clearly indicated that offenders who were not assessed as a 'risk' to society and could be 'corrected' should be supervised in the community. A plea of mercy then was specifically reserved for certain offenders in an attempt to reduce the prison population (Bochel 1976; McWilliams 1983, 1985; Radzinowicz and Hood 1986) and to 'correct' offenders through moral education.

The use of a plea of mercy by a police court missionary to correct and to educate a wayward soul increased with the *Summary Jurisdiction Act 1879* (Eng.) (McWilliams 1983). This Act extended the range of offences that could be dealt with by a magistrate but also extended the common law doctrine of recognisance[4] from young and petty offenders to adult offenders. This, along with the *Probation First Offenders Act 1887* (Eng.) encouraged extensive use of recognisance in 'appropriate cases' and an informal social inquiry into an offender's 'lifestyle' for those whom it was thought probation was a suitable disposal. Whilst the pledge by the Police Court mission to work for the reformation of an increasing number of offenders' souls through 'religious' supervision continued to grow, no formal application for probation could take place until January 1908 when the *Probation of Offenders Act 1907* (Eng.) came into force (McWilliams 1985).

Now officially a penalty of the magistrates' court, probation had taken its first step away from solely being a religious and/or philanthropic mission. This step did not change the moral mission of the newly formed probation service. However, it could be seen as the start of a 'public' service rather than simply a voluntary *ad hoc* provision, because the state offered to pay probation officers a wage instead of relying on voluntary 'religious' workers. However, the Home Office only offered to pay probation officers a low wage and not fund the local running cost of probation, leaving the local community, religious and philanthropic organisations to continue the funding of probation.

As soon as probation became official, however, it was thought 'professionals' should take the place of missionary workers in supervising offenders in the community. Due to the low wage on offer and the continuing influence of the Police Court mission, many of those who took up the new probation officer post had previously been voluntary workers. A sense of mission, regardless of the new official standing of the probation service, therefore continued. Instead of being usurped by the 1907 Act, missionary zeal infused probation working practice and the 'newly' formed probation committees with its *raison d'etre*. Whilst the *Criminal Justice Act 1925* (Eng.)

gave the Home Secretary the legislative power to 'restructure the provision of probation' and to fund the probation service for the first time, the 'dual control' (McWilliams 1985, pp. 271–3) between the Police Court mission and probation committees lasted until 1936. The Home Office eventually abolished 'dual control' only when it came increasingly to recognise probation officers as 'professionals' with a particular 'scientific practice' and body of knowledge above and beyond a 'moral mission'.

Laying claim to a specialised knowledge to 'treat the sick', the role of probation officers began to change from that of a servant of the court to that of 'experts', able to guide and 'educate' the lay magistrate into identifying the 'correct' disposal in the interests of 'objective' science (McWilliams 1986, p. 257). With the increasing and significant importance placed upon 'diagnostic science' by the probation service, and official recognition of a distinctive working practice by the Home Office (1936), its claim to be a 'professional' service began to firmly take hold. It was not until after the Second World War, however, that the 'appliance of science' and 'professionalism' and particularly 'casework' gave the probation service its own special role in the criminal justice system.

## The 'Appliance of Science' in Probation

As the 'warfare' state gave way to the 'welfare' state in England and Wales in the late 1940s and early 1950s, the relationship between the magistrates' court, the Home Office and the probation service began to alter critically (Garland 1985). Three major changes began to take place that affected the role, position and status of the probation service in the criminal justice system during this era of the 'appliance of science'.

First, the *Criminal Justice Act 1948* (Eng.) extended the early release of various categories of offenders from prison on licence to be supervised by probation officers in the community. Prior to this, the probation service mainly dealt with offenders on probation but was now confident of its ability to 'correct' and supervise a variety of offenders after a period of custody. Second, and possibly to help carry out its new expanded role, the Home Office increased its level of funding to cover at least 50 per cent of probation service expenditure (Brownlee 1998). Third, its self-assured confidence that it could deal with a variety of offenders was based upon its unwavering allegiance to a 'body of knowledge' and a 'casework' method of 'treatment' that had gained political credibility and acceptance.

This 'faith' in a scientific diagnostic approach no doubt encouraged the chairman of the National Association of Probation Officers to assert that the 'modifying body of knowledge on casework...together with the professional standards built up through the years...entitles us to our claim to constitute a profession' (Corner 1956, p. 54).

Demanding professional recognition similar to that of a physician (McWilliams 1985), the probation service appeared to be an altruistic caring service. Due to its close allegiance to a diagnostic problem-solving approach to 'crime' and 'criminality', offenders seemed to be cured rather than simply 'corrected'. This image of the probation service, however, has been called into question (Cohen 1975; Haxby 1978). Probation has always contained an element of control with the threat of coercion. Be it moral approbation and religious exhortation or scientific diagnosis, 'correcting behaviour' has been the mainstay of the probation service no matter how altruistic and humane the motives of individual officers. With the gradual introduction of a more scientific approach, and an increasing emphasis on diagnosis and treatment, the possibility of control and coercion did not disappear, it 'merely altered the form of intervention' with which it might be associated (McWilliams 1986, p. 257).

Whilst the *Criminal Justice Act 1948* (Eng.) was a liberal measure aimed at reducing the severity of punishment (Rawlings 1999), it unwittingly also widened the net of social control (Cohen 1985). The release of offenders on licence in the community marked the beginning of a clear link between the prison, the Home Office and probation service. This is not to say that this 'link' had not previously existed. In fact, working in a custodial regime has become part of most probation officers' careers (Haxby 1978; May 1991). From its early origins, however, probation has been seen as a way of diverting certain 'types' of offenders away from prison. Whilst this has changed throughout the history of the probation service, any 'supervision in the community' has always been set against the unchanging backdrop of the prison. The one constant threat throughout the history of probation has been the possibility of a period of imprisonment for the offender(s) who violate the condition(s) of their penalty.

Having secured a virtual monopoly on supervising offenders in the community based on an accepted political and scientific credibility, the probation service gradually began to move away from being a servant of the court(s) to become a servant of the 'executive' (McWilliams 1987, p. 103). This 'professional' self-characterisation was accompanied by, and in part was legitimated upon, the standardisation of administration and increasing legislative bureaucracy. However, this increasing bureaucracy was a double-edged sword. It gave the probation service and its officers a basis upon which to make a claim of 'professionalism' while at the same time relinquishing some of the 'local' power it possessed to the central governing body of the Home Office. In doing so it gave the Home Office the opportunity to 'guide' probation working practice through the creation of policy.

Wasting no time, the Home Office began to recommend working practice through a variety of routes. The Home Office (1961) recommended that the writing of a social inquiry report (now pre-sentence report)[5] should not be left to the discretion of local individual probation officers but should follow a set national formula. Two years later, it recommended that compulsory aftercare should be extended to as many offenders as possible (Home Office 1963). Swiftly following on from this, the Home Office began to issue circulars and rejected the proposal by the National Association of Probation Officers that offenders who failed to observe to the condition(s) of aftercare should be reported to the judiciary. Instead the Home Office preferred principal probation officers to report directly to the Home Office. This did not go unrecognised at the time as Goslin claimed that 'it seems clear that power properly resting with the judiciary is being transferred to the executive, via our good selves...' (cited in McWilliams 1981, p. 103).

At this time, however, the majority of the cases the probation service had to deal with were offenders sentenced to probation by the courts and not those released on licence or seeking aftercare (McWilliams 1981). This situation was to rapidly change as probation officers began to act as 'agents' of the executive by taking on more and more people to supervise in the community. As this workload increased, so did the bureaucracy and recruitment of officers to support and sustain this period of unprecedented growth. In the early 1960s there was one principal or senior probation officer managing six basic grade officers, but by the mid-1970s there was one to every three (McWilliams 1981). This significant rise in the ratio of supervisory to mainstream grades (Haxby 1978) enabled the hierarchical professional structure that already existed in the probation service to gradually become a hierarchical and bureaucratic administrative structure. This no doubt enabled the future goals of policy to be pursued with rational efficiency when a shift in the philosophy of punishment changed from one of predominantly 'caring' to one of 'punishment in the community' (Home Office 1988).

This shift, according to May (1994), had already begun in England in the early 1970s. It was recommended by the Home Office Advisory Committee (1974) that a new non-custodial sentence for young adults called a 'supervision and control order' should be used to punish offenders in the community. It appeared that the probation service had lost much of the confidence of the judiciary due to its overriding concern with pathological diagnosis based upon its unwavering allegiance to a specific 'body of knowledge' and use and application of scientific 'jargon'.[6] Many probation officers reacted with horror at being asked to 'punish in the community' and resisted the application of a 'supervision and control order' claiming it would turn them into 'screws on wheels' (Haxby 1978, p. 2).

Even though the probation service resisted the 'supervision and control order', the early 1970s 'nothing works' research of Martinson (1974) found a growing and sympathetic audience emphasising social discipline (Walker and Beaumont 1985) after years of 'applying science' and welfare to the problem of crime. This in itself is not surprising as neither the prison nor the probation service seemed capable of stemming the rising tide of officially recorded crime as more and more offenders seemed to be dragged into the widening net of a unwieldy bureaucratic criminal justice system (Cohen 1985).

For main grade probation officers, the bureaucratic system which helped develop and support a claim to professionalism was now beginning to erode the range and substance of an officer's decision-making. The 'individual' competence of professional probation officers came to clash with the bureaucratic competence of the 'service'. As offenders have become 'units' and categories to manage bounded by a policy framework, officers have become defined by the service rather than by a professional 'diagnostic knowledge' that was once so popular. The formation of this professional class of 'probation mangers' in the criminal justice system due to earlier legislation has helped facilitate the institutionalisation of strategies that have led to the supervision of offenders now being joined by the management of officers in the community.

## National Standards and the Management of Probation Officers

Since the establishment of an 'official' national probation service in 1907, the Home Secretary has had statutory authority to make rules and to issue 'guidelines' to local area committees.[7] As a consequence the Home Office has always had the opportunity to promote a fundamental alteration in the philosophy and practice of probation. With the rise in 'law and order' and the punishment of stigmatised 'out-groups' in the ascendancy in the early 1980s (Worrall 1997, p. 22), a crucial change in probation working practice began to take place. In such a climate the social work diagnostic approach of casework used predominantly by the probation service began to be replaced by an ethos of punishment and apportioning blame to the individual. The primary aim of the probation service became 'to punish' and not to diagnose through 'science' a social or psychological malaise excusing offending and offenders. The offence became the focus of punishment and the offender had to take responsibility for his or her actions.

The probation service, then, was not expected to supervise but now punish in the community.[8] This alteration in its working practice was not one that the probation service willingly subscribed to and resisted the emphasis placed upon the controlling aspects of its work (Bottoms and McWilliams 1979; Walker and Beaumont 1981). It nonetheless became part of the 'system' of 'bifurcated' crime control signalled in the *Criminal Justice Act 1982* (Eng.) (May 1994). This emphasis upon punishment continued to increase as the *Statement for National Objectives and Priorities* (Home Office 1984) for the probation service moved the focus of their work away from assisting minor offenders 'in need' toward working with categories of offenders thought to be a risk to society (Audit Commission 1989; 1991). Now under intense pressure from the Home Office to punish in the community and unable to mount a credible challenge to the popular political rhetoric of punishment, the probation service had to 'reconfigure', albeit grudgingly, into a more 'punitive agency' in order to survive (Garland 1997, p. 3).

Part of this reconfiguration was accepting the imposition of National Standards. First introduced in 1988 (Brownlee 1998) to make Community Service Orders (CSOs) consistently tough and demanding on offenders, National Standards have developed to cover and provide detailed instruction about all probation working practice. Set by the Home Office and extremely prescriptive in character, they restrict professional discretion and require probation officers to adhere to practice 'guidelines'. Expected to adhere to set standards, probation officers are held accountable by the Home Office to reach set targets and be 'competent' *in* their work rather than 'knowledgeable' *of* its practice.

This is clearly apparent in the latest set of National Standards where little is said about the role of probation officers other than that they must ensure that 'the Standards must be adhered to in all but exceptional individual circumstances', and if a decision is to be taken which will depart from the Standards is should be 'endorsed by the designated line manager' and the reason(s) given should be clearly recorded and justified 'on the offender's record'. Furthermore, all probation officers are expected to 'respond fully and promptly to any Home Office request for information and statistical returns' (Home Office 2000a, p. 2). Under such close examination it is hardly surprising that in the eyes of some probation officers, control over working practice has reduced the role, position and status of professional probation officers to that of criminal justice operatives concerned only with the technicalities of a bureaucratic job (Worrall 1997).

This role is a long way from its original mission to 'save souls' and 'advise, assist and befriend' and/or diagnose a social or psychological pathology through casework. The view that the 'appliance of science' could produce a society free of crime has faded as we have seemingly reached a stage where we accept that crime cannot be eliminated or brought under complete control. Instead of attempting to control all criminal activity, the state has withdrawn to manage that which it can control. Consequently, whilst much criminal activity is beyond the reach of the state, the working practice of its 'criminal justice practitioners' is within its grasp. Now under close scrutiny, probation officers are held accountable and expected to perform in a 'competent' manner within guidelines set by the Home Office.

Criminal justice, then, is now concerned less with the diagnosis and treatment of individuals and more with the new penology and actuarial techniques of risk management to assess and manage a permanently dangerous segment of the population while maintaining the system at minimum cost (Feeley and Simon 1992; 1994). However to maintain this 'system' at a minimum cost, those probation officers working in the field must be controlled and held accountable by the Home Office, the Audit Commission and Her Majesty's Inspectorate of Probation. The new penology, then, is not simply about the management and classification of offenders; it is also about the management of the system of criminal justice and its practitioners according to set standards based on formal rationality.

In this way it is easy to see that National Standards for the probation service are part of the new penology. They clearly indicate to officers that set standards must be maintained and targets reached. Individual independent officers with a specific body of knowledge are becoming anachronistic as set guidelines predominantly determine working practice. Instead of professional autonomy, set standards provide a benchmark against which the successful administration of probation can be judged where the numbers of orders completed are seen as the ultimate mark of success.[9] This bureaucraticisation and standardisation of probation working practice, however, started some years ago (Pease 1980) when probation officers began to follow a national formula and individual offenders were only assessed in reference to the categories they 'fitted' created by national policy.

Whilst many senior members of the probation service could adapt and become managers of practice, the majority of basic grade officers who had been trained to use generic social work skills in dealing with offenders were now at a disadvantage. The appliance of science and particularly probation 'social work' training, whereby officers were trained to 'advise, assist and befriend' has changed to 'confront, control and monitor' (Worrall 1997, pp. 63–77).[10] By eroding professional autonomy with National Standards and questioning the use of social work skills when expected to punish in the community, the demand by the Home Office for 'competent' uncritical employees (Nellis 1996, p. 14) to keep offenders under surveillance has become increasingly important (Drakeford and Vanstone 1996, p. 5). The culmination of this change is a shift towards a more intellectually restrictive, competence-orientated and managerial culture that infuses not only the probation service but also much of contemporary society (Gailbraith 1992; Nellis 1996).

It now appears that probation officers are regulated and subjected to continuous monitoring. Seen predominantly as part of the problem of crime and its 'control' rather than as a solution, the working practice of probation officers is less to do with the application of social work skills with offenders in the community and more to do with 'system(s) management' (Harris 1994, p. 34; Nellis 1995, p. 28). The relentless pursuit of efficiency, predictability and control is producing a dehumanised, rationalised, techno-bureaucratic service that is part of the industry of crime control (Christie 1993). Under 'new' management and infused with a private value for money ethos above and beyond 'treatment' or 'punishment', probation officers are moving away from being professional autonomous agents to becoming prison officers *in* and *of* the community as they follow a rigid set procedure determined by the Home Office.[11]

## New Public Management and the Probation Service

While management of any kind may be a reasonably recent innovation in the criminal justice system, the probation service, as we have already seen, did gradually develop an administrative and supervisory hierarchy during its 'diagnostic' era. This has meant that there was already in place a professional management structure that could respond to the challenge of a 'new' style of public management. This 'new' style of management came to prominence in 1979 when the 'market' was extolled by the Conservative Party as a panacea for our economic and social decline. They made a virtue out of the necessity to rein in public spending and downgrade the 'social' aspects of government policy (Brownlee 1998). Rather than 'treat' offenders, they preferred to punish them but also control 'criminal justice practitioners' by measuring their performance against set 'standards' within a centrally controlled limited expenditure. Seen as part of the problem of criminal justice, the 'new' style of public management helped measure the performance of the probation service and its officers by holding them accountable to reach set 'national' standards and be efficient and effective whilst providing value for money.

This has led to employing 'managers' who know nothing about the probation service but have a management style more attuned to the commercial sector (Hood 1991, pp. 4–5). Yet, as Peters (1996) has pointed out, this is where a 'value system' that is extraneous to the influence of NPM and its parsimonious approach to crime control has been pushed on to the periphery of criminal justice. In this position, instead of 'saving', 'treating' and/or managing offenders, the probation service seems to spend more of its time on scrutinising its own internal working practice where the social values of its success have been downgraded and replaced by objectives which can be measured.

For the Home Office these objectives become 'outputs' that can be quantified and measured by a range of instrumentally constructed 'key indicators' so as to be susceptible to external audit. In this way they are controlling and keeping the probation service a 'servant of the executive' whilst at the same time managing to distance itself from any failure in practice. In addition, the probation service is also reliant on the Home Office for 100 per cent of its funding (Home Office 2000b) and must perpetually prove that it is a viable service providing punishment in the community where its economy, efficiency and effectiveness is not in doubt. It could be argued that by elevating the importance of demonstrating cost-efficiency, value for money and better use of resources, probation officers are becoming managers of 'budgets' rather than assisting or even punishing offenders in the community.

However, this economic approach to crime and its control does little more than encourage practice that neglects the diversity and complexity of real life (Hudson 1993). This in turn has reduced the need for 'professional' officers to work in the community. The policy, planning and coordination of criminal justice have become of paramount importance as the new penology has abandoned rehabilitation without necessarily encouraging punishment as it seems devoid of any *raison d'etre* other than to manage that which it can control. Due possibly to its vulnerable position in the 'system' and discredited diagnostic scientific approach to offenders, however, the probation service is under increasing pressure to adhere to set National Standards and reach set targets within set budgets. In this way the probation service and particularly its officers are increasingly restrained if not regulated in the community.

## The Regulation of Officers in the Community

This chapter began by claiming that the probation service has moved away from its 'moral mission' of assisting offenders and 'applying science' to managing its own officers in the community. This, arguably, is due to a variety of factors that have built up over the years rather than any one overriding reason. To illustrate this, an examination was made of the changing role and underlying philosophy of the probation service, its relationship with the magistrates' court and the Home Office, and its claim to be a 'profession' based on a particular body of knowledge.

As has been seen, the underlying philosophy of probation has changed from one based on the religious exhortation of offenders to the scientific diagnosis of a pathological disorder. Whilst elements of both still exist within the probation service (McWilliams 1987), the use and popularity of cognitive behavioural psychology has begun to take hold. This is not because of its usefulness in reducing crime but because of its 'fit' with managerialism (Garland 2001) on how it can mould and control offender(s) and/or staff. Therefore it has had to become pragmatic to survive in the present punitive penal climate. Rather than confidently assert that it has a specific body of knowledge that it once did, it now seems to spend much of its time discussing how it can be of use in preventing crime (Harris 1992) and what should be the value based around which probation is organised (Nellis 1995; James 1995; Spencer 1995).

With this in mind, it is suggested that it might be time to update McWilliams' work (1981, 1983, 1985, 1986, 1987) that charted the development and history of the probation service. To what McWilliams (1987) termed the phase of special pleading (1870s–1930s), the phase of diagnosis (1930s–1970s) and the phase of pragmatism (1970s–late-1990s), should now be added the 'phase of management'.[12] This phase, however, began during the diagnostic era when probation officers started to move away from being servants of the courts to becoming servants of the 'executive'. Whilst this may have gradually eroded local autonomy, the probation service gained recognition from the Home Office to be a professional organisation with a particular 'scientific practice' and body of knowledge above and beyond a 'moral mission'.

This situation has changed, however, as the penal climate has become decidedly punitive. Unable to persuade the probation service to become punitive (Bottoms and McWilliams 1979; Walker and Beaumont 1981), the Home Office has become involved in the setting and issuing of 'guidelines' to cover all aspects of probation working practice. As part of the many 'guidelines' now issued by the Home Office, National Standards clearly state not only what is required of probation officers but also how they should perform (May 1991). Expected to be 'competent' rather than 'knowledgeable', National Standards are only one part of the 'new controls' that probation officers now have to deal with. In this way it is debatable whether the probation service can still claim to be a profession, as probation officers are beginning rapidly to lose their professional status as their working practice starts to resemble prison officers *in* and *of* the community.

## Notes

1   The new National Probation Service for England and Wales came into being on 1 April 2001. The reform of the service was originally proposed in the Criminal Justice and Court Service Bill 1998 but did not receive Royal Assent and become the Criminal Justice and Court Services Act until 15 March 2000.

2   By 'professional', it is meant that probation officers possess an approved qualification, commitment to a code of practice, a specific 'body of knowledge' and the capacity to attract the support of a lay clientele.

3   In 1877, those arrested for a drunk and disorderly offence represented over 50 per cent of all crime in London (McWilliams 1983).

4   Recognisance was a bond or promise made by an offender(s) to a local magistrate to keep the peace. For more information see Samaha (1991) and Simon (1993).

5   Not only did the 'social inquiry report' change in name to become the 'pre-sentence report' in the *Criminal Justice Act 1991* (Eng.), it also changed its focus from the welfare of the 'client' to the offence committed by the offender(s).

6   For a useful and enlightening example of the change from a 'moral' to a 'scientific technical' use of language in probation officers' 'social inquiry reports' see (McWilliams 1983, pp.100–1).

7   With the formation of a new National Probation Service, the Home Secretary reduced the previous 55 probation areas down to 42, making the boundaries coterminous with the Police Service and Crown Prosecution Service. More importantly, though, was the shift in the balance of power away from the probation service and into the hands of the Home Secretary to determine and direct local boards on the required outcomes and standard(s) of service delivery, to appoint the members of the local probation boards and to hold each Chief Probation Officer accountable to the Secretary of State for local administration and management.

8    In fact, since 1 April 2001 the probation service strengthened the enforcement of community sentences by initiating breach proceedings after the second rather than third 'unacceptable' breach after its recommendation in the National Standards for the Supervision of Offenders in the Community (Home Office 2000a).

9    This can be clearly illustrated with the Home Office setting and dictating that the new probation service should reduce the reconviction rate of those under its supervision by five per cent by at least 2004.

10   In February 1995, Michael Howard repealed the legal requirement for all new probation officers to hold a Diploma in Social Work. Whilst this has been partially reversed by Jack Straw, the Labour Party Home Secretary from 1997–2001, he continued to maintain that new probation officers 'should no longer be linked to social work education' (Brownlee 1998a, p. 94).

11   The link between the probation and prison service can be clearly seen not only historically but most recently with the 'Joining Forces: Prison–Probation Review' (Home Office 1998). Emphasising a more integrated approach between prison and probation and working towards common goals with similar standards, a clear continuum of punishment from custody to 'resettlement' (not through care) in the community is developing, with the potential for working practice to blur rather than remain distinct.

12   By this phase it is not only meant the 'management' of offenders but also the 'management' of probation officers.

Chapter 15

# The Regulation of Professionals in the Digital Age

Russell G. Smith

## Introduction

As we have seen in previous chapters, the nature of professional work has changed considerably in recent times. Perhaps the most profound changes have been due to the increasing reliance which professionals place upon computing and communications technologies for their daily practice. Professionals' use of information technologies extends from simple reliance upon telephones, through communications by facsimile and electronic mail, to the most advanced forms of communication and the dissemination of information using the Internet and teleconferencing facilities. Professional records relating to clients and billing are also now regularly recorded on computerised databases.

These developments have enabled professionals to have greater personal control over their work-related communications than in the days when they relied upon secretaries and administrative assistants. They have also extended the geographical boundaries of practice across jurisdictional borders both within and across countries, enabled practitioners to deal with a better-informed clientele and provide information and advice to them electronically. Finally, these developments have permitted professionals to carry out the business side of practice using computers and electronic funds transfer systems, thereby enhancing the speed and administrative efficiency of practice.

Each of these changes, however, has provided new opportunities for professionals to act illegally or in breach of accepted standards of professional conduct. This chapter examines such opportunities by focusing upon six areas of crime and unprofessional conduct in the digital age: electronic registration fraud; unregistered practice; online advertising; breach of confidentiality; theft and dishonesty; and some other specific forms of online unprofessional practice.

## Crime and Unprofessional Conduct in the Digital Age

Professionals are able to, and have throughout history, committed most forms of crime and unprofessional behaviour. As the twenty-first century unfolds, it may be predicted that as new forms of online illegality emerge, professionals will take up the opportunity to commit these as well. In the digital age the following six areas, in particular, are likely to create the greatest opportunities for illegal and unprofessional conduct to occur.

*Electronic Registration Fraud*

Information technologies have the potential to facilitate greatly the fraudulent registration of professionals. Desktop publishing facilities, for example, can be used to counterfeit certificates of examination results as well as entire degree and diploma testamurs which can then be used to obtain professional registration. Manipulation of databases held by Universities and licensing authorities could also be used to ensure that checks which are made on a practitioner's identity or academic performance are able to be validated.

The Internet is now being used for higher-educational purposes with entire courses being offered online. Students simply enrol in the course and receive educational materials electronically and communicate with lecturers via electronic mail. Seminars may be conducted through the use of chat rooms and newsgroups, and assignments can be sent electronically with examiners' comments provided by return electronic mail using 'revisions' software. There have, however, been instances of online universities failing to provide recognised, or indeed any, valid qualifications, or occasionally failing to deliver any educational programs at all.

In the United States, 19 people were defrauded when a web site calling itself 'Loyola State University' advertised Bachelors, Masters and Doctoral degrees for between US$1,995 and $2,795. All that candidates were required to do was to send details of their life experiences along with the payment and they would receive their degree within a month (Denning 1999, p. 132; Rothchild 1999, p. 908, n. 61).

*Unregistered Practice*

Traditionally, the work of unqualified and unregistered 'quack' medical practitioners was able to be detected simply by inspecting public registers in which the details of acceptably qualified individuals were published. In the digital age, however, although access to such registers may be enhanced if they are made publicly available on the Internet by licensing authorities—which rarely seems to occur—the ability of individuals to practice electronically without registration is made much easier than in the past where one's physical presence made detection easier.

Conducting professional work through the use of information technologies greatly enhances the ability of individuals to escape the requirements for professional registration. It is easy, for example for anyone to create an online investment advisory service without complying with the registration requirements of bodies such as the Australian Securities and Investments Commission. Other novel questions of registration have also been created by digital technologies. Is, for example, the creator of investment advisory software required to be registered as an investment adviser, or is the software merely a tool by which advice can be sought from others?

In addition, digital technologies easily permit individuals to disguise their identities online through the use of fabricated information published on professional-looking web sites, or by using anonymous electronic re-mailing services to thwart attempts at discovery of their true identity and location. Unqualified practitioners are, accordingly, able to provide online services to the public with little chance of detection.

Online professional practice also has the tendency to cross state and territory borders—not to mention international jurisdictional boundaries. For example, legal advice may be given by telephone, facsimile, electronic mail, the Internet or by video-conferencing in which solicitors, barristers and clients may be located in three separate jurisdictions. Telemedicine procedures are also specifically designed to enable doctors, nurses and patients to be present at different locations at the same time. Unless those involved in providing such professional services are registered in each jurisdiction in which the service is provided—which may be two or more—the practitioner may have committed offences of unregistered practice if representations are made that he or she holds registered status.

Where professional registers are created digitally and made available for public perusal online, it will be necessary to ensure that entries cannot be manipulated either from within or outside registration authorities. The use of appropriate levels of encryption and cryptographic keys for user authentication would be necessary safeguards to help protect databases of registration information. Computers do, however, have the benefit of being able to process information much more readily than in the past. It would be possible, therefore, for the fact of a practitioner's erasure from a Register to be placed on the licensing authority's web site minutes after the decision was actually made. This could then be inspected by all other licensing authorities which might have an interest in that practitioner's registration standing.

## Advertising

Throughout the early twentieth century, most established professions prohibited advertising and canvassing for work. Such rules were said to be in the public interest as clients were not well placed to assess the quality of practitioners' work and might make a choice solely on the basis of the lowest price. This could then lead to standards being eroded through undue price competition (Baxt 1994, p. 4).

Prohibitions on advertising had the effect of distinguishing a profession from a purely commercial activity which was profit-driven and intent on seeking out new business. Advertising was considered to be unethical for doctors and lawyers to engage in except in highly limited circumstances which did not detract from the decorum of the profession. Having a 'sandwich man' parade through the centre of town, advertising a medical practice was considered to be 'infamous conduct in a professional respect' until very recently and, indeed, could still result in the practitioner's conduct being examined, albeit possibly for other reasons (see Smith 1994).

In the 1980s and 1990s, however, the effects of competition policy and the changing nature of professional practice led to rules against advertising and touting being relaxed. All that remained illegal and unprofessional was advertising that infringed general community laws against misleading and deceptive practices and certain specific rules which prevented professionals from comparing themselves with other colleagues.

In Victoria, for example, subsection (1) of section 64 of the *Medical Practice Act 1994* (Vic.) provides:

A person must not advertise a medical practice or medical or surgical services in a manner which:
  (a) is or is intended to be false, misleading or deceptive; or
  (b) offers a discount, gift or other inducement to attract patients to a medical practitioner or medical practice unless the advertisement also sets out the terms and conditions of that offer; or
  (c) refers to or quotes from testimonials or purported testimonials; or
  (d) unfavourably contrasts medical or surgical services provided by a medical practitioner or medical practice with services provided by another medical practitioner or medical practice.

This has led to a proliferation in advertising of medical services such as treatments for bladder problems, impotence, anxiety, penile enlargement, cosmetic surgery, tattoo removal and laser treatment. As Walton (1998, p. 3) observes: 'today much of the promotional activity is generated by medical entrepreneurs who target particular sections of the community. The services are profit-driven and dependent on a high turnover of patients.'

Because the Internet, in particular, provides such a comprehensive and efficient medium for advertising, it is being used to market a wide variety of health care products and services. Various frauds involving health care products and services have already been identified including a number of alleged cures for cancer (Varney 1996). These are much the same as other fraudulent health product scams but may be carried out much more extensively on the Internet with approaches being made to substantial numbers of individuals.

The problem has also arisen of professionals constructing their own web sites in order to advertise their professional activities or provide information to the public, but failing to do so ethically and in accordance with standards of acceptable practice. In one case, for example, a famous doctor in the United States maintained a web site which contained material advertising particular health products. It was alleged, however, that he had failed to disclose a commercial interest in the products being advertised and sold through the web site (see Noble 1999). Although this form of non-disclosure of commercial interests has always been considered unethical practice, the blurring of advertising and information which takes place on the Internet is more pervasive, easier to perpetrate and, arguably, more convincing.

Online professional advertising also creates problems where goods and services are offered which would infringe local laws in jurisdictions where the information is read and consumed. In one case, for example, a human kidney was offered for auction with bidding reaching US$5.7 million in an Internet auction site. The sale clearly infringed local laws and the sale was later withdrawn. Similarly, for doctors in the Netherlands to offer information and advice about euthanasia via the Internet to patients in Australia, may infringe local laws in Australia, although not in the Netherlands. There is, however, a substantial body of information available through the Internet concerning assisted suicide and euthanasia (see, for example, DeathNet <http://www.rights.org/~deathnet/open.html> and the Hemlock Society <http://www.hemlock.org/>).

*Breach of Confidentiality*

A fundamental ethical duty imposed on most professionals is to keep client affairs confidential. This arises out of a respect for the client's privacy and also helps to encourage clients to be frank when communicating with their professional advisers in the knowledge that their confidences will not be disclosed elsewhere.

Although some professionals might not realise it, communications carried out via telephones and computer networks are vulnerable to interception for both lawful as well as unlawful purposes. There have been numerous instances in Australia and overseas, for example, of doctors' private telephone conversations having been intercepted and used in legal proceedings (Smith 1998).

Where online services are used for professional communications, such as for the transmission of confidential information about clients, the security risks take on great importance. In the case of medicine, electronic data transmission may involve patients' medical records, reports from consultants to general practitioners, pathology test results as well as online telemedicine procedures which are now becoming available. Perhaps the greatest area of concern arises where intimate images of patients being examined are transmitted electronically. Although data may pass along systems in encrypted form, this is by no means entirely secure and medical practitioners could well breach confidentiality by transmitting personal information across computer networks (see Stanberry 1997).

Professional communications between solicitors, barristers, judges and clients could also be compromised if they are sent electronically. The use of electronic mail in legal practice is now common and it is often assumed that highly sensitive information will be safe if sent electronically. In addition, the changing nature of legal practice in which specialist practitioners contract out their services to large corporations creates an environment in which disclosure of professional confidences to business rivals could have profound consequences (Gray 1999, p. 73). One could imagine that the failure to make use of an appropriate level of encryption when transmitting sensitive material between lawyers and their clients could result in professional disciplinary action resulting. Education of professionals regarding the need for online security should be present in every professional practice course, if not in undergraduate studies as well (Celler, Lovell and Chan 1999).

Apart from confidential communications between a professional and client being overheard, or intercepted electronically, the possibility arises that confidential material held on electronic databases could be compromised and the information used for illegitimate purposes (see Carter, M. 2000).

Intercepted communications could, for example, be used for commercial purposes. In one case in the United States, a bank manager paid a health official to check computerised health records of loan applicants, thus requiring the official to breach confidentiality (Anonymous 1996). In another case, a banker on a state health commission obtained access to a list of all the patients in the state diagnosed as suffering from cancer and cross-referenced it with the bank's client list. He then arranged for these patients' loans to be called in (Anonymous 1993; Commonwealth of Australia, House of Representatives Standing Committee on Family and Community Affairs 1996 submission of Computer Sciences Corporation Australia, vol. 4, p. 892).

In the United States, a panel of the National Research Council has also identified a number of security risks associated with electronic patient records and recommended greater use of access restriction devices (Leary 1997). An example of such risks which recently took place in Pinellas County, Florida, involved the leak of a confidential computer disk which contained the names of almost 4,000 individuals suffering from AIDS (United States, General Accounting Office 1997, p. 63). In another incident at the University of Michigan Medical Centre, thousands of patient records were disclosed on public Internet sites for two months before the problem was rectified (Carter M. 2000, p. 29, n. 16).

A variety of solutions has been suggested to authenticate messages transmitted electronically. Public key cryptographic systems have been developed which permit the recipients of electronic data messages to be sure that they have come from an identifiable source and that the content of the message has not been interfered with. The use of so-called 'hashing algorithms' in conjunction with biometric user authentication systems would create a much higher degree of security for electronic transmissions than occurs with paper-based systems. It will take a considerable time, however, before such technologies are readily available throughout the community.

In the meantime, enhanced education of practitioners about the security risks associated with using information technologies is needed. In the United Kingdom, for example, medical education rarely deals with computer security and confidentiality, instead focusing on clinical applications of information technology. Ellis and Kidd (2000, p. 24), for example, submit that even the simplest measures such as the use of screen savers and not sharing passwords, are often poorly understood and not regularly enforced by British general practitioners. Much more extensive education of practitoners will be needed to ensure that they adopt appropriate security procedures when dealing with confidential patient/client data transmitted electronically (Celler, Lovell and Chan 1999, p. 520).

## *Theft and Dishonesty*

Digital technologies have greatly facilitated the commission of crimes of theft and dishonesty and it is likely that professionals will be involved in making use of the opportunities which have been created in the same way as others in the business community. Arguably, because many professional activities rely heavily on information processing, the opportunities for the commission of electronic theft may be greater than for others whose work does not rely on such technologies to the same extent.

Dishonest practices may relate to the online advertising of professional services, as we have seen, and to attempts to secure the payment of fees by manipulating electronic payment systems. One of the greatest areas of vulnerability relates to the creation of false documents through the use of the digital technologies of scanning and printing using desktop personal computers.

These technologies have already been used to forge cheques, benefit claim forms and payment vouchers. One of the most frequently used means of carrying out computer-based fraud at present involves the creation and use of false identities. In the health care context, the possibility arises of providers creating phantom referrals in respect of legitimate patients. This has already taken place through the use of paper-based documents and the same type of fraud would be facilitated in an electronic system. In one recent case being prosecuted by the Health Insurance Commission, a psychiatrist is alleged to have made claims amounting to more than $1 million in respect of false referrals received from more than 100 general practitioners over approximately a six-year period. The phantom referrals were, in fact, never made by general practitioners but fabricated by the psychiatrist through forging signatures and creating false referrals and benefit assignment forms (see Cauchi 1999).

In the future, electronic funds transfer systems are likely to become the principal means by which payments are made to and from professionals. One can imagine the situation developing in which most professional services will be paid for using electronic cash of one form or another.

Such systems are likely to be targets for fraud and illegality in the same way as other electronic funds transfer systems have been used to steal funds. Because of the substantial sums of money which governments provide for public health care, those who provide services and those who receive payments may be tempted to steal such funds. In Australia between 1 July 1997 and 30 June 1998, for example, 128,023 Medicare services amounting to $7,461,353 were processed by electronic funds transfer. Although this represents a relatively small proportion of the 202.2 million Medicare services billed worth $6,334 million in the same year, the proportion of payments made electronically will increase considerably in the future (Health Insurance Commission 1998).

As the use of electronic processing of claims increases, so the risk of fraud will also increase, perhaps facilitated by the computer technologies adopted. Risks relate to the possibility of electronic claim forms being electronically counterfeited or manipulated, signatures being forged and electronic funds transfers being altered or diverted away from legitimate recipients (Smith 1999a). The Health Insurance Commission has already been subject to fraud perpetrated by insiders and the possibility exists that those with the technological skills could attack the Commission's electronic claiming system internally. In 1997, for example, two former Health Insurance Commission employees were convicted of defrauding the Commonwealth by creating false provider accounts and making illegal claims to the combined value of more than $45,000 (Health Insurance Commission 1997, p. 23).

## Online Unprofessional Conduct

If one examines the various Codes of Professional Conduct which are published by state and territory professional registration boards and professional associations, it is apparent that practitioners who make use of online services could infringe many of these ethical rules in a variety of ways.

In the case of medicine, conducting professional examinations or prescribing drugs through the use of communications technologies without having conducted a proper examination of the patient has previously resulted in findings of guilt of professional misconduct (Smith 1994) and the use of telemedicine will create further risks of this nature. Already instances have emerged of doctors being paid to write prescriptions for drugs such as Viagra for patients who have requested the drug online. The doctors base their judgment of information provided by patients without ever having met or physically examined them (see, for example, *SafeWeb Medical*, <http://www.safewebmedical.com/> visited 10 March 2000). Online pharmacies are also beginning to emerge which have been used to sell drugs through web sites, sometimes in breach of local laws which prevent particular unapproved drugs from being dispensed in certain jurisdictions (Stolberg 1999). In the future when the Australian Department of Industry, Science and Tourism's (1998) Pharmaceutical Electronic Commerce and Communication Project becomes operational, paper prescriptions for drugs will be replaced by an online prescribing and distribution network (Abernethy 2000). Although this is predicted to result in considerable savings for the health care budget, it could open the way to unauthorised persons obtaining access to drugs for improper purposes.

Failure to respond to a patient's requests for assistance made by electronic mail, for example, could also be unprofessional if the practitioner has inadequate systems in place to record, monitor and respond to incoming messages. Improper delegation of professional duties to inadequately trained colleagues may occur where practitioners are not directly involved in providing online treatment themselves.

Serious negligence in the use of computer-based procedures may also give rise to professional liability and, in extreme cases, criminal liability. In North America, for example, there are numerous reports of patients being severely burnt by receiving excessive doses of radiation from the computer-controlled radiation therapy system, Terac-25 (Neumann 1995, pp. 68–70).

## Professional Regulatory Issues in the Digital Age

These few examples of illegal and unprofessional conduct arising out of the use of information technologies present those seeking to prevent and to control such conduct with a range of novel problems. Some relate to legal difficulties in seeking to take action in respect of laws which are unsuited to digital crime, whilst others concern the practical problems associated with obtaining evidence of what has taken place in electronic transactions. Still other difficulties relate to the determination of the appropriate jurisdiction in which the conduct has taken place and the choice of an appropriate forum in which the matter may be dealt with.

### Cross-Border Practice

Cross-border practice will affect all professionals in the digital age where advice and professional services are delivered electronically. Systems of professional regulation are invariably restricted territorially in that the registration body only has jurisdiction over those practitioners who are registered with it and or who practise within a specified geographical area.

This gives rise to problems where practitioners engage in cross-border practice, either between different states and territories or internationally, as they would be required to be registered in every location where the work is performed. Already this is becoming problematic for a number of professions. In the case of architecture in Australia, for example, it has been estimated that 22 per cent of architectural fees come from services delivered offshore (Peck 1999).

The practice of nursing may also require practitioners to travel across state boundaries. This may occur in places where the nurse practices close to a state or territory border and an emergency situation, such as a road traffic accident or a national disaster, requires the nurse to care for a patient located across the border. Some Nurses Acts have specific provisions to deal with these so-called emergency treatment situations which enable a nurse registered in one state or territory to render treatment in another state or territory for short periods (in New South Wales, for example, not exceeding 24 hours: *Nurses Act 1991* (NSW) s. 25(c)).

Some states and territories also enable nurses to engage in procedures relating to the retrieval of organs or tissues from people for transplantation purposes which take place in jurisdictions other than those in which they are registered. Thus, a nurse who is registerd in Victoria who, for example, is required to accompany a donor from Victoria to Tasmania for a transplantation procedure which is to be conducted in Tasmania, will not infringe the Tasmanian *Nurses Act 1995* (s. 94(c)). In the Australian Capital Territory, a similar exemption is given for nurses involved in quarantine procedures which cross borders (*Nurses Act 1998* (ACT) s. 78(b)).

These exceptions in relation to temporary practice, organ retrieval procedures, emergencies and quarantine are, however, not uniform throughout all of the Australian states and territories, with some jurisdictions not even providing for them at all (for example, the Northern Territory and Western Australia).

In the case of telemedicine procedures which take place across jurisdictional boundaries, it is necessary for all those involved, be they general practitioners, surgeons or nurses, to be registered in each jurisdiction involved. Difficult questions arise as to the precise place at which a telemedicine procedure takes place and so, arguably, those involved should be registered in the jurisdiction in which they, themselves, are physically located at the time of the procedure, as well as the jurisdiction in which the patient is located. Specific legislation could, of course, make such multiple registration unnecessary.

Legal practice which makes use of information technologies can also involve crossing jurisdictional boundaries. Advice may be given by telephone, facsimile, electronic mail or video-conferencing in which solicitors, barristers and clients may be located in three separate jurisdictions. If the advice given is negligent or otherwise involves unprofessional practice, questions would arise as to which licensing authority would take action, and on the basis of which code of practice.

Advertising legal services on the Internet, for example, could infringe local laws in some jurisdictions in which the data are received, but not in others. In addition, the provision of legal advice via an Internet site raises various problems of professional indemnity insurance where there are no controls placed on access to the information provided. The lawyer might not, for example, know to whom the information has been provided, and the purposes for which it is being used. In addition, problems arise in keeping information up to date (Gray 1999, p. 89). Again, questions would arise as to the appropriate jurisdiction in which proceedings should be brought.

Questions of taxation law might also arise where services are provided by professionals electronically. Under Australia's new tax system, for example, in order to be taxable, a supply must be connected with Australia (s. 9-5, *A New Tax System (Goods and Services Tax) Act 1999* (Cth)). A supply will be connected with Australia if it is done in Australia or if the supplier makes the supply through an enterprise that the supplier carries on in Australia (s. 9-25(5)). If supplies are exported to non-residents for consumption outside Australia, however, GST will not be payable (s. 38-190). If, for example, a lawyer provides legal advice by electronic mail to a client outside Australia, that service will not incur GST if the advice does not concern Australian goods or property. If the advice was merely about the client's business practices in an overseas country, the services provided would be GST-free. If, however, the advice concerned property within Australia, GST would be payable. The main regulatory difficulty with such a situation concerns the identification of the transaction which contains the services, as the advice may be given electronically and payment made by electronic funds transfer direct to the supplier's bank account.

*Standards of Practice*

Determining appropriate standards of practice is also problematic in the digital age where practitioners may be required to comply with multiple, sometimes conflicting, laws and codes of conduct in a variety of jurisdictions.

Codes of conduct should, ideally, be uniform throughout the various jurisdictions to which they apply in Australia, and be in conformity with any internationally recognised principles which exist. National bodies such as the Law Council of Australia and the Australian Medical Council may be able to assist in preparing and disseminating uniform guidelines for professional practice which makes use of information technologies in Australia.

Already uniform standards are starting to be developed for professionals within Australia. National Nursing Competency Standards for registered and enrolled nurses are now published by the Australian Nursing Council Inc. (1994) and have been accepted by all Nurses Boards in Australia as the basis for determining eligibility for registration and enrolment. The Council has also developed other documents including the *Code of Ethics for Nurses in Australia* (1993) and the *Code of Professional Conduct for Nurses in Australia* (1995) which represent agreed national standards of practice (Fletcher 1998).

Agreed standards for telemedicine procedures are also beginning to be developed. Standards Australia (1995), for example, already has a Standard on Personal Privacy Protection in Health Care Information Systems, while various standards are being developed by the European Standardisation Committee, Technical Committee on Medical Informatics (CEN TC251) which was established in March 1990 (see de Moor 1997).

## Some Solutions

*Mutual Recognition*

The digital age brings with it the need for people to be able to practise their profession in a variety of geographical locations. Telemedicine, for example, often involves practitioners participating in joint consultations in order to treat a patient who might not be physically present but, perhaps, assisted by a nurse. Legal and accounting practitioners may also be called upon to offer advice by telephone or electronic mail to clients resident overseas. As a result it is arguably necessary for all those involved to be registered to practise in each of the jurisdictions concerned.

In Europe, the free movement of people was one of the central tenets of the establishment of the Community with the Treaty of Rome in 1960. The legal device by which freedom of movement for professionals has been achieved is that of mutual recognition of qualifications and the right to practise in different countries within the Union. The European Commission began working on the question of mutual recognition in 1958, but by 1982 only six professions had achieved mutuality in full or in part: medicine, nursing, dentistry, veterinary science, midwifery and law.

Legally, the European Court of Justice has confirmed the right of any professional practitioner who is a national of a member state to set up in practice in another Member State or to provide a service there from his own member state. In practice, however, certain conditions must first be fulfilled which has meant that, practically, mutuality has not been achieved in full. The European Commission must examine and be satisfied of the mutuality of training requirements, ethical standards and professional status for every member state for which mutuality is to be applicable—clearly an onerous obligation (de Crayencour 1982, p. 12).

Of particular importance is the need for mutuality to be present with respect to practitioners' good character and good repute on admission to practise as well as in relation to matters of professional discipline. This is necessary in order to prevent those who have been found guilty of professional misconduct in one member's state simply setting up practice in another and being able to reoffend.

In Australia, professional mutual recognition was achieved with the passage of uniform legislation in each state and territory as well as the Commonwealth (see chapter 1). In order to be able to practise in another jurisdiction, practitioners must notify the registration board in the new jurisdiction, provide evidence of current registration and pay the prescribed fee. The practitioner then becomes subject to the legislative regime which applies in the new jurisdiction which include professional conduct matters.

If a practitioner's registration is subject to conditions or restrictions in the original jurisdiction, then any subsequent registration in another jurisdiction will be subject to the same conditions or restrictions. Suspension or cancellation of registration in one jurisdiction also suspends or cancels registration in the other jurisdiction. The effectiveness of this system is obviously dependent upon immediate notification of any orders which affect a practitioner's registration from one jurisdiction to another.

Although the mutual recognition scheme achieves its objective of allowing the mobility of practitioners between jurisdictions, it is necessary for practitioners to apply separately to the registration board in the state or territory in which they seek to practise, comply with the formal requirements and pay appropriate fees. This, in practice, is both time-consuming and expensive.

In order to facilitate the process of mutual recognition for lawyers in Australia, a scheme is being implemented in which all practitioners will be provided with a so-called 'National Travelling Practising Certificate'. When agreed upon by each state and territory, this will allow lawyers to practise throughout Australia without having to make a separate application for registration in each jurisdiction (Dixon 1999, p. 75; Parker 1997, p. 14, discussing the *Legal Profession Amendment (National Practising Certificates) Act 1996* (NSW)). Practitioners who practise in another jurisdiction will be required to adhere to local rules of professional conduct and fulfil trust account requirements and also carry adequate professional indemnity cover. Procedures will also ensure that disciplinary sanctions cannot be duplicated across jurisdictions (Harley 1998).

The system of mutual recognition of professional qualifications and registration, although facilitating cross-border practice in the digital age, does not solve the problems identified above of state and territory-based systems of professional regulation.

*National Regulation*

*Intra-professional regulation*  Many of the problems associated with the regulation of cross-border professional practice could be resolved if professional regulation were undertaken on a national basis. The idea of a national regulatory body with registration and disciplinary powers for each profession has been recommended for a number of professions in recent years (for example, see Clifton-Steele 1994 regarding law; see Peck 1999 regarding architecture). In the words of the immediate past President of the Law Council of Australia:

> It is time the legal profession became truly national: one governing body; the issuing of one practising certificate; one national set of cohesive disciplinary rules which recognise the right to practise as a barrister, a solicitor or both; a single national appraisal committee in relation to legal education; and even one monthly legal journal for the whole of Australia (Dixon 1999, p. 77).

Although some progress has been made in this regard, a good deal remains to be accomplished. There are, however, a variety of national professional bodies such as the Law Council of Australia which was established in 1933 and which has actively pursued matters of national importance for the profession (Dixon 1999). More recently, in July 1992, the Australian Nursing

Council Inc. (ANCI) was established with representatives from, and funding by, each state and territory. The purpose of the Council is to establish and to maintain national standards and processes for the regulation of nursing within Australia (Fletcher 1998).

The ANCI maintains the National Nurses Administrative Database, which is a database used to facilitate the collection of consistent national statistical data relating to the registration of nurses. The database is located at the offices of ANCI and provides a central repository which facilitates the mutual recognition of nurses' qualifications amongst Nurses Boards. The database allows for an indicator to be shown against the names of nurses who are the subject of investigation of their professional conduct or who have had conditions placed on their practice. This indicator enables a Nurses Board in one state to contact boards in other states and territories should a nurse apply for registration under mutual recognition. At present five regulatory authorities are online and using the database (Fletcher 1998).

Establishing a single national system of professional regulation for practitioners within a given profession would provide the most effective way of resolving the problems associated with cross-border registration and practice. Such a national professional conduct body has existed for almost a century and a half in the United Kingdom in the form of the General Medical Council which draws its members from across Britain and has jurisdiction over all British medical practitioners (see Smith 1994). In Australia, the infrastructure of the Australian Medical Council or the ANCI could be adapted to fulfil this wider professional function.

A single national regulatory body for each profession would be able to impose one uniform standard for education of practitioners, procedures for registration, standards of conduct and disciplinary inquiries. Already some of these functions are carried out by national professional bodies such as the Law Council of Australia and the ANCI.

The achievement of this objective would require each state and territory to request the Commonwealth Parliament to pass appropriate legislation and for each state and territory to abolish their own professional legislation. The result would be in accordance with the competition policy of the government and would enhance cross-border professional labour movements. Such a proposal would, however, represent a significant movement of power away from the states and territories and to the Commonwealth which might be opposed at the local level. State and territory boards have always had a particular desire to control professional regulation and this may be seen as an inappropriate loss of state and territory involvement.

Professional conduct proceedings could either be conducted at a central location in Canberra or by individual state and territory committees. Centralising proceedings in Canberra would, however, be costly in terms of travel for those involved in proceedings, and a centralised system may be out of touch with the highly specific issues which arise in local settings. The use of video presentation of evidence may, however, provide a solution to these concerns. Generally, however, it may be preferable for national professional bodies to maintain locally staffed Professional Conduct Committees in each population centre.

A variation on this idea would be for a national system of registration to be established, but for each state and territory to limit its functions to the investigation and adjudication of professional conduct matters. Practitioners would, therefore, only be required to obtain national registration, similar to the National Practising Certificate for lawyers, with all registration fees being payable to the national registering authority which would then be required to subsidise state and territory-based professional conduct activities.

The advantages of such a system would be that local expertise and knowledge of local conditions would continue to be available for the conduct of professional conduct inquiries, and that those involved in inquiries would not need to travel to Canberra. The single system of registration and standard-setting would, however, resolve the issues associated with cross-border practice as every practitioner would be registered for practice anywhere in Australia at all times.

Again, this proposal would require the states and territories to confer legislative authority on the Commonwealth Parliament with respect to national registration, but not the investigation and adjudication of professional conduct matters.

A less drastic approach would involve the retention of the existing state and territory-based registration boards with their existing functions, but entail the enactment of uniform legislation in each jurisdiction which would deem practitioners who are registered in one state to be registered in another state for the specific purpose of carrying out cross-border procedures. In drafting suitable legislation, care would be needed to ensure that it remained 'technology-neutral' and also that jurisdiction for the purposes of disciplinary investigations was specified. Arguably, the place at which the consumer of professional services is located should be the *prima facie* consideration in determining place of registration for practitioners, applicable rules of conduct and jurisdiction of disciplinary bodies (see Commonwealth of Australia, House of Representatives Standing Committee on Family and Community

Affairs 1996, submission by the Australian Medical Council, vol. 1, p. 110). This would ensure that consumers do not have to take action in a jurisdiction other than that in which they reside, and that one set of rules would govern services which involve a number of practitioners who are located in several different jurisdictions.

*Inter-professional regulation* The development of multidisciplinary practice, coupled with cross-border practice using information technologies may, in the future, see the creation of inter-professional regulatory bodies. Arguably, disciplinary proceedings could be conducted by a single national body, perhaps with state and territory-based committees, with jurisdiction over a number of agreed professions. Standards would, however, remain within the power of each profession to determine. The composition of disciplinary committees would vary depending upon the profession of the person being investigated, with common membership to provide lay and legal input into proceedings.

Although it may take some time before a single system were developed which could regulate the professional conduct of doctors and lawyers together, the advent of multidisciplinary practices for business professionals could see interprofessional tribunals develop for law and accountancy in the near future.

*Global Regulation*

One important consequence of the globalisation of professional practice has been the creation of international codes of ethics which are able to be used as standards for national and local codes. In the case of architecture, for example, it has been recommended that Australian regulatory legislation should follow the draft Guidelines for Registration/Licensing/Certification of Architects published by the International Union of Architects (see Peck 1999).

Although some principles such as confidentiality and honesty may exist across national borders, other more specific rules of conduct and etiquette are bound to vary according to local circumstances. For example, the different legal cultures embodied by the common law, civil law and Islamic law traditions make the establishment of a truly international code of legal practice difficult (see Boon and Levin 1999, p. 403).

In Europe, the cross-border activities of lawyers are governed by the Council of the Bars and Law Societies of the European Union's *Code of Conduct for Lawyers in the European Community* while lawyers who practise in different jurisdictions globally are bound by the International Bar

Association's *International Code of Ethics* and its *General Principles of Ethics*. These documents set out general principles which local codes of professional practice and etiquette should follow.

In addition, the increasing incidence of cross-border criminal conduct has resulted in the establishment on 1 October 1999 of Europol, a European agency charged with coordinating the law enforcement efforts of police services in individual member states within the European Union. Arguably, a comparable coordinating authority could be established to focus the activities of professional regulatory bodies within the Union.

As an alternative to global regulation of practice within specific professions, international regulation could focus upon the specific types of conduct engaged in, regardless of the discipline concerned. The use by professionals of information technologies is a case in point. Already there exist a number of codes of practice which govern specific online activities, mainly relating to misleading, deceptive and unethical conduct involving the Internet.

Internet service providers, for example, have established a variety of industry-based organisations, a number of which have their own codes of practice. In Australia, the Internet Industry Association, for example, has a code of practice (Version 4.2 of 12 February 1999) which was based on generally accepted international standards, such as Australian Standard AS-4269–1995, a wide range of existing and related codes, the Ministerial Council of Consumer Affairs' Guide to Fair Trading Codes of Conduct and various regulatory schemes in related industries.

In addition, the need to protect the privacy of personal information in the digital age has led to the establishment of a number of self-regulatory initiatives. In February 1998, for example, the Federal Privacy Commissioner released the *National Principles of the Fair Handling of Personal Information* which set out a number of rules for the collection and release of personal information (see Field 1999). Although compliance with such principles is voluntary, wilful disregard of them could be taken into account in determining whether or not a professional person has acted improperly.

Professionals, like other users of online technologies, are required to adhere to such codes of practice simply by reason of their use of the technology. Failure to comply would, however, not only result in the sanctions specified in the various codes of practice being imposed, but could also result in the practitioner being dealt with by his or her own professional regulatory body. The unprofessional conduct would, accordingly, arise out of non-compliance with an international standard, but would be dealt with by a local authority.

## Technology-based Regulation

Technology may also provide some of the answers to professional regulation in the digital age. Technology-based solutions extend from preventive techniques to sophisticated detection and monitoring activities which are able to enhance existing controls. Although these may venture into the realm of what has been described as 'digital rule', in which the technologies of power come to dominate our lives (Jones 1999), technology-based regulation could provide an effective solution to some forms of online professional misconduct.

*Identification technologies*  Authentication of one's identity is crucial in preventing computer-based fraud and is likely to be central in the prevention of digital professional misconduct as well. At present, most authentication procedures involve the use of passwords or personal identification numbers (PINs). Ensuring that these are used carefully and are not able to be compromised represents a fundamental crime prevention measure.

In addition to education of professionals about the need to use systems correctly, a variety of innovative ideas have been developed to protect passwords and to enhance user authentication (see Alexander 1995). Systems are available which change passwords regularly, or which deny access after a specified number of consecutive tries using invalid passwords. Terminals have been devised with automatic shutdown facilities which operate when they have not been used for specified periods of time. Single-use passwords, challenge-response protocols and call-back systems have also been devised as a means of carrying out user authentication. Finally, space geodetic methods can authenticate the physical locations of users.

In the future, many user authentication systems will make use of so-called biometric identifiers which make use of an individual's unique physical characteristics. Common examples include fingerprints, voice patterns, typing patterns, retinal images, facial or hand geometry and even the identification of a person's subcutaneous vein structures or body odours (Johnson 1996). Although such systems achieve much higher levels of security than those which rely upon passwords, they are expensive to introduce and raise potential problems in terms of privacy and confidentiality of the personal data stored on government computer networks. An initiative designed to reduce social security fraud in Toronto has been the enactment of legislation which would enable welfare benefit recipients to use fingerprint authentication when dealing with the Ontario government in Canada. Detailed privacy protections are built into the legislation which includes requirements for all biometric data to be encrypted and for the original biometric to be destroyed after the encryption process has been completed (Cavoukian 1999).

*Data-matching technologies* Maintaining extensive databases of individuals is another way of being able to validate identities and thus prevent fraud. Data-matching is being used extensively by government agencies to identify inappropriate claims made in respect of state-funded benefit programs. In Australia in the early 1990s, a complex database was created by the federal government in an attempt to prevent taxation and social security fraud, by identifying individuals who made claims for benefits from government funds to which they were not entitled. In the year 1996–97, the program resulted in direct savings of $157 million for two departments: Social Security, and Employment, Education, Training and Youth Affairs (Centrelink 1997).

*Neural networks* Individuals' use of computers and their online activities can also be monitored through the use of software which logs usage and allows regulators to know if computers have been used for inappropriate purposes. It is also possible to monitor the activities of individuals, sometimes covertly such as through video surveillance or checking electronic mail and files transmitted through servers. Filtering software may also be used to prevent users from engaging in certain behaviours. 'Surfwatch', for example, can be customised to deny access to specified content.

The use of computer software to monitor online business activities also provides an effective means of detecting fraud and deterring individuals from acting illegally. The Australian Health Insurance Commission, for example, employs artificial neural networks to detect inappropriate claims made by health care providers and members of the public in respect of various government-funded health services and benefits. In 1997–98, this technology contributed to the Health Insurance Commission locating $7.6 million in benefits which were paid incorrectly to providers and the public (Health Insurance Commission 1998).

Such technologies could, for example, have identified the unusual patterns of prescribing and patient deaths associated with the practice of Dr Harold Shipman, who was convicted on 31 January 2000 at Preston Crown Court in England, of murdering 15 female elderly patients, in similar circumstances, and sentenced to life imprisonment in respect of each conviction (Carter, H. 2000).

Although the use of such technologies clearly has benefits in terms of detecting illegality, questions of infringement of privacy and confidentiality of data transmission arise. If such monitoring technologies were used covertly by professional registration authorities, this could give rise to infringement of confidentiality of communications between professionals and their clients. In order to avoid such problems, monitoring technologies can be adapted to analyse anonymous data in order for practitioners to regulate their own patterns of conduct. This has, for example, proved to be highly effective in preventing over-servicing in the health care sector.

## Conclusions

Digital technologies will greatly enhance the ability of people to infringe professional rules of practice and other laws in the twenty-first century. Already a range of instances of such conduct has begun to emerge. Many security risks simply replicate traditional forms of professional misconduct, but make use of computers to enhance the speed and efficiency with which they may be carried out. Others are directed at computer systems themselves, such as by using computers to transfer funds illegally.

A wide range of strategies exist to prevent and to control such conduct, some of which make use of well-established control practices such as risk assessment and the provision of information to those most at risk, while others make use of the most recent digital technologies to prevent systems from being put to improper purposes or to detect illegal conduct immediately it takes place.

To reduce the risk of professional misconduct and crime in the twenty-first century, it will be essential for all those involved to work cooperatively in making use of the latest technologies of computer crime control.

Where preventive strategies have failed to work, it may be necessary to devise new regulatory structures to deal with technology-related unprofessional conduct. As globalisation of professional activities continues to expand, it is likely that the most appropriate response would be to enhance national, and indeed international, regulatory structures.

The development of international codes of practice among professional groups, and also between professions, will become essential in the years to come. In the age of multidisciplinary practices which make use of online services, it may well be appropriate to see international professional regulatory bodies created, or at least for national and internal bodies to agree on common standards of conduct and procedures to deal with unprofessional behaviour. In Europe this is now becoming a reality. The various jurisdictions within Australia should consider further the establishment of regulatory bodies which cross geographical boundaries as well as boundaries between professional groups. It would then be easier to harmonise procedures with those adopted in other countries.

Chapter 16

# Raising the Standard: An Integrated Approach to Promoting Professional Values and Avoiding Professional Criminality

Charles Sampford and Sophie Curzon Blencowe

## Introduction

People view crime by professionals as particularly abhorrent, particularly heinous. When an accountant steals from a client, a lawyer perverts justice and a doctor murders a patient, these crimes seem even more offensive. An examination of what it means to be a professional provides an insight into society's reaction to professional criminality. It also provides an insight into the lesser (but related) mischief of inadequate professional behaviour and the greater virtue of exemplary professional conduct. A central theme of this chapter is that improving the emphasis on, and rewards for, exemplary professional conduct will reduce the extent of both professional crime and inadequate behaviour.

Accordingly, we argue that society should not make a fetish out of crime in the professions, and suggest a more positive coordinated approach to raising professional standards; an approach that recognises that professional work falls into a normative continuum of which crime is only a small part. Whilst emphasising the essential 'backstop' role for shaming and punishment, we suggest that praise and rewards for high professional standards are more important. Our approach also recognises that there are many distinctions among professionals important for ethical issues and that incentives must be tailored to the particular profession and type of practice, to encourage members of each to embrace a critical morality. We use the legal profession as an example and examine two problems that impede the attainment of higher standards by lawyers. In particular, we suggest that institutions must be redesigned so that they support and uphold the public values that justify the existence of the professions.

**Why do we find Criminal Behaviour by Professionals so Offensive?**

Recent writers on the subject of professionalism have, in near universal agreement, raised their voices in alarm. The Dean of the Yale Law School, Professor Kronman, for example, has claimed that the legal profession has been overtaken by a 'crisis of values' (see Sutton 1994), while Maddox (1998) points to an ethical malaise so deep that many professions may have lost their meaning altogether and become little more than self-interested economic units functioning in a world of crass commercialism. But this begs the question of *how to define what a profession is,* the answer to which will shed light on why society (rightfully) views criminal behaviour by professionals as especially abhorrent.

Technical definitions of professions and professionalism abound. Most authors point out that although the diverse nature and variety of professions excludes any single definition, there are at least three characteristics historically common to all. First, an individual must embark upon a course of extensive and intellectually demanding training in order to be admitted into a profession. Second, a profession is characterised by the provision of advice or service rather than things. Third, a professional is able to maintain a high degree of autonomy over his or her work. The above characteristics stem from society's acceptance of the profession's right to exist as an entity in the form of a voluntary association, to engage in self-regulation and to exercise monopolistic or at least significant control over both entry to the profession and the provision of services (see Bayles 1981, pp. 7–8; Constantinides 1991, p. 1333; and Longstaff 1995, p. 26).

One of the themes of this volume is the extent to which the traditional (substantive and structural) characteristics of a profession, particularly autonomy and self-regulation, still hold true or are even desirable in the modern corporate and bureaucratic world (see chapter 3, Western). However, we would like to place these issues to one side and focus instead on the normative or ideational features of professions. Kultgen (1998), for example, distinguishes between substantive, structural and ideational characteristics of professions. It is our argument that a profession's right to exist, along with the power and privileges its members enjoy, rests upon the profession's *upholding of public values through the development, transmission and application of a body of knowledge.* The creation of this body of knowledge and its concentration in the hands of a few creates a knowledge gap between the professional and client. That gap gives the profession power. One of the criticisms of professions is that occupational knowledge is 'mystified' and access to it is restricted, thus perpetuating the power of professionals over other groups in society (see Coady 1997, p. 75). Such power is reinforced by differential access to other resources—technological, physical and organisational. For example, it is not just medical knowledge but access to medical technology that gives the medical profession its capacity to heal. It is the institutional links to courts that make barristers so effective.

We do not suggest that the knowledge differential is deliberately created and increased to further the power of the profession. However, once power differentials are created, for whatever reason, there is a reluctance to give them up and there remains a temptation to use them for personal gain, either at the expense of the client or in some cases to the mutual enrichment of the professional and client at the expense of the wider public. Controlling the use and abuse of that power is one of the principle concerns of the community and one of the principle purposes for professional ethics. The fundamental question concerning any profession receiving public support and privileges is how can that support, and its continuation, be justified. That justification cannot be in terms of the benefits the profession confers on its members but the benefits the profession confers on the general public. The argument is that an educated group of specialists developing, transmitting and applying a specialist body of knowledge will use that knowledge to benefit the broader community.

This argument builds upon the ideal that the establishment and sustenance of a profession involves a social compact with society, granting privileges such as autonomy, self-regulation, monopolistic rights and public funding of professional education in return for the provision of desirable social goods. The proviso is that the profession place 'the public interest foremost, even if serving the public interest may at times be at the professionals' own expense' (Longstaff 1995, p. 27). Recently, some of the privileges granted to professions are being challenged. The Australian National Competition Council, for example, is currently examining monopoly rights of the legal profession. The Law Council of Australia has responded by making specific claims about the public benefits of the legal profession to defend its monopolies. This debate and questioning is healthy because it forces the profession to justify its contemporary relevance and benefit to society (see Law Council of Australia 1999).

Crucially, different public values and interests will apply to different professions and should be seen as embodied in the very definition of these professions (Coady 1997, pp. 76–7). Coady goes on to warn against promoting myths about the higher moral behaviour of professionals as opposed to individuals in non-professional occupations. To do this, she argues, is to 'undervalue the particular moral expectations which are rightly attached to occupations and roles which have a lower status but are as essential to our society as are those which have professional status'. An example is the child-care worker, entrusted with the care of the next generation but not granted 'professional' status (Coady 1997, p. 77, see also chapter 7 in this volume).

In the case of the medical profession, its privileges are justified by the values of preserving life and health. The privileges of the legal profession are justified by the values of upholding justice, the rule of law and the rights of the individual. It is easy to be cynical about such claims but there is little doubt that most professionals believe them and, for the most part, try to act upon them. Thus Davis and Elliston assert that:

> One of the tasks of the professional is to seek the social good. It follows from this that one cannot be a professional unless one has some sense of what the social good is…each profession seeks the social good in a different form, according to its particular expertise…Without such knowledge professionals cannot perform their social roles (cited by Longstaff 1995, p. 29).

The reason why crime committed by professionals in the course of their work is rightly considered so heinous is that each profession is socially justified as a body of trained individuals who are committed to serving the public in one or more ways. In a sense, the knowledge and power gap of professionals is only tolerated by the rest of the community on the basis that the professional will use this knowledge and power to the benefit of the public. As Justice Hayne observes in this volume, the public put their *trust* in professionals to use their knowledge and access to resources and institutions to pursue the values that justify the existence of the profession (chapter 2, Hayne). It is important, however, to note Coady's (1997, p. 73) critique of the assumption that trust is central to every relationship between professional and client. Although this may have been true in the past, some clients (especially corporate clients) can hardly be described as vulnerable. Crime by professionals invariably abuses the trust between professional and client, and fundamentally denies and subverts those values that are at the heart of their professions and define their activities. Crime by professionals negates what should be viewed as the central tenet of professionalism: to 'practise within a moral frame of reference' (Henry 1994, p. 145).

However, the existence of professional crime and the many lesser failings discussed below does not mean that we should follow the lead of power theorists such as Larson who cynically reject the idea of professionals upholding important public values as either a self-serving ideology masking social inequality or a public relations exercise (see Kultgen 1998; Newton 1998). We acknowledge that professions often do not live up to their ideals. But this does not mean that we should throw away the ideals or completely do away with the concept of professionalism as suggested by Elkins (1984) or Rhode, who argues that the legal profession is 'dead or dying' (see Maddox 1998, p. 327). Instead, we need to think of ways to breathe new life into old ideals and to encourage members of professions to embrace a critical morality. In particular, each profession must creatively consider how to avoid the temptations to misuse its power. It is no surprise that one of the key themes of this volume is the need to (re)design professional institutions to achieve this goal (see chapter 8, Day).

## Crime as Only the Tip of the Iceberg: The Behavioural Continuum

Participation in crime can be viewed as the worst failure of the professional in terms of behaviour antithetical to the public values of his or her profession. However, crime represents only the tip of the iceberg of activities that fail to further the public values that justify a particular profession. Professional crime can be seen as the tip of an iceberg of unproven crimes, unethical, questionable and/or antisocial behaviour. Attention to professional misbehaviour is not primarily about chasing down the criminals. It is about attempting to ensure that professionals live up to the high standards that justify the existence of the profession. Our aim should not be to concentrate on the worst forms of professional behaviour. The fact that professional behaviour is not bad enough to justify prosecution hardly equates to fulfilling the ideal of professionals upholding the social good.

One of the authors has long argued that improving professional or institutional behaviour (and avoiding misbehaviour) requires a coordinated approach based on a 'trinity'[1] of ethical standard setting, legal regulation (of which criminal law is only a part) and institutional reform (see Sampford 1991, p. 186 and, for an application of these ideas to the legal profession, Sampford and Parker 1995). Such an approach recognises that professional behaviour falls into a normative continuum from the highest professional standards, through good work, sub-par work, misconduct and criminality. It also recognises that there is a professional practice continuum from solo to large group settings and that there are many distinctions among professionals important for ethical issues (Bayles 1989, p. 201). The goal of the 'trinity' is to raise individual professionals as far up the normative continuum as possible, using means appropriate to the particular profession and work setting. The Australian Nursing Council's use of individual self-assessment as the basis for determining continuing competence of nurses, as discussed by Leanne Raven in this volume, is a good example of a focus on continually lifting standards within a profession (chapter 6, Raven). Such a strategy is far more likely to be successful than a policy of deterrence based on punitive sanctions. Not only is it obviously better to avoid the opportunity for ethical failings than to deal with their consequences, there is some evidence that punishment can in fact be counterproductive (Bayles 1989, p. 185; Braithwaite 1999, p. 1739). We would argue that in imposing criminal sanctions, society should not primarily emphasise community disgust at the behaviour condemned. Rather, society should emphasise the positive values of the profession (and society) that have been betrayed. This is the reason why the individual has received a higher level of punishment than others who were not professionally committed to those values.

Recourse to the criminal law should be only a backstop, not the principle means of tackling the problem. This is not to deny that criminal prosecutions have an important place in the improvement of standards. As Durkheim (1964, pp. 70–110) observed, criminal sanctions have powerful symbolic value, emphasising in the most public way the unacceptability of certain actions.

More pragmatically, legal sanctions underwrite the other means of avoiding illegal behaviour. Braithwaite (1993, 1999) famously conceptualises the various responses to illegal and unethical behaviour as an 'enforcement pyramid'. He argues that for the majority of individuals (the 'virtuous actors'), an appeal to reason (persuasion) will be sufficient. Braithwaite places deterrence in the middle of his pyramid, dealing with a lesser number of cases. The assumption is that the threat of deterrence in its various forms will be sufficient for the 'rational actor'. The apex of the pyramid, representing the implementation of various sanctions to 'incapacitate' the 'incompetent or irrational actor', is the focus of least frequent regulatory activity. However, Braithwaite notes that the existence of criminal sanctions (albeit rarely or never used) is crucial. 'This is the paradox of the pyramid. Lop the top off the pyramid and one might destroy the capacity of the pyramid to channel the regulatory action down to the co-operative base of the pyramid' (Braithwaite 1993, p. 95). Similarly, Braithwaite (1999, p. 1729) notes that the most effective business regulatory agencies 'carry big sticks' (possess strong capabilities to apply sanctions) but 'speak softly' (rarely use them).

One needs sanctions, including serious criminal sanctions, as a backstop and ultimate guarantor of the more positive normative systems higher up the pyramid that outline positive values for the profession. Developing the analogy, backstops may be important, even vital, but they are not the main game. The skills of the backstop are necessary but only when the keeper and slips fail for one reason or another. You may place a backstop if the bowler is wayward or the keeper is lacking in the skills to take chances or stop byes. However, you cannot win the game through the backstop and the main focus of the game is with bowler, batsmen and keeper. If the backstop is the first line of defence, the game is already lost. If the fielding team is doing well, the backstop may never be used. Returning to our theme, sanctions are not the primary control mechanism and avoiding them should never be seen as the rationale behind professional values.

What is vital is the coordination of the various approaches to improving behaviour to shift as much behaviour as high up the behavioural continuum as possible. Ethical standards should set out the aspirational goals at the highest levels of the behavioural continuum; disciplinary codes and criminal sanctions should be addressed to the lowest levels of the behavioural continuum. Even for those who do not reach the highest ideals of the profession, other means should underpin and reward higher standards at all levels. The more successful a coordinated approach based on ethical standard-setting, legal regulation and institutional reform, the higher the overall standards of the profession and the fewer professionals at the lower levels committing crimes and ethical breaches. Thus, in a well-ordered profession, the aspirations of most practitioners will be to strive for the highest standards of the profession and this focus will keep individuals so far from the sanctionable minimum that there will be very few breaches, even by those who fall below the average. Criminal behaviour will also be rarer if the occurrence of institutional temptations or dilemmas is reduced. The more effective is ethical standard-setting and ethical education, the lesser the opportunity to resort to the excuse of ignorance. And the more effective is institutional reform, the less likely the profession's acceptance of the excuse that the individual faced an ethical dilemma, alone and unsupported.

In short, criminal behaviour will be easier to detect for two reasons. First, individuals engaging in such behaviour will be more easily visible and more readily subject to peer condemnation because they will be more obviously out of the mainstream. Second, the more limited number of breaches means that the resources of regulatory and disciplinary agencies can be concentrated on a small number of more isolated miscreants. With most professionals falling well above the line of potential misconduct, the profession can join the community and external regulators in what we will suggest should be the 'pitiless pursuit of the few offenders'. In terms of our own analogy, the iceberg will be smaller, and its tip will be miniscule and easier to get at.

## Setting, Interpreting and Reinforcing Values

We will now examine more closely the relationship between the values at various levels along the behavioural continuum and the means for their articulation and advancement or enforcement. A critical part of this strategy is to bring the values at different points on the continuum into sync so that the norms for each type of behaviour (the highest professional standards, good work, sub-par work, misconduct and criminality) are mutually supportive and broadly consistent. This is not as simple as it sounds because the norms at different levels are set by different groups, for overlapping but not entirely consistent reasons. To have the norms at each level set by the same body would change the nature and undermine the effectiveness of norms at different levels. For example, if the norms of good practice within an organisation were set by statute, they would cease to be the norms of the organisation and might be narrowly construed. What each profession needs to do is to have a clear appreciation of the different normative systems involved, the way they interact and the way they can be mutually reinforcing.

At each stage of the behavioural continuum we must look at the means by which values are articulated, enforced and *reinforced*. We emphasise the latter because praise and rewards are the most important means of promoting and realising values. We must also identify temptations, conflicts and dilemmas specific to the type of profession, the type of practice and the individual's standing within the behavioural continuum. It is important to highlight the fact that different levels of the continuum require different levels of specificity, different sanctions (positive and/or negative) and different institutional interpretation and enforcement.

### *Criminal Behaviour and Legal Sanction*

At the lowest levels of the behavioural continuum, the sanctions are greatest— including fines, imprisonment and public opprobrium. The criminal law is designed as a means for indicating the opprobrium of society for certain kinds of actions and the attachment of that opprobrium to those who are

**Table 16.1  The normative/behavioural continuum**

| Level | Set | Interpreted | Enforced | Reinforced rewarded/ praised |
|---|---|---|---|---|
| Highest aspiration | Self/society/ profession | Self | Self | Society/ profession |
| Standard aspiration | Profession/ firm | Firm (courts) | Firm | Firm |
| Minimal aspiration | Profession | Profession/ firm (courts) | Profession/ firm | |
| Criminal behaviour | Society | Courts | Courts | |

'Firm' means the place in which a professional works such as an agency, firm, practice, company or hospital.

proven to have performed them. To be effective and just, formal sanction and social opprobrium require clear and prior statements of the maximum possible precision, endorsed by the highest authority (which is, in a democracy, at the very least the representative parliament and sometimes an elected president as well). The authoritative interpretation and enforcement of these rules must be by a justice system on which the highest standards of procedural fairness are imposed.

*Minimal Professional Standards and Professional Enforcement*

The profession will set minimum standards for membership of the profession and procedures for detecting breaches (see, for example, chapter 10, Wilson). These minimal values are those of the profession so that the profession is, in general, the appropriate body to define, interpret and enforce them. These minimal professional standards will obviously be higher than those required to escape criminal sanction. The requirements of precise (and prior) definition, social endorsement and procedural fairness do not apply so rigidly to the policing of minimal professional standards. However, in recognition of the costs both financial and to reputation of being expelled from a profession, there needs to be procedural fairness, independence and precision in the definition and application of those norms whose breach can lead to expulsion or suspension. It is not necessary for the court to actually enforce these norms, although it may act in its supervisory capacity to ensure that the profession's procedures reach appropriate standards of fairness and legality.

There is room for a significant variety of techniques for dealing with both individuals and institutions where their conduct has fallen below the requisite minimal levels of professional behaviour (see, in general, Fisse and Braithwaite 1993; Braithwaite and Mugford 1994). Firms should be expected to enforce minimal professional standards and, indeed, higher ones (as will be seen below). They will do this through their own internal monitoring and disciplinary procedures—including dismissal. However, the professional disciplinary bodies should always have a disciplinary role where their standards have been breached. This does not mean that all transgressions should lead to disbarment. Braithwaite's proposals for 'reintegrative shaming' in the corporate context may have an important role, forcing those responsible for harm to encounter their victims in a face-to-face encounter and to acknowledge and learn from their wrongs. An example of the application of reintegrative shaming in the corporate world concerned the fraudulent behaviour of Colonial Mutual life insurance agents in selling insurance policies to impoverished Aboriginal people in remote communities. During the settlement process, senior executives were forced to meet the victims of the scam and to endure living in the same third-world conditions as the rest of the community (Fisse and Braithwaite 1993, p. 236).

Most of the profession's norms will deal with the conduct of members to avoid the abuse of power created by the 'knowledge gap' and the differential access to relevant resources provided by the profession. However, an important set of norms should always be those that attempt to *reduce* the knowledge gap or reduce the possibilities of its abuse. For example, most legal professionals see it as a sign of good practice to explain legal options in lay terms and to provide options to the client. The latter standards have an important role in the next level of behaviour discussed below.

*Standard Aspirations and the Role of the Firm*

As we move up the scale of professional behaviour to the 'standard aspiration' of good practice, the profession should retain an important role in setting such standards, particularly those that improve service to clients and realise the values that justify the profession's existence. Although it is not the role of the profession to punish an individual for failing to meet these higher standards, the profession should be involved in encouraging all its members to aspire to these ideals. Institutions that can play a vital role in this regard include all the places in which professionals work, including the agency, firm, practice, company and hospital. For the purposes of this chapter we will rather inaccurately refer to all these institutions as the 'firm'. As institutions they will generally be concerned to ensure that 'best practice' is, as far as possible, promoted and achieved. They have a clear financial and legal interest in monitoring both overall performance and the work of individual professionals as employees.

In pursuing these objectives, how much attention should the firm give to the goal of furthering values of the profession? The answer is that if the profession is to move up the normative and behavioural continuum from 'just good enough to avoid prosecution or disbarment' towards the aspirational standards of good practice, the firm must pay much more attention to furthering the values of professions. It is at this level that there is a great deal of criticism of professions. For example, the structure of legal institutions, especially law firms, is a major impediment to individual reflection and the realisation in daily practice of the higher values of the profession. The modern catch-cry that 'law is big business' encapsulates the potential for conflict between professional values and business interests/maximisation of profits. Adams and Albert (1999), for example, argue that law firms are 'hybrid organisations', with their identity composed of two distinct and often incompatible components: a profession and a business. The authors formulate a set of management guidelines to enable law firms to restore a healthy balance between these two identities.

The rise of the American practice of monitoring and judging the performance of employee solicitors (and later partners) on the basis of the number of 'billable hours' rightly raises concerns about the temptation to overcharge or otherwise engage in sharp practice. The problem is strikingly simple. Whatever the firm's public position on professional values, if it judges and promotes its own employees on the basis of their money-raising ability, then it is very obviously pursuing profit maximisation at the expense of professional values. We would argue that such a firm should forfeit the right to be seen as an organisation of professionals and to enjoy the associated regulatory privileges.

Schneyer (1992, p. 10) rightfully observes that the 'ethical infrastructure' of law firms may have at least as much to do with causing and avoiding unjustified harm as do the individual values and practice skills of individual lawyers. Firms must involve their staff in a collective and educational process of determining the ethical dilemmas, challenges and temptations that arise and determining the norms, sanctions and institutional supports required to minimise the dilemmas and temptations (Sampford 1998). New theories of moral and participatory leadership, based on engagement and dialogue rather

*Crime in the Professions*

than control, with the 'ability to shape and alter not just ideals but motives, desires or valuings' of members of the organisation, are also important (see Rosenthal and Buchholz 2000, p. 193). Professional firms need to recognise their role in promoting, articulating, interpreting and realising professional values that justify the existence of the profession. They need to be explicit about the values their firm stands for, consistent with the values of the profession and reflecting the work of that firm, with its own clients and areas of specialty.

It is at the point of designing internal processes to encourage higher standards of practice that we want to emphasise the importance of reward. Moving up the behavioural continuum, what is relevant is the extent of praise that is received. We would like to build upon Bayles' (1989, p. 201) argument that 'in general, people act the way they think they are expected to act and for which they are rewarded by praise or money'. Firms need to adopt institutional means to ensure that internal rewards are not available to those who weaken, compromise or avoid professional values. In conjunction with firms, professions should require the establishment of an 'ethical regime', processes for ethical leadership and processes that ensure that the highest rewards go to those who are furthering the values of the profession rather than merely making more money for the firm. The profession might, itself, reward professional firms that take this exercise seriously with 'integrity ratings'. If they do not, some independent body might seek to do this. Ultimately, this should not cost the firm, as a reputation for integrity is a vital asset in today's marketplace. If firms distinguish themselves on pursuing higher standards and others fail to match them, the latter should not be surprised if they, and their clients, are subject to greater external scrutiny.

*Highest Aspiration*

The firm is the best place in which to pursue the 'standard aspiration' of current best practice. However, the higher up the aspirational scale, the more room for variation and interpretation, as with all normative standards. This degree of variation and uncertainty in the definition and application of the highest professional aspirations is to be embraced. Firms that allow employees to exercise their critical faculties to examine how they may best, as individuals, promote the highest aspirations of the profession and best realise its values in their own work recognise the importance of thinking 'outside the square'. One of the authors has elsewhere written about the importance of critical morality in questioning and developing the positive morality of professional groups (Sampford and Wood 1992).

At this level, it is the individual who is interpreting professional values. If we fail to meet our highest aspirations, we may chastise ourselves but no one else should do so. The profession, firm and society cannot sanction someone for failing to achieve the highest standards of the profession. This would, by definition, require the punishment of most of the profession, including all those merely following good practice. While negative sanctions will only be imposed internally, this does not mean that the pursuit and achievement of the highest standards should not be rewarded externally. In many cases, there are social rewards (public recognition and formal honours) for those who uphold and extend the highest standards of the profession. Rewards to those, and only those, who have reached the top of the behavioural continuum according to at least one publicly defensible interpretation, should be encouraged.

All of the above measures are designed to push as many professionals as possible up the continuum of behaviour—not just avoiding the most unethical behaviour that leads to criminal sanction or professional disbarment, but seeking the highest standards of behaviour. If these measures are moderately successful, the number of professionals who are tempted into professional crime, or whose behaviour is even close, will be reduced. However, cultural and economic/structural impediments to change within each profession need to be overcome to achieve this goal. The following section deals with two problems within (but not confined to) the legal profession.

## Impediments to Higher Professional Standards Within the Legal Profession

*Reluctance to Report Colleagues*

According to Professor John Western, lawyers are more inclined than other professionals to take no action against colleagues suspected of misconduct (chapter 3, Western). We suspect that one of the reasons for lawyers' reluctance to report a colleague for misconduct is the recognition that the particular temptation or pressure that the individual has succumbed to is one shared by many others in the competitive commercial environment of legal practice. However, this provides even more reason for dealing with these issues openly and within an institutional context. The profession should not stick together to protect members who have betrayed the values espoused by the profession. Indeed we would argue that one who has betrayed these values has lost the right to be called a professional. In particular, professionals engaging in criminal behaviour can be compared to soldiers ripping off their uniforms to reveal the ensigns of an opposing army. Their behaviour is a betrayal of the values of the profession and does not call for sympathy but the most forceful institutional reaction. This is not to deny the possibility of the rehabilitation of those professionals who have offended against the law or engaged in lesser forms of misconduct, but merely to argue that their colleagues should not protect them from disclosure and disciplinary action.

However, the tendency of many professionals and their associations has been to view colleagues who have engaged in misconduct as merely straying too far over the line dividing minimum standards from misconduct and even criminal behaviour. Ideally, under the coordinated approach to professional standards that we propose, individuals will be seen as falling so far below the standards of the profession that there will be no room for emphatic feelings of 'but for the grace of God and/or the vigilance of the regulators, go I'. A lack of professional toleration for misconduct in conjunction with institutional encouragement of reporting will make it more likely that colleagues will report misbehaviour without fear of being victimised as whistleblowers. As Bayles (1989, p. 196) asserts, a primary issue is that of motivation: 'both attitudes toward reporting violations and the structure of the workplace will have to change' (see also Kultgen's suggestions for reform, 1998, pp. 287–9).

## *It is the Client Who Pays*

For the legal profession, perhaps the biggest problem is that the justification of the profession is in terms of public values but the financial rewards come from clients. The (perceived) conflict between the lawyer's role as zealous advocate for his or her client and the lawyer's broader duties to legal institutions, the rule of law and serving justice in the community are commonplace. We have previously argued that most lawyers are genuinely committed to ethical principles because they believe it is in their long-term interest to act ethically or because they believe there are higher, independent reasons for doing so. But the danger is that commercial pressures, the desire to advance within a firm, to retain wealthy clients and to maximise billable hours, means that ethical values take second place or are neglected altogether (Sampford and Blencowe 1998; Sampford and Parker 1995, p. 14; Sampford, Blencowe and Condlln 1999). One strategy that law firms could adopt would be to set a ceiling on the annual number of hours each lawyer could bill, thus hopefully reducing the temptation both to overcharge and to neglect ethical considerations (Adams and Albert 1999, p. 1162).

Clients of lawyers will often want them to undermine the effectiveness of laws—especially in areas of taxation and corporate responsibility. Part of the answer lies in the need for each lawyer to critically analyse and then publicly justify how serving a particular client to achieve particular ends supports one or more public values that justify the profession (for a critique of the client advocate model's rejection of the lawyer's giving of ethical advice, see Sampford and Blencowe 1998). But institutional measures, and in particular financial incentives, are required to prevent collusion by lawyers with the immoral and/or illegal objectives of clients. The usual response of a professional when requested to do something contrary to the values of the profession, is to refuse to act. Such clients are passed on to another professional. At best, clients, having been told why you cannot act for them, are savvier about what to say next time. At the worst clients may find the next professional more amenable. This unfortunate fact may be used as a self-serving justification by professionals who say that if they do not act for such clients, others will. They will at least console themselves that they are not handing the client to someone less ethical than themselves.

The professional who wants to preserve a self-image as an ethical professional will find a form of practice which meets the client's desires without breaching either the criminal law or professional ethical rules. This will generally lead to an approach that becomes in fact, if not in rhetoric, serving the client in any way that is not unethical or illegal. Ethics is treated as a set of restrictions on behaviour in the same way as the criminal law. In order to further the primary value of serving the client, ethical standards start being read as narrowly as a tax statute. This is a recipe for driving professional behaviour *down* the behavioural continuum rather than up it.

One answer is to impose costs on clients who attempt to seek the same outcome elsewhere and on lawyers who accept that business. The client's file should travel to the new lawyer, and with it the first lawyer's advice that what was requested was illegal or unethical. Lawyers who have refused to act for such a client and then see the client shopping elsewhere should be able to alert a disciplinary panel that would be able to ask questions of the new lawyer. This would reduce the incentive for clients to move away from lawyers who insisted on being ethical and for other lawyers to take them on. By breaking the wall of silence between professionals (while still preserving any client's confidence outside of a current lawyer–client relationship) it would make it difficult for a client to modify his story the second time around. This would involve some variation to the existing confidentiality provisions, but nothing that contradicts the principles underlying them.

The Professional Conduct and Practice Rules of the Law Society of New South Wales, made under the *Legal Profession Act 1987* (NSW), for example, provide exceptions where the client authorises disclosure or the practitioner is compelled by law to disclose. Disclosure could be made a requirement of lawyers taking on work, although a statutory modification might be more appropriate. There could always be a provision that the solicitor or client might seek court approval for a non-disclosure occasions in which justice would not be served.

The legal profession would then become, in a sense, a 'conspiracy of virtue'. This goal is best pursued by the profession as a whole. However, a group of firms could agree to follow specific principles; namely eschewing certain kinds of business and refusing to take on a matter in which all files from the previous lawyer were not brought to them. In relation to the first principle, if a group of firms insisted that they would not offer tax avoidance or regulatory avoidance work, this would attract clients who did not want to engage in such practices and wanted to be identified as ethical. The remaining lawyers, and clients, would be rather obviously seen as more likely to engage in tax or regulatory avoidance and be justified targets for audits and inspections. The second principle, which assumes that the client can authorise the disclosure, can be accommodated within existing rules. The successful implementation of both principles is a matter of institutional will power.

## Conclusion

Professional crime is the tip of an iceberg of unproven crimes, unethical, questionable and/or antisocial behaviour. Icebergs do not float on seawater. There is something underneath. The community should be as concerned by this as well. Attention to professional misbehaviour is not primarily about chasing down the criminals. It is about attempting to ensure that professionals live up to the high standards that justify the existence of the profession. This can only be achieved via the 'trinity' of ethical standard setting, legal regulation and institutional design.

A coordinated approach calls for professionals to use their power responsibly for the purposes for which it was given. As one of the authors has argued elsewhere (Sampford 1998, p. 49):

> the key…is to look to the justification of our professional activity and use that justification to provide the values that inform our ethics, the principles guiding the laws that regulate us and the design of the institution in which we work.

Crucial to this process is the need for critical reflection and dialogue among members of a profession and among junior and senior employees of organisations about setting aspirations and ensuring they are vigorously pursued. But even more is required—the courage to question corporate and professional practices and to revise ethical standards in response to the rapidly changing nature of professional work and social values. Podgor (1996, p. 328), for example, argues that 'it is self-defeating [for the legal profession] to maintain an aspirational paradigm of "public spirit" unless ample consideration is devoted to rectifying the inherent bias within the profession', including discrimination based on gender.

This calls for a 'conspiracy of virtue' rather than a 'conspiracy of professionalism'. The latter can be viewed as the tendency of individuals to uncritically accept the practices/standards of their profession or, worse, to hide an agenda of personal wealth creation behind the myth that any professional work in and of itself fulfils the social good (for the argument that there are inherent virtues in professions, see Meilander 1991). It also requires what Kultgen (1998, p. 289) terms 'a sense of limits' (of the profession's rightful claims to money, resources, power and expertise). Professions will be judged on how well they perform those tasks and should expect little public sympathy if they fail. They should certainly not expect the continuation of privileges accorded to them by the community and its laws.

## Note

1   The term 'trinity' was coined in response to a colleague who referred to it as a trilogy—emphasising the idea that the three are not to be pursued in sequence (as is often the case in real life) but as three parts of a common and inseparable whole.

# Bibliography

Abeles, N. 1998, 'Commentary on "Scientific Societies and Whistleblowers: The Relationship between the Community and the Individual"', *Science and Engineering Ethics*, vol. 4, pp. 115–17.

Abernethy, M. 2000, 'Quack Goes the Mouse', *Bulletin*, 29 February, pp. 66–8.

Adams, E.S. and Albert, S. 1999, 'Law Redesigns Law: Legal Principles as Principles of Law Firm Organization', *Rutgers Law Review*, vol. 51, pp. 1133–206.

Alexander, M. 1995, *The Underground Guide to Computer Security*, Addison-Wesley Longman Inc., New York.

*Allinson v. General Council of Medical Education and Registration* [1894] 1 QB 750 at pp. 760–1 per Lord Esher MR (United Kingdom Court of Appeal, 23 February 1894).

Anderson, D.S. and Western, J. 1970, 'Social Profiles of Students in Four Professions', *Quarterly Review of Australian Education*, vol. 3, no. 4, pp. 1–28.

—— 1976, 'The Professions: Reason and Rhetoric', in Boreham, P., Pemberton, A. and Wilson, P. (eds), *The Professions in Australia: A Critical Appraisal*, University of Queensland Press, St Lucia, pp. 42–55.

Annas, G.J. and Grodin, M.A. 1992 (eds), *The Nazi Doctors and the Nuremberg Code: Human Rights in Human Experimentation*, Oxford University Press, New York.

Anonymous 1993, 'RMs Need to Safeguard Computerised Patient Records to Protect Hospitals', *Hospital Risk Management*, vol. 9, pp. 16–19.

Anonymous 1996, 'Medical Records Face Hacker Risk', *Security Australia*, vol. 16, no. 10, p.18.

Association of Massage Therapists Australia Inc. 1999, *Background Paper: Registration of the Massage Industry*, Association of Massage Therapists Australia Inc., Melbourne.

Audit Commission 1989, *The Probation Service Promoting Better Value for Money*, HMSO, London.

—— 1991, *Going Straight: Developing Good Practice in the Probation Practice*, HMSO, London.

Australian Associated Press 1999, 'AMA Rejects ALP Call for Suspect Doctors' Names', 29 December.

Australian Bureau of Statistics 1996, *Census of Population and Housing: Selected Family and Labour Force Characteristics for Statistical Local Areas* (Cat. Nos. 2017.0–8), Australian Bureau of Statistics, Canberra.

——— 1997, *Australian Standard Classification of Occupations*, Second Edition and ASCO Coder, ABS No. 1220.0.30.001, Australian Bureau of Statistics, Canberra.

Australian College of Acupuncturists 1994, *Submission for AHMAC's Criteria on the Regulation of Health Occupations: Acupuncture.*

Australian Competition and Consumer Commission (ACCC) 1998, *Statement: Cooperation and Leniency in Enforcement*, ACCC, Canberra.

Australian Council of Homoeopathy Ltd 1998, *The Australian Council of Homoeopathy Certification Program for Homoeopathic Practitioners: Executive Summary*, Australian Council of Homoeopathy Ltd, Brisbane.

*Australian Financial Review* 2000, 'Great One Day...Scammed the Next', 24 January, p. 21.

Australian Health Ministers Advisory Council 1995, *Criteria for Assessing the Need for Statutory Regulation of Unregulated Health Occupations*, Australian Health Ministers' Advisory Council, Canberra.

——— 1997, *Working Group Advising on Criteria and Processes for Assessment of Regulatory Requirements for Unregulated Health Occupations: Final Report*, Australian Health Ministers' Advisory Council, Canberra.

Australian Institute of Health and Welfare 1999, *Nursing Labour Force 1998*, Cat. No. HWL 14, AIHW National Health Labour Force Series, Australian Institute of Health and Welfare, Canberra.

Australian Nursing Council Inc. 1993, *Code of Ethics for Nurses in Australia*, ANCI, Canberra.

——— 1994, *National Competencies for the Registered and Enrolled Nurse in Recommended Domains*, ANCI, Canberra.

——— 1995, *Code of Professional Conduct for Nurses in Australia*, ANCI, Canberra.

——— 1996, *Principles for Dealing with Professional Conduct Issues*, ANCI, Canberra.

——— 1999, *Summary of Decisions at ANCI Meeting in November*, ANCI, Canberra.

Australian Securities and Investments Commission 1999, *Media Release 99/473.*

Australian Securities and Investments Commission and the Financial Planners Association 1999, *Don't Kiss Your Money Goodbye*, <http://www.asic.gov.au/consumer/index.htm> (visited 27 March 2000).

Australian Society of Certified Practising Accountants 1998, 'Professional Conduct', *Australian CPA*, June, p. 83.

——— 1999, 'Professional Conduct', *Australian CPA*, December, p. 80.

Baker, J. 1996, *Conveyancing Fees in a Comparative Market*, Justice Research Centre and Law Foundation of New South Wales, Sydney.

Barnett, T., Cochrane, D.S. and Taylor, G.S. 1993, 'The Internal Disclosure Policies of Private Sector Employers: An Initial Look at their Relationship to Employee Whistleblowing', *Journal of Business Ethics*, vol. 12, p. 127.

Baxt, R. 1994, 'Professions and the Challenge of Competition: Why the Hilmer Report and its Endorsement Create New Opportunities for the Professions', *Corporate and Business Law Journal*, vol. 8, no. 1, pp. 1–25.

Bayles, M. 1981, *Professional Ethics*, Wadsworth Publishing Co, Belmont.

Bayley, D. 1966, 'The Effects of Corruption in Developing Nations', *Western Political Quarterly*, December, pp. 719–23.

Bensoussan, A. and Myers, S. 1996, *Towards a Safer Choice: The Practice of Traditional Chinese Medicine in Australia*, University of Western Sydney Macarthur, Faculty of Health, Campbelltown.

Bhojani, S. 1997, *'Public Benefits' Under the Trade Practices Act*, Australian Competition and Consumer Commission, Sydney.

Bird, S.J. 1998, 'The Role of Professional Societies: Codes of Conduct and their Enforcement', *Science and Engineering Ethics*, July 4, pp. 315–20.

Blossfeld, H.P. and Shavit, Y. 1993, 'Persisting Barriers: Changes in Educational Opportunities in Thirteen Countries', in Shavit, Y. and Blossfeld, H.P., *Persistent Inequality: Changing Educational Attainment in Thirteen Countries*, Westview Press, Inc., Colorado.

Bochel, D. 1976, *Probation and Aftercare: Its Development in England and Wales,* Scottish Academic Press, Edinburgh.

Boon, A. and Levin, J. 1999, *The Ethics and Conduct of Lawyers in England and Wales*, Hart Publishing Limited, Oxford.

Borruso, M.T. 1991, 'Sexual Abuse by Psychotherapists: The Call for a Uniform Criminal Statute', *American Journal of Law and Medicine*, vol. 17, pp. 289–311.

Bottoms, A. and McWilliams, W. 1979, 'A Non-Treatment Paradigm for Probation Practice', *British Journal of Social Work*, vol. 9, no. 2, pp. 159–202.

Boudon, R. and Bourricaud, F. 1989 (English edition By Hamilton, P.), *A Critical Dictionary of Sociology*, University of Chicago Press, Chicago.

Braithwaite, J. 1993, 'Responsive Regulation for Australia', in Grabosky, P. and Braithwaite, J. (eds) *Business Regulation and Australia's Future*, Australian Institute of Criminology, Canberra.

—— 1999, 'A Future Where Punishment is Marginalized: Realistic or Utopian?', *UCLA Law Review*, vol. 46, pp. 1727–50.

Braithwaite, J. and Mugford, S. 1994, 'Conditions of Successful Reintegration Ceremonies: Dealing with Juvenile Offenders', *British Journal of Criminology*, vol. 34, pp. 139–68.

Brault, S. 1997, *Collective Reflections on the Changing Workplace*, Department of Labour, Ottawa.

Breen, K., Plueckhahn, V. and Cordner, S. 1997, *Ethics, Law and Medical Practice*, pp. 98–107, Allen & Unwin, St Leonards.

British Medical Association 1992, *Medicine Betrayed: The Participation of Doctors in Human Rights Abuses*, Report of a Working Party, Zed Books Ltd, London.

Brown, B. 1998, *Scams and Swindlers*, ASIC and the Centre for Professional Development, Sydney.

Brown, M. 1999, 'Accounting for Change', *Law Institute Journal*, vol. 73, no. 10, pp. 30–1.

Brownlee, I. 1998, *Community Punishment: A Critical Introduction*, Longman, Harlow.

Bryant, R. 1999, 'Nurse Regulation: An Inquiry into Culpability', *Joan Durdin Oration*, Paper Series No. 5, The University of Adelaide Department of Clinical Nursing, Adelaide.

Callister, D.J. and Bythewood, T. 1995, *Of Tiger Treatments and Rhino Remedies: Trade in Endangered Species Medicines in Australia and New Zealand*, TRAFFIC Oceania, Sydney.

Campbell, J. 1857, *Lives of the Lord Chancellors and Keepers of the Great Seal of England*, 4th ed., vol. iii, William Clowes & Sons, London.

Cant, S. 2000, 'Max Green Linked to Gun-Running', *The Age*, February 8, p. 3.

Carchedi, G. 1977, *The Economic Identification of Social Classes*, Routledge and Kegan Paul, London.

Carlton, A-L. 1998, 'Review of Traditional Chinese Medicine in Victoria', in Smith, R.G. (ed.), *Health Care, Crime and Regulatory Control*, pp. 80–95, Hawkins Press, Sydney.

Carr-Saunders, A.M. and Wilson, P.A. 1933, *The Professions*, Clarendon Press, Oxford.

Carter, H. 2000, 'How Many Patients Did This Doctor Kill?', *Guardian Weekly*, vol. 162, no. 6, pp. 1, 10.

Carter, M. 2000, 'Integrated Electronic Health Records and Patient Privacy: Possible Benefits But Real Dangers', *Medical Journal of Australia*, vol. 172, no. 1, pp. 28–32.

Cauchi, S. 1999, 'Psychiatrist Accused of $1m Fraud', *Age* (Melbourne) 6 January, p. 5a.

Cavoukian, A. 1999, 'Privacy and Biometrics', Paper presented to the 21st International Conference on Privacy and Personal Data Protection, Hong Kong, 13 September <http://www.pco.org.hk/conproceed.html> (visited 17 December 1999).

Celler, B.G., Lovell, N.H. and Chan, D.K.Y. 1999, 'The Potential Impact of Home Telecare on Clinical Practice', *Medical Journal of Australia*, vol. 171, no. 10, pp. 518–21.

Centrelink 1997, *Data-Matching Program: Report on Progress 1996–97*, Data-Matching Agency, Canberra.

Chester, N. 1981, *The English Administrative System 1780–1870*, Oxford University Press, Oxford.

Christie, N. 1993, *Crime Control as Industry: Towards Gulags, Western Style* (2nd ed.) Routledge, London.

Clear, T. and Karp, D. 1999, *The Community Justice Ideal: Preventing Crime and Achieving Justice*, Westview Press, Boulder, Colorado.

Cleek, M.A. and Leonard, S.L. 1998, 'Can Corporate Codes of Ethics Influence Behaviour?', *Journal of Business Ethics*, vol. 17, no. 6, pp. 619–30.

Clifton-Steele, R. 1994, 'Peak Law Bodies Tell TPC the Legal Profession is Already Most Competitive: Developing a National Competition Policy', *Law Society Journal*, vol. 32, no. 2, pp. 66–7.

Coady, M.M. 1996, 'The Moral Domain of Professionals', in Coady, M.M. and Bloch, S. (eds), *Codes of Ethics and the Professions*, pp. 28–51 Melbourne University Press, Melbourne.

—— 1997, 'Just How Ethical Should Professionals Be?', in Alexandra, A., Collingridge, M. and Miller, S. (eds) *Proceedings of the Third Annual Conference of the Australian Association for Professional and Applied Ethics*, pp. 72–8, Keon Publications, Wagga Wagga.

Cohen, S. 1975, 'Its Alright for You to Talk: Political and Sociological Manifestos for Social Work Action', in Bailey, R. and Brake, M. (eds), *Radical Social Work*, Edward Arnold, London.

—— 1985, *Visions of Social Control: Crime, Punishment and Classification*, Polity Press, Cambridge.

College of Physicians and Surgeons of Ontario 1993, *Sexual Abuse and Mandatory Reporting Survey*, Insight Canada Research, Toronto.

Collis, B.W. 1996, '"Tort and Punishment" – Exemplary Damages: The Australian Experience', *Australian Law Journal*, vol. 70, no. 1, pp. 47–53.

Commonwealth Department of Aged Care 1997, *Aged Care Principles*, Department of Aged Care, Canberra.

Commonwealth Department of Health and Aged Care 1999, *Unpublished Response to AHMAC on Progress Report on Implementation of Recommendations of Victorian Ministerial Advisory Committee Report on Regulation of Traditional Chinese Medicine*, 6 June.

Commonwealth of Australia, House of Representatives Standing Committee on Family and Community Affairs 1996, *Inquiry into Health Information Management and Telemedicine: Submissions and Evidence*, Australian Government Publishing Service, Canberra.

Commonwealth of Australia, Model Criminal Code Officers Committee of the Standing Committee of Attorneys-General 2000, *Damage and Computer Offences: Discussion Paper, Chapter 4*, Commonwealth Attorney-General's Department, Canberra.

Commonwealth of Australia, *Parliamentary Debates, House of Representatives*, 3 November 1992, vol. 186, pp. 2432–5.

Competition Policy Taskforce (Victoria) 1996, *National Competition Policy Guidelines for Review of Legislative Restrictions on Competition*, Department of Premier and Cabinet, State Government of Victoria, Melbourne.

Condren, C. 1995, 'Code Types: Functions and Failings and Organisational Diversity', *Business and Professional Ethics Journal*, vol. 14, no. 4, pp. 69–88.

Constantinides, C.A. 1991, 'Professional Ethics Codes in Court: Redefining the Social Contract Between the Public and the Professions', *Georgia Law Review*, vol. 25, pp. 1327–73.

Corner, E.P. 1956, 'Chairman's Address to the Annual Conference of the National Association of Probation Officers', *Probation*, no. 8, pp. 22–4.

Corones, S. 1998, 'Solicitors' Liability for Misleading Conduct', *Australian Law Journal*, vol. 72, pp. 775–85.

Curtis, L. 1980, 'Freedom of Information: the Australian Approach', *Australian Law Journal*, vol. 54, pp. 525–35.

Dahrendorf, R. 1959, *Class and Class Conflict in Industrial Society*, Stanford University Press, Stanford.

Darley, J.M. 1996, 'How Organisations Socialize Individuals into Evildoing', in Messick, D.M. and Tenbrunsel, A.E. (eds), *Codes of Conduct: Behavioural Research into Business Ethics*, pp. 13–44, Russell Sage Foundation, New York.

Davies, M. and Makkai, T. 2000, *Professions in Australia Study*, Australian National University, Canberra.

Davis, M. 1991, 'Thinking Like an Engineer: The Place of a Code of Ethics in the Practice of a Profession', *Philosophy and Public Affairs*, vol. 20.

de Crayencour, J-P. 1982, *The Professions in the European Community: Towards Freedom of Movement and Mutual Recognition of Qualifications*, Commission of the European Communities, Brussels.

de Moor, G.J.E. 1997, 'European Standards Development in Healthcare Informatics: Actual and Future Challenges', <http://miginfo.rug.ac.be:8001/mim/mim_94_2/mim0001h.htm>.

Denning, A. 1981, 'Misuse of Power', *Australian Law Journal*, vol. 55, pp. 720–7.

Denning, D.E. 1999, *Information Warfare and Security*, ACM Press, New York.

Department of Industry Science and Tourism 1998, *Pharmaceutical Electronic Commerce and Communication: The Way Forward*, Department of Industry Science and Tourism, Canberra.

Department of the Environment 1998, *Wildlife Protection (Regulation of Exports and Imports) Amendment Bill Regulation Impact Statement*, Department of the Environment, Canberra.

Dix, A. 1998, 'Disciplinary Regulation', in Smith, R.G. (ed.), *Health Care, Crime and Regulatory Control*, pp. 48–58, Hawkins Press, Sydney.

Dixon, F. 1999, 'The State of the Profession', *Law Institute Journal*, vol. 73, no. 12, pp. 75–7.

Dixon, Sir O. 1965, *Jesting Pilate and Other Essays and Addresses*, Law Book Company, Melbourne.

Doig, A. 1994, 'Honesty in Politics and Public Spending: The Ethical Environment', paper presented to the *Second Seminar on the Status and Prevention of Corruption*, Santiago, Chile, 4–6 July.

*Dr Noel Rodney Campbell v The Dental Board of Victoria*, 14 December 1999.

Drakeford, M. and Vanstone, M. 1996, *Beyond Offending Behaviour*, Arena, Aldershot.

Drury, B. 1996, 'Blame and Claim: Litigation in Australia', *Sydney Morning Herald*, September, p. 11.

Dunn, I.M. 1996, 'Medicine and the Law: Crisis or Beat Up?', *Medical Journal of Australia*, vol. 164, pp. 180–2.

Durkheim, E. 1964, *The Division of Labour in Society*, Free Press, New York.

Eccleston, R. 1999a, 'Clinical Error', *The Australian*, 8–9 May, p. 21.

—— 1999b, 'Chaos if Scan Scam is Proved: Doctors', *The Australian*, 28 December, p. 3.

Editorial 1964, *Times of India* 10 May, p. 6.

Editorial 1994, 'US Physicians and the Death Penalty', *Lancet*, vol. 343, p. 743.

Elkins, J.R. 1984, 'Ethics, Professionalism, Craft and Failure', *Kentucky Law Journal*, vol. 73, pp. 937–65.

Ellis, N.T and Kidd, M.R. 2000, 'General Practice Computerisation: Lessons from the United Kingdom', *Medical Journal of Australia*, vol. 172, no. 1, pp. 22–24.

Evatt, H.V. 1945, *Australian Labour Leader*, 3rd ed., Angus & Robertson, Sydney.

Feeley, M. and Simon, J. 1992, 'The New Penology: Emerging Strategy of Corrections and its Implications', *Criminology*, vol. 30, no. 4, pp. 449–74.

—— 1994, 'Actuarial Justice: The Emerging New Criminal Law', in Nelken, D. (ed.), *The Futures of Criminology*, pp. 173–201, Sage, London.

Fels, A. 1997a, *Can the Professions Survive Under a National Competition Policy? The ACCC's View*, Australian Competition and Consumer Commission, Sydney.

—— 1997b, *Competition Health: Two Years On*, Australian Competition and Consumer Commission, Sydney.

Field, A. 1999, 'Electronic Commerce and the Internet: Which Government is Doing What?' *Law Institute Journal*, April, pp. 56–62.

Finn, P. 1978, 'Official Misconduct', *Criminal Law Journal*, vol. 2, p. 307.

Finn, P. and Smith, K.J. 1992, 'The Citizen, the Government and "Reasonable Expectations"', *Australian Law Journal*, vol. 66, pp. 139–51.

Fisse, B. and Braithwaite, J. 1993, *Corporations, Crime and Accountability*, Cambridge University Press, Cambridge.

Fitzgerald Report 1989, *Report of a Commission of Inquiry Pursuant to Orders in Council*, Government Printer, Brisbane.

Fletcher, J. 1998, 'National Influences on the Regulation of Professional Conduct', in Smith, R.G. (ed.), *Health Care, Crime and Regulatory Control*, Hawkins Press, Sydney, pp. 72–79.

Freckelton, I. 1996, 'Enforcement of Ethics', in Coady, M.M. and Bloch, S. (eds), *Codes of Ethics and the Professions*, pp. 130–65, Melbourne University Press, Melbourne.

—— 1998, 'The Criminalisation "Solution" to Medical Misconduct', in Smith, R.G. (ed.), *Health Care, Crime and Regulatory Control*, pp. 26–47, Hawkins Press, Sydney.

Freidson, E. 1970a, *Profession of Medicine*, University of Chicago Press, Chicago.

—— 1970b, *Professional Dominance*, Atherton Press, New York.

—— 1986, *Professional Powers*, The University of Chicago Press, Chicago.

—— 1994, *Professionalism Reborn*, Polity Press, Cambridge.

Frye, T. 1993, 'Caveat Emptor: Institutions, Credible Commitment and Commodity Exchanges in Russia', in Weimer D. (ed.), *Institutional Design*, Kluwer, Dordrecht.

Gailbraith, J. 1992, *The Culture of Contentment*, Penguin, Harmondsworth.

Garland, D. 1985, *Punishment and Welfare*, Gower, Aldershot.

—— 1996, 'The Limits of the Sovereign State: Strategies of Crime Control in Contemporary Society', *British Journal of Criminology*, vol. 36, no. 4, pp. 445–71.

—— 1997, 'Probation and the Reconfiguration of Crime Control', in Burnett, R. (ed.), *The Probation Service: Responding to Change. Proceedings of the Probation Studies Unit First Colloquium*, pp. 1–10, Centre for Criminological Research, Oxford.

—— 2001, *The Culture of Control: Crime and Social Order in Contemporary Society*, Oxford University Press, Oxford.

Gawande, A. 1999, 'When Doctors Make Mistakes', *The New Yorker*, 1 February, p. 40.

Gawler, M. 1999, 'MDPs: What in the World is Going On?', *Law Institute Journal*, vol. 73, no. 10, p. 3.

General Medical Council 1999, 'Bold New Proposals for Restoration Procedures', *GMC News* Winter, pp. 1, 3.

Glass, M. 1993, *Tommy Bent: 'Bent by Name, Bent by Nature'*, Melbourne University Press, Melbourne.

Goode, W. 1960, 'Encroachment, Charlatanism and the Emerging Professions: Psychology, Sociology and Medicine', *American Sociological Review*, vol. 25, no. 6, pp. 902–14.

Gorlin, R.A. 1999, *Codes of Professional Responsibility*, 4th ed. Bureau of National Affairs, Washington.

Gray, D. 1999, 'Doctors in the Firing Line', *The Age*, December 24, pp. A1–A2.

Gray, G. 1999, 'The Changing Face of Legal Practice and Implications for Professional Indemnity Insurance', *Insurance Law Journal*, vol. 11, no. 1, pp. 72–90.

Greenwood, E. 1957, 'Attributes of a Professional', *Social Work*, vol. 2, pp. 45–55.

Hall, T. 1979, *White Collar Crime in Australia*, Harper & Row, Sydney.

Halsbury's Laws of Australia, *Criminal Law*, Butterworths, Sydney.

Hammond, S.B. 1956, *Draft Report of the First Year Student Survey*, University of Melbourne, Melbourne.

Hanlon, G. 1999, *Lawyers: The State and the Market: Professionalism Revisited*, Macmillan Press Limited, London.

Harley, J. 1998, 'Mutual Recognition a Step Closer', *Law Society of South Australia Bulletin*, vol. 20, no. 6, pp. 6–7.

Harris, R. 1992, *Crime, Criminal Justice and the Probation Service*, Tavistock, London.

—— 1994, 'Continuity and Change: Probation and Politics in Contemporary Britain', *International Journal of Offenders Therapy and Comparative Criminology*, vol. 31, no. 1 pp. 33–45.

Harrison, B. 1971, *Drink and the Victorian Temperance Question in England 1815–1872*, Faber and Faber, London.

Haxby, D. 1978, *Probation: A Changing Service*, Constable, London.

Health Insurance Commission 1997, *Annual Report 1996–97*, Professional Review Supplement, Australian Government Publishing Service, Canberra.

—— 1998, *Annual Report 1997–98*, Australian Government Publishing Service, Canberra.

Henderson, P. 1996, 'The Plaintiff's Perspective', in *Medical Negligence: Crisis or Beat-up?*, Business Law Education Centre, Melbourne.

Hennessy, P. 1990, *Whitehall*, Fontana, London.

Henry, C. 1994, 'Professional Behaviour and the Organisation', in Chadwick, R.F. (ed.), *Ethics and the Professions*, pp. 145–55, Aldershot, Brookfield.

Hilmer, F. 1993, *National Competition Policy Review*, Australian Government Publishing Service, Canberra.

Hoedeman, P. 1991, *Hitler of Hippocrates: Medical Experiments and Euthanasia in the Third Reich*, Book Guild, Lewes.

Home Office 1936, *Report of the Departmental Committee on the Social Services in Courts of Summary Jurisdiction*, Cmd 5122, HMSO, London.

—— 1961, *Report of the Interdepartmental Committee on the Business of the Criminal Courts (the Streatfield Report)*, Cmnd 1289, HMSO, London.

—— 1963, *The Organisation of Aftercare (the Wooton Report)*, HMSO, London.

—— 1974, *Report on the Advisory Council on the Penal System: Young Adult Offenders* (3rd ed.), HMSO, London.

—— 1984, *The Probation Service in England and Wales: Statement for National Objective and Priorities*, HMSO, London.

—— 1988, *Punishment, Custody and the Community (Green Paper)*, Cm 424, HMSO, London.

—— 1995, *National Standards for the Supervision of Offenders in the Community*, HMSO, London.

—— 1998, *Joining Forces: The Prisons–Probation Review*, HMSO, London.

—— 2000a, ' National Standards for the Supervision of Offenders in the Community 2000', <http://www.homeoffice.gov.uk/cpd/probu/natstds.htm> (visited 6 March 2000).

——2000b, *The Criminal Justice and Court Services Act*, HMSO, London.

Hood, C. 1991, 'A Public Management for All Seasons?', *Public Administration*, vol. 69, pp. 3–19.

Hudson, B. 1993, *Penal Policy and Social Justice*, Macmillan, Basingstoke.

Illich, I. 1977, 'Disabling Professions', in Illich, I., Zola, I.K., McKnight, J., Caplan, J. and Shaiken, H., *Disabling Professions*, pp. 11–39, Marion Boyars Publishers Limited, London.

In re a Solicitor; Ex parte The Law Society [1912] 1 KB 302 (United Kingdom High Court of Justice, King's Bench Division, 8 November 1911).

Institute of Chartered Accountants in Australia 1999, 'Institute Disciplinary', *Charter*, vol. 70, no. 10, p. 98.

Jackson, J.A. 1970, *Professions and Professionalism*, Cambridge University Press, Cambridge.

James, A. 1995, 'Probation Values for the 1990s—and Beyond?', *Howard Journal*, vol. 34, no. 4, pp. 326–43.

Jennings, B., Callahan, D. and Wolf, S. 1987, 'The Professions: Public Interest and Common Good', in *The Public Duties of the Professions* The Hastings Report Special Supplement, February, The Hastings Institute, Hastings on Hudson NY.

Johnson, A.G. 1995, *The Blackwell Dictionary of Sociology*, Blackwell Reference, Oxford.

Johnson, E. 1996, 'Body of Evidence: How Biometric Technology Could Help in the Fight Against Crime', *Crime Prevention News*, December, pp. 17–19.

Johnson, T.J. 1972, *Professions and Power*, Macmillan Press Limited, London.

Johnstone, M.J. 1999, *Reporting Child Abuse: Ethical Issues for the Nursing Profession and Nurse Regulating Authorities*, RMIT University, Melbourne.

Jones, J.B. 1996, 'Whistleblowing: No Longer Out of Tune', *Australian Accountant*, August, pp. 56–7.

Jones, R. 1999, 'Digital Rule', *Punishment and Society*, vol. 2, no. 1, pp. 5–22.

Kamenetsky, C. 1984, *Children's Literature in Hitler's Germany*, Ohio University Press, Athens, Ohio.

Kamvounias, P. 1999, 'Health Sector Liability Under the Trade Practices Act', *Australian Health Review*, vol. 22, no. 1, pp. 81–96.

Kane, A.W. 1995, 'The Effects of Criminalization of Sexual Misconduct by Therapists: Report of a Survey in Wisconsin', in Gonsiorek, J.C. (ed.), *Breach of Trust: Sexual Exploitation by Health Care Professionals and Clergy*, Sage Publications, Thousand Oaks, pp. 317–37.

Kaufman, D. 1994, 'Diminishing Returns to Administrative Controls and the Emergence of the Unofficial Economy: A Framework of Analysis and Applications to Ukraine', *Economic Policy*, December, pp. 51–69.

Keaney, M.A. 1996, 'Medicine and the Law: Is Litigation Increasing?', *Medical Journal of Australia*, vol. 164, pp. 178–9.

Kermode, S., Brown, C. and Emmanuel, N. 1995, 'National Competition Policy: A Review of the Significance of the Hilmer Report for Nursing', *Collegian*, vol. 2, no. 4, pp. 15–2.

Kinnear, P. and Graycar, A. 1999, 'Abuse of Older People: Crime or Family Dynamics?', in *Trends and Issues in Crime and Criminal Justice*, No. 113, Australian Institute of Criminology, Canberra.

Klitgaard, R. 1988, *Controlling Corruption*, University of California Press, Berkeley.

Komesaroff, P. 1999, 'Ethical Implications of Competition Policy in Healthcare', *Medical Journal of Australia*, vol. 170, no. 6, pp. 266–8.

Kriegler, R. 1999, 'LIV Annual Survey of Legal Practitioners', *Law Institute Journal*, March, pp. 52–7.

Kultgen, J. 1988, *Ethics and Professionalism*, University of Pennsylvania Press, Pennsylvania.

—— 1995, *Autonomy and Intervention*, Oxford University Press, New York.

—— 1998, 'The Ideological Use of Professional Codes', in Sticker, R.N. and Hauptman, R. (eds.), *Ethics, Information and Technology: Readings*, pp. 273–90, McFarland, Jefferson.

Ladd, J. 1992, 'The Quest for a Code of Professional Ethics: An Intellectual and Moral Confusion', in Rhode, D. and Luban, D. (eds.), *Legal Ethics*, pp. 121–7, Foundation Press, Westbury, NY.

Larson, M. 1977, *The Rise of Professionalism: A Sociological Analysis*, University of California Press, Berkeley.

Law Council of Australia 1999, 'Policy Statement on the Reservation of Legal Work for Lawyers', <http://www.lawcouncil.asn.au/rlwpol.htm/> (visited 17 February 2000).

Law Reform Commission 1993, *Scrutiny of the Legal Profession: Complaints Against Lawyers*, New South Wales Law Reform Commission, Sydney.

Law Society of New South Wales 2000, 'Professional Conduct and Practice Rules made under the *Legal Profession Act 1987*', <http://www.lawsocnsw.asn.au/resources/solrules/solrules/> (visited 17 February 2000).

Leary, W.E. 1997, 'Panel Cites Poor Security on Medical Records', *New York Times Fax*, 6 March.

Lever, J.W. 1971, *The Tragedy of State*, Methuen & Co, London.

Levitt, A. 2000, 'Investing With Your Eyes Open', Remarks of Chairman Arthur Levitt at the *Los Angeles Times* 4th Annual Investment Strategies Conference, Los Angeles, California, February 12.

Lewis, C.S. 1965 (originally published 1946), *That Hideous Strength*, MacMillan, London.

Lichtenberg, J. 1996, 'What Are Codes of Ethics For?', in Coady, M.M. and Bloch, S. (eds.), *Codes of Ethics and the Professions*, pp. 13–27, Melbourne University Press, Melbourne.

Lifton, R.J. 1986, *The Nazi Doctors*, Macmillan, London.

Long, M., Carpenter, P. and Hayden, M. 1999, *Participation in Education and Training*, Australian Council for Educational Research, Hawthorn.

Longstaff, S. 1995, 'The Lawyer's Duty to the Community', in Miller, S. (ed.), *Professional Ethics: Proceedings of the Professional Ethics Workshop held at the School of Humanities and Social Sciences, Charles Sturt University*, pp. 23–40, Keon Publications, Wagga Wagga.

Lupton, D. 1996, 'Your life in their hands: trust in the medical encounter', in Gabe, J. and James V. (eds), *Health and the Sociology of Emotion* (*Sociology of Health and Illness* Monograph Series) pp.157–172.

Maddox, Hon. A.H. 1998, 'Lawyers: The Aristocracy of Democracy Or "Skunks, Snakes and Sharks"?', *Cumberland Law Review*, vol. 29, pp. 323–46.

Madison, J. 1780, *Federalist Papers*.

Mahoney, D. 1996, 'The Criminal Liability of Public Officers for the Exercise of Public Power', *The Judicial Review*, vol. 3, p. 3.

Manzetti, L. 1994, 'Economic Reform and Corruption in Latin America', *North–South Issues*, vol. 3, pp. 1–6.

Marshall, P.J. 1965, *The Impeachment of Warren Hastings*, London.

Martinson, R. 1974, 'What Works?', *The Public Interest*, March, pp. 22–54.

Mathiesen, T. 1983, 'The Future of Control Systems: The Case of Norway', in Garland, D. and Young, P. (eds) *The Power to Punish*, pp. 130–145, Heinemann, London.

Matthew, H.C.G. 1986, *Gladstone 1809–1874*, Clarendon Press, Oxford.

May, T. 1991, *Probation, Politics and Practice*, Open University Press, Milton Keynes.

—— 1994, 'Probation and Community Sanctions', in Maguire, M., Morgan, R. and Reiner, R. (eds) *The Oxford Handbook of Criminology*, pp. 861–87, Oxford University Press, Oxford.

May, W. 1980, 'Professional Ethics: Setting, Terrain and Teacher', in Callahan D. and Bok, S. (eds), *Ethics Teaching in Higher Education*, pp. 205–41, Hastings Center, Plenum Press, New York.

McWilliams, W. 1981, 'The Probation Officer at Court: From Friend to Acquaintance', *Howard Journal*, vol. 20, pp. 97–116.

—— 1983, 'The Mission to the English Police Courts 1876–1936', *Howard Journal*, vol. 22, pp. 129–47.

—— 1985, 'The Mission Transformed: Professionalisation of Probation between the Wars', *Howard Journal*, vol. 24, no. 4, pp. 257–74.

—— 1986, 'The English Probation System and the Diagnostic Ideal', *Howard Journal*, vol. 25, no. 4, pp. 241–60.

—— 1987, 'Probation, Pragmatism and Policy', *Howard Journal*, vol. 26, no. 2, pp. 97–121.

Meilander, G. 1991, 'Are There Virtues Inherent in a Profession?', in Pellegrino, E, Veatch, R.M. and Langan, J.P. (eds) *Ethics, Trust and the Professions: Philosophical and Cultural Aspects*, pp. 139–53, Georgetown University Press, Washington DC.

Mills, C.W. 1959, *The Sociological Imagination*, Oxford University Press, New York.

Milstein, R.D. 1999, 'Telehealth: Opportunities and Liabilities', *Medical Journal of Australia*, vol. 171, no. 10, pp. 561–2.

Mishkin, B. 1995, 'Ethics, Law and Public Policy', *Professional Ethics Report*, Spring, pp. 4–7.

Montias, J.M. and Rose-Ackerman, S. 1981, 'Corruption in a Soviet-type Economy: Theoretical Considerations', in Rosefielde, S. (ed.), *Economic Welfare and the Economics of Soviet Socialism: Essays in Honor of Abram Bergson*, Cambridge University Press, Cambridge.

Murphy, M.D. 1997, 'The Public Interest as the Exemplar of Good Administration', paper presented to Victorian Administrative Appeals Tribunal Conference, 30 October.

Murugason, R. and McNamara, L. 1997, *Outline of Criminal Law*, Butterworths, Melbourne.

Nellis, M. 1995, 'Probation Values for the 1990s', *Howard Journal*, vol. 34, no. 1, pp. 19–41.

—— 1996, 'Probation Training: The Links with Social Work', in May, T. and Vass, A. (eds), *Working with Offenders: Issues, Contexts and Outcomes*, pp. 7–31, Sage, London.

—— 2000, 'Renaming Probation', *Probation Journal*, vol. 47, no. 1, pp. 39–44.

Neumann, P. 1995, *Computer Related Risks*, Addison-Wesley, Reading, MA.

New South Wales Parliament Joint Committee on Health Care Complaints Commission 1998, *Unregistered Health Practitioners: The Adequacy and Appropriateness of Current Mechanisms for Resolving Complaints*, New South Wales Parliament, Sydney.

New South Wales, Health Department 1997, *Circular 97/80*, Issued 11 August.

—— 1998, *Review of the Medical Practice Act—Final Report*, New South Wales, Health Department, Sydney.

Newton, L. 1998, 'The Origin of Professionalism: Sociological Conclusions and Ethical Implications', in Stickler, R.N. and Hauptman, R. (eds), *Ethics, Information and Technology: Readings*, pp. 261–72, McFarland, Jefferson.

*NIBA Gazette* 2000, 'Investors Burned in Fake MLC Scam', February, p. 3.

Niesche, C. and Marris, S. 1999, 'Specialists Attack "Unfair" Scanner Slurs', *The Australian*, December 24, p. 6.

Nisselle, P. 1996, 'Medicine and the Law: Is There a Crisis?', *Medical Journal of Australia*, vol. 164, pp. 178–9.

Noble, H.B. 1999, 'Hailed as a Surgeon General, Koop Criticised on Web Ethics', *New York Times*, September 4.

Northcote–Trevalyn Report 1851, House of Commons Papers, Cmn 3638, HMSO, London.

Nurses Board of Victoria 1999, *Annual Report*, Nurses Board of Victoria, Melbourne.

—— 1999, *Code of Practice for Midwives in Victoria*, Melbourne.

Nurses Board South Australia 1999, *Annual Report*, Nurses Board South Australia, Adelaide.

Nurses Registration Board New South Wales 1999, *Annual Report*, Nurses Registration Board New South Wales, Sydney.

Nursing Board of Tasmania 1999, *Annual Report*, Nursing Board of Tasmania, Hobart.

Office of Regulatory Reform 1995, *Regulatory Impact Statement Handbook*, Victorian Department of State Development, Melbourne.

Office of the Prime Minister 1999, 'Changes to Goods and Services Tax', *Press Release*, 31 May.

Painter, M. 1998, 'Public Sector Reform, Intergovernmental Relations and the Future of Australian Federalism', *Australian Journal of Public Administration*, vol. 57, no. 3, pp. 52–63.

Parker, C. 1997, 'Justifying the New South Wales Legal Profession 1976 to 1997', *Newcastle Law Review*, vol. 2, no. 2, pp. 1–29.

Parliament of the Commonwealth of Australia, Senate 1998, *Wildlife Protection (Regulation of Exports and Imports) Amendment Bill 1998. Explanatory Memorandum*, Australian Government Publishing Service, Canberra.

Parliament of Victoria, Social Development Committee 1986, *Inquiry into Alternative Medicine and the Health Food Industry*, Parliament of Victoria, Melbourne.

Parsons, T. 1939, 'The Professions and Social Structure', *Social Forces*, vol. 17, pp. 457–67.

Pascoe, J. 1994, 'Professional Regulation after the Hilmer Report', *Australian Accountant*, March, pp. 35–40.

Paterson, A.A. 1996, 'Professionalism and the Legal Services Market', *International Journal of the Legal Profession*, vol. 3, nos. 1–2, pp. 139–48.

Pease, K. 1980, 'Community and Prison: Are They Alternatives?', in Pease, K. and McWilliams, W. (eds), *Community Service by Order*, pp. 27–43, Scottish University Press, Edinburgh.

Peck, M. 1999, 'Competition Policy and the Regulation of the Professions', *Australian Construction Law Newsletter*, vol. 68, Oct/Nov, pp. 30–31.

Peters, A. 1996, 'Main Currents in Criminal Law', in Van Dijk, P. (ed.) *Criminal Law in Action*, pp. 19–36, Gouda Quint, Arnham.

Podgor, E.S. 1996, 'Lawyer Professionalism in a Gendered Society', *University of South Carolina Law Review*, vol. 47, pp. 323–48.

Pope, J. (ed.) 1996, *National Integrity Systems: The TI Source Book*, Transparency International, Berlin (<http://www.transparency.org> visited: 9 May 2000).

Poulantzas, N. 1975, *Classes in Contemporary Capitalism*, New Left Books, London.

Pritchard, D. and Morgan, M.P. 1989, 'Impact of Ethics Codes on Judgments by Journalists: A Natural Experiment', *Journalism Quarterly*, vol. 66, no. 4, pp. 934–41.

Quah, J.S.T. 1989, 'Singapore's Experience in Curbing Corruption', in Heidenheimer A.J. (ed.) *Political Corruption: A Source Book*, Transaction Publishers, New Brunswick.

Queensland Nurses Council 1999, *Annual Report*, Queensland Nurses Council, Brisbane.

*R v. Armstrong* [1922] 2 KB 555 (United Kingdom Court of Criminal Appeal, 16 May 1922).

Radzinowicz, L. and Hood, R. 1986, *A History of Criminal Law and its Administration Since 1750*, vol. v, Stevens, London.

Rawlings, P. 1999, *Crime and Power: A History of Criminal Justice 1688–1988*, Longman, London.

Reasons, C.E. 1982, 'Crime and the Abuse of Power: Offenses and Offenders Beyond the Reach of the Law', in Wickman, P.M. and Dailey, T. (eds), *White-Collar and Economic Crime*, pp. 59–72, Lexington Books, Massachusetts.

Rennie, D. 1997, 'Editorial: Thyroid Storm', *Journal of the American Medical Association*, vol. 277, no. 15, pp. 1238–43.

Rhodes, R. 1994, 'The Hollowing Out of the State: The Changing Role of Public Service in Britain', *The Political Quarterly*, vol. 65, no. 2, pp.138–51.

Robertson, G. 1998, *The Justice Game*, Penguin, London.

Rodwin, M.A. 1993, *Medicine, Money and Morals*, Oxford University Press, New York.

Rose-Ackerman, S. 1978, *Corruption: A Study in Political Economy*, Academic Press, New York.

—— 1994, 'Reducing Bribery in the Public Sector', in Trang D.V., ed., *Corruption and Democracy*, pp. 21–8, Institute for Constitutional and Legislative Policy, Budapest.

Rosenberg, S. 1996, 'Secrecy in Medical Research', *New England Journal of Medicine*, vol. 334, pp. 392–4.

Rosenthal, S.B. and Buchholz, R.A. 2000, *Rethinking Business Ethics: A Pragmatic Approach*, Oxford University Press, Oxford.

Rothchild, J. 1999, 'Protecting the Digital Consumer: The Limits of Cyberspace Utopianism', *Indiana Law Journal*, vol. 74, pp. 893–989.

Roy Morgan Research Centre 1999, Morgan Poll, finding No. 3199.

*Royal Commission on Administration of the Lands Department*, New South Wales Parliamentary Papers, 1906, Government Printer, Sydney.

Samaha, J.B. 1981, 'The Recognisance Bond in Elizabethan Law Enforcement', *American Journal of Legal History*, vol. 25, pp.189–204.

Sampford, C. 1991, 'Law, Institutions and the Public/Private Divide', *Federal Law Review*, vol. 20, pp. 185–22.

—— 1998, 'What's a Lawyer Doing in a Nice Place Like This? Lawyers and Ethical Life', *Legal Ethics*, vol. 1, no. 1, pp. 35–50.

Sampford, C. and Blencowe, S. 1998, 'Educating Lawyers to be Ethical Advisers', in Economides, K. (ed.), *Ethical Challenges to Legal Education and Conduct*, pp. 315–40, Oxford University Press, Oxford.

Sampford, C. and Parker, C. 1995, 'Legal Regulation, Ethical Standard-Setting and Institutional Design', in Parker, C. and Sampford, C. (eds), *Legal Ethics and Legal Practice: Contemporary Issues*, pp. 11–24, Oxford University Press, Oxford.

Sampford, C. and Wood, D. 1992, 'The Future of Business Ethics: Legal Regulation, Ethical Standard Setting and Institutional Design', *Griffith Law Review*, vol. 1, pp. 58–72.

Sampford, C., Blencowe, S. and Condlln, S. (eds) 1999, *Educating Lawyers for a Less Adversarial System*, Federation Press, Sydney.

Santen, J. van 1999, 'Dr QQ: How an Innocent GP Became a Media Target', *Medical Observer*, 12 November, pp. 36–7.

Sawer, G. 1968, *Ombudsmen* (2nd ed.), Melbourne University Press, Melbourne.

Schneyer, T. 1992, 'Professional Discipline for Law Firms', *Cornell Law Review*, vol. 77, pp. 1–46.

Schön, D.A. 1983, *The Reflective Practitioner*, Basic Books Inc., London.

Schoner, G., Milgram, J. and Gonsiorek, J. (eds) 1989, *Psychotherapists' Sexual involvement with Clients: Intervention and Prevention*, Walk In Counselling Centre, Minneapolis.

Sharp, D. 1994, 'US Execution Protocols', *Lancet*, vol. 343, p. 785.

Shaw, G.B. 1925, *The Doctor's Dilemma: A Tragedy*, Constable and Company Limited, London.

—— 1931, *Doctors' Delusions*, Constable & Co. Limited, London.

Shleifer, A. and Vishney, R. 1992, 'Pervasive Shortages under Socialism', *Rand Journal of Economics*, vol. 23, pp. 237–46.

—— 1993, 'Corruption', *Quarterly Journal of Economics*, vol. 108, pp. 599–617.

Shonell, F.J., Rowe, E. and Meddleton, I.G. 1962, *Promise and Performance: A Study of Student Progress at University Level*, University of Queensland Press, Brisbane.

Siggins, I. 1996, 'Some Historical Precedents', in Coady, M.M. and Bloch, S. (eds), *Codes of Ethics and the Professions*, pp. 55–71, Melbourne University Press, Melbourne.

Simon, J. 1993, *Poor Discipline: Parole and the Social Control of the Underclass, 1890–1990*, The University of Chicago Press, Chicago.

Simon, J. and Feeley, M. 1995, 'True Crime: The New Penology and Public Discourse on Crime', in Blomberg, T. and Cohen, S. (eds), *Punishment and Social Control, Essays in Honour of Sheldon L. Messinger*, pp. 147–80, Aldine de Gruyter, New York.

Simpson, J.A. and Weiner, E.S.C. (eds) 1989, *Oxford English Dictionary*, 2nd ed., Oxford University Press, Oxford.

Sinclair, A. 1996, 'Codes in the Workplace: Organisational Versus Professional Codes', in Coady, M.M. and Bloch, S. (eds), *Codes of Ethics and the Professions*, pp. 88–108, Melbourne University Press, Melbourne.

Smith, R.G. 1993, 'The Development of Ethical Guidance for Medical Practitioners by the General Medical Council', *Medical History*, vol. 37, pp. 56–67.

—— 1994, *Medical Discipline: The Professional Conduct Jurisdiction of the General Medical Council, 1858–1990*, Clarendon Press, Oxford.

—— 1998, 'The Regulation of Telemedicine', in Smith, R.G. (ed.), *Health Care, Crime and Regulatory Control*, Hawkins Press, Sydney, pp. 190–203.

—— 1999a, 'Electronic Medicare Fraud: Current and Future Risks', *Trends and Issues in Crime and Criminal Justice*, no. 114, Australian Institute of Criminology, Canberra.

—— 1999b, *In Pursuit of Nursing Excellence: A History of the Royal College of Nursing, Australia 1949–1999*, Oxford University Press, South Melbourne.

Somervell of Harrow 1959, 'The State as Defendant', *Australian Law Journal*, vol. 33, pp. 148–53.

Southwick, J. 1997, 'Australian Council of Professions' View', paper delivered at a joint conference on competition law and the professions, *Can the Professions Survive Under a National Competition Policy?* 11 April, Perth, Western Australia, published by Australian Government Publishing Service, Canberra.

Spencer, H. 1896, *Principles of Sociology*, Appleton and Company, New York.

Spencer, J. 1995, 'A Response to Mike Nellis: Probation Values for the 1990s', *Howard Journal*, vol. 34, no. 4, pp. 344–9.

Stanberry, B. 1997, 'The Legal and Ethical Aspects of Telemedicine. 1: Confidentiality and the Patient's Rights of Access', *Journal of Telemedicine and Telecare*, vol. 3, pp. 179–97.

Standards Australia 1995, *Personal Privacy Protection in Health Care Information Systems*, Australian Standard 4400, Homebush, Standards Australia.

Starke J.G. 1992, 'Recent Cases', *Australian Law Journal*, vol. 66, pp. 50–1.

Starr, P. 1982, *The Social Transformation of American Medicine*, Basic Books, New York.

Steketee, M.1999, 'Greed En Masse a Stain on Medicos', *The Australian*, December 24, p. 6.

Stephenson, C. and Marchman, F.G. 1937, *Sources of English Constitutional History*, Harper, New York.

Sternberg, E. 2000, *Just Business*, second edition, Oxford University Press, Oxford.

Stewart, J. 1999, *Blind Eye: How the Medical Establishment Let a Doctor Get Away with Murder*, Simon and Schuster, New York.

Stolberg, S.G. 1999, 'Internet Drug Deals: A Regulation Dilemma', *New York Times*, 27 June.

*Sunday Program*, Channel 9, Television Broadcast, 13 February 2000.

Sutton, J.F. 1994, 'Book Review: Lawyers Today: Wise Professionals Or Mere Skill Technicians?', *South Texas Law Review*, vol. 35, pp. 741–51.

Swindle, O. 1999, Remarks of President Ronald Reagan quoted in a speech on 23 February for Pillsbury, Madison & Sutro Anti Trust Program, 'A Common Sense Approach to High Tech', <http://www.ftc.gov/speeches/swindle/pillspch.htm> (visited 27 March 2000).

Sykes, E.I., Lanham, D.J., Tracey, R.R.S. and Esser, K.W. 1997, *General Principles of Administrative Law* (4th ed.), Butterworths, Melbourne.

Tanzi, V. 1994, in International Monetary Fund, *Corruption, Governmental Activities and Markets*, IMF Working Paper, Washington DC.

Tawney, R.H. 1920, *The Acquisitive Society*, Harcourt Brace, New York.

Temby, I. 1985, 'Prosecution Discretions and the Director of Public Prosecutions Act 1983', *Australian Law Journal*, vol. 59, pp. 197–203.

*The Australian* 1998, 'Scan Scandal Betrays Trust in Doctors', 28 December, p. 8.

*The Labourforce Australia Historical Summary 1966–1984*, ABS, Cat. No. 6204.0, Australian Bureau of Statistics, Canberra.

Tillman, R. and Pontell, H.N. 1992, 'Is Justice "Collar-Blind"?: Punishing Medicaid Provider Fraud', *Criminology*, vol. 30, no. 4, pp. 547–74.

Tonking, A.I. 1995, 'Implications for the Legal Profession in Competition Policy Reforms', *Law Society Journal*, vol. 33, no. 7, pp. 38, 40–2.

Trade Practice Commission 1994, *Study of the Professions: Legal – Final Report*, Trade Practices Commission, Sydney.

Transparency International 1999, 'Corruption Perception Index 1999', *TI Newsletter*, December (<http://www.transparency.org> visited: 9 May 2000).

Travis, A. 1999, 'Straw's Tough on Probation Order', *The Guardian (London)*, 8 December, p. 11.

Trebilcock, M.J., Dewees, D.N. and Duff, D.G. 1990, 'The Medical Malpractice Explosion: An Empirical Assessment of Trends, Determinants and Impacts', *Melbourne University Law Review*, vol. 17, pp. 539–65.

United Kingdom 1995, *Nolan Commission*.

United Kingdom, House of Commons, First Special Report from the Committee of Public Accounts, Session 1980–81, *The Role of the Comptroller and Auditor-General*, Report, vol. i, HMSO, 4 February 1981.

United States, General Accounting Office 1997, *Telemedicine: Federal Strategy is Needed to Guide Investments*, Report to Congressional Requesters No. GAO/NSIAD/HEHS-97–67, Washington, General Accounting Office.

Varney, C. 1996, 'Regulating Cyberspace: An Off the Record Interview with Federal Trade Commissioner Christine Varney', *Computer Underground Digest*, 25 March, no. 8(24).

Victorian Government Department of Human Services 1998, *Review of Nurses Act 1993 and Medical Practice Act 1994 Discussion Paper*, Victorian Government Department of Human Services, Melbourne.

Victorian Government Department of Human Services Ministerial Advisory Committee on Traditional Chinese Medicine 1998, *Traditional Chinese Medicine: Report on Options for Regulation of Practitioners*, Victorian Government Department of Human Services, Melbourne.

Victorian Register of Certified Homoeopathy Practitioners Inc. 1997, *The Certified Homoeopathic Practitioner. Holistic Healthcare*, Brochure.

Vocino, M. and Tyler, G. 1996, 'The Library and the FBI: Ethical Decision making under Pressure in Pasquerella', in Lynn, A.G.K. and Vocino, M. (eds), *Ethical Dilemmas in Public Administration*, pp. 49–57, Praeger, Westport, Conn.

Wade, H.W.R. and Forsyth, C.F. 1994, *Administrative Law*, 7th ed., Oxford University Press, Oxford.

Walker, H. and Beaumont, B. 1981, *Probation Work: Critical Theory and Socialist Practice*, Blackwell, Oxford.

—— 1985, *Working with Offenders*, Macmillan, London.

Wallis, E. 2001, *A New Choreography: Integrated Strategy for the National Probation Service for England and Wales, Strategic Framework 2001–2004*, Home Office, London.

Walton, M. 1998, 'Competition Policy and the Regulation of the Medical Profession', *Journal of the Health Care Complaints Commission*, vol. 1, no. 6, pp. 1–5.

—— 1998, 'The Problem of Reporting Sexual Misconduct by Colleagues and Patients', in Smith, R.G. (ed.), *Health Care, Crime and Regulatory Control*, pp. 118–134, Hawkins Press, Sydney.

Webb, S. and Webb, B. 1917, 'Special Supplement on Professional Associations: Parts 1 and 2', *New Statesman*, vol. 9, no. 211, pp. 1–24; vol. 9, no. 212, pp. 25–48.

Western Australia 1992, *Royal Commission into Commercial Activities of Government*, Report, vol 1, Government Printer, Perth.

Wijesinghe, C.P. and Dunne, F. 1999, 'Impaired Practitioners Notified to the Medical Practitioners Board of Victoria from 1983 to 1997', *Medical Journal of Australia*, vol. 171, pp. 414–17.

Wilensky, H.L. 1964, 'The Professionalisation of Everyone', *American Journal of Sociology*, vol. 70, pp. 137–58.

Williams, E.N. 1960, *The Eighteenth Century Constitution: 1688–1815 Documents and Commentary*, Cambridge University Press, London.

Williams, D. 1999, 'Law and the Government: Past, Present and the Future', *Law Institute Journal*, vol. 73, no. 12, pp. 62–6.

Williams, G. 1983, *Textbook of Criminal Law*, 2nd ed., Butterworths, London.

Wilson, B. 1999, 'Health Disputes "A Window of Opportunity" to Improve Health Services', pp. 179–192, in Freckelton, I. and Petersen, K., *Controversies in Health Law*, Federation Press, Sydney.

Wilson, B., Jackson, K. and Punshon, T. 1998, 'Conciliation', in Smith, R.G. (ed.), *Health Care, Crime and Regulatory Control*, pp. 59–71, Hawkins Press, Sydney.

Worrall, A. 1997, *Punishment in the Community: The Future of Criminal Justice*, Longman, Harlow.

Wright, E. 1985, *Classes*, New Left Books, London.

Yellowlees, P.M. and Brooks, P.M. 1999, 'Health Online: The Future Isn't What it Used to Be', *Medical Journal of Australia*, vol. 171, no. 10, pp. 522–5.

Zinn, C. 2000, 'Australian Radiologists Face Prosecution for Fraud', *British Medical Journal*, vol. 320, p. 140.

# Index

289